MORNING STAR RISING

INDIGENOUS PACIFICS

SERIES EDITORS

Noelani Goodyear-Ka'ōpua
and April K. Henderson

FACING THE SPEARS OF CHANGE:
THE LIFE AND LEGACY OF JOHN PAPA ʻĪʻĪ
Marie Alohalani Brown

FOUND IN TRANSLATION:
MANY MEANINGS ON A NORTH AUSTRALIAN MISSION
Laura Rademaker

THE PAST BEFORE US: MOʻOKŪʻAUHAU AS METHODOLOGY
Edited by Nālani Wilson-Hokowhitu

EVERYTHING ANCIENT WAS ONCE NEW:
INDIGENOUS PERSISTENCE FROM HAWAIʻI TO KAHIKI
Emalani Case

MORNING STAR RISING

The Politics of Decolonization in West Papua

CAMELLIA WEBB-GANNON

UNIVERSITY OF HAWAIʻI PRESS
HONOLULU

Paperback edition 2022

Printed in the United States of America

Library of Congress Cataloging-in-Publication Data

Names: Webb-Gannon, Camellia, author.
Title: Morning star rising : the politics of decolonization in West Papua / Camellia Webb-Gannon.
Description: Honolulu : University of Hawaiʻi Press, 2021. | Series: Indigenous pacifics | Includes bibliographical references and index.
Identifiers: LCCN 2020046918 | ISBN 9780824887872 (hardcover) | ISBN 9780824888893 (adobe pdf) | ISBN 9780824888909 (epub) | ISBN 9780824888916 (kindle edition)
Subjects: LCSH: Decolonization—Indonesia—Papua Barat—History. | Papua Barat (Indonesia)—History—Autonomy and independence movements.
Classification: LCC DU744.5 .W43 2021 | DDC 325/.309951—dc23
LC record available at https://lccn.loc.gov/2020046918

ISBN: 9780824888886 (paperback)

University of Hawaiʻi Press books are printed on acid-free paper and meet the guidelines for permanence and durability of the Council on Library Resources.

Cover art: *Freedom Fighter.* Illustration by Channell Anivai (Shawk23).

For Victor, Ronny, Rosa, Wensi, Benny, Rex, Peter, Jim,
Wendy, Joe, Anne, Jill, Geoff, Michael, Ellen, and Tim.
I couldn't have written this book without you.

CONTENTS

Acknowledgments

I have been working on this book in one form or another for thirteen years. Many people enabled my research and writing over this time, and I owe them tremendous thanks.

Thank you to the many Papuans inside West Papua who supported me as I carried out this research, included me in their gatherings, allowed me to interview them, took me into their homes, looked out for me, taught me, and shared their hopes, fears, and dreams with me. To protect their identities, I will not name them here, but their sacrifices and generosity are at the heart of this book.

I am grateful to the countless West Papuans living in diaspora who welcomed me into their communities and enthusiastically supported this project, including Ronny Kareni, Rex Rumakiek, Leah Rumwaropen, Petra Rumwaropen, Rosali Rumwaropen, Henk Rumbewas, Jacob Rumbiak, Amatus Douw, Herman Wanggai, Benny Wenda, Octo Mote, Paula Makabory, Frank Makanuey, John Tekwie, Wensi Fatubun, Joseph and Jacob Prai, Oridek Ap, Nancy Jouwe, Michael Kareth, Sonny Karubaba, and Freddy Waromi. I would also like to pay my respects to the West Papuan activists, politicians, and intellectuals whom I had the privilege of interviewing for this book before they passed away: Viktor Kaisiepo, Otto Ondawame, Clemens Runawery, Andy Ajamiseba, Seth Rumkorem, Zachi Sawor, and Neles Tebay. Their legacy continues to inspire me.

Earlier versions of chapter 1 and part of chapter 4 were previously published and then significantly revised for inclusion in this book. Some of chapter 5 originally appeared in a coauthored article and is now in this book with my coauthors' consent. I am immensely indebted to my intellectual mentors: the late Peter King, Jim Elmslie, Wendy Lambourne, Eben Kirksey, John Braithwaite, Rebecca Spence, Ted Wolfers, Stephen Hill, Stuart Kirsch, Andrew McWilliam, Stephanie Lawson, Michael Webb, and Clive Moore. They read drafts of sections, chapters, or the entire manuscript and challenged my thinking while offering critical insights into theoretical worlds I had not previously considered. Of course, I take responsibility for any errors that remain.

My thanks also go to the series editors of Indigenous Pacifics, April Henderson and Noelani Goodyear-Kaʻōpua, for believing in this book and to University of Hawaiʻi Press editor Emma Ching for guiding it to publication. I am also most grateful to the anonymous reviewers of the manuscript for generous and insightful feedback.

I am inspired by Sydney-based activists Joe Collins' and Anne Noonan's indefatigable commitment to justice in West Papua and am indebted to Joe's daily e-mail digest with news from and about West Papua, which is an invaluable research resource.

I am obliged to Papua New Guinean artist Chan Anivai for allowing me to use his powerful illustration as the cover of this book.

Finally, I thank my family for their love and support. My father, Michael Webb, put me on this path. My mother, Ellen Webb, and mother-in-law, Jill Gannon, helped raise my children. My father-in-law, Geoff Gannon, has supported my interest in social justice for two decades. My husband, Tim Gannon, has been my partner through the joy and pain of this advocacy journey. My daughter has been attending Free West Papua rallies since before she was born, and we are teaching my infant son to say "*merdeka.*"

List of West Papuan Political Factions

AMPTPI, Asosiasi Mahasiswa Pegunungan Tengah Papua Se-Indonesia (Central Highlands Student Association)
DAP, Dewan Adat Papua (Papuan Customary Council)
DEMMAK, Dewan Musyawarah Masyarakat Koteka (Koteka Tribal Assembly)
FORDEM, Forum Demokrasi (Democracy Forum)
Fourteen Star Movement
Free West Papua Campaign
IYCLWP, International Youth Coalition for the Liberation of West Papua
KNPB, Komite Nasional Papua Barat (National Committee for West Papua)
MRP, Majelis Rakyat Papua (Papua People's Assembly)
NRFPB, Negara Republik Federal Papua Barat (Federal Republic of West Papua)
OPM, Organisasi Papua Merdeka (Free Papua Movement)
PDP, Presidium Dewan Papua (Papua Presidium Council)
PNWP, Parlemen Nasional West Papua (National Parliament of West Papua)
TPN, Tentara Pembebasan Nasional (National Liberation Arm)
ULMWP, United Liberation Movement for West Papua
WPNCL, West Papua National Coalition for Liberation
WPNGNC, West Papua New Guinea National Congress

INTRODUCTION

The Morning Star

> It is darkest before the Morningstar dawns. The silence awaits the purest first light of the Morningstar to fight back the deepest of darkness. As the world lights up and all life wakes on earth, will also those who are prisoner by darkness be free.
>
> —*Joseph Prai, "Special Tribute to Late Kelly Kwalik"*

Starlight and Unity

When Captain James Cook first set sail in the Pacific in 1768, it was, ostensibly, to observe the passage of the planet Venus across the sun. According to the Royal Society and the Royal Navy at that time, the best vantage point from which to observe this rare event, which occurs approximately once every 120 years, was in Tahiti (Thomas 2016, 10). During the voyage, Cook ventured past the territory now known as West Papua.[1] The territory's population had previously encountered navigators from Europe and Asia, beginning in the early 1500s with sporadic contact with Portuguese explorers pursuing the spice trade in the nearby Maluku Islands. Nearly one century later, the Dutch also sought to establish trade links in west New Guinea and later searched the island's western shores for gold. Finding little success with either mission, Dutch interest in New Guinea waned, although it was piqued briefly again in 1699 as a consequence of rival English exploratory expeditions to the island. Following in the wake of Cook's first Pacific voyage on the HMS *Endeavour,* however, a more marked tension between the Dutch and the British in New Guinea emerged as each power pursued settlement and trade opportunities in the region, vied for more influence in the western half of the island, and sought unfettered access to shipping routes in west coast waters. Information gathered from Cook's South Pacific voyages assisted the British in establishing a penal colony in New South Wales on the Australian east coast in 1788. From that point on, British interest in New Guinea, the island lying immediately to the north of Australia, intensified (Moore 2003, 89). This competition led, in time, to a more established colonial presence on the island. In 1848, New Guinea was divided along the 141st meridian east, demarcating the territory west of the meridian as Dutch (and to the east, later, as British and German).

Since the time of early European–West Papuan encounters, West Papua's history of colonization and its subsequent decolonization journey have been backlit with the glow of Venus, the planet known by West Papuans as the enigmatic Morning Star—the symbolic beacon of their independence movement. Although the allure of Venus/the Morning Star did contribute to the Pacific expedition of the HMS *Endeavour* and the formalization of colonialism that followed in West Papua and elsewhere in the Southwest Pacific, the light of the Morning Star, in the view of West Papuans, will also ultimately guide them out from under their ongoing colonization, which, under Indonesian rule, has become increasingly brutal. This is alluded to in the epigraph above, written by one West Papuan independence advocate, Joseph Prai, as part of a tribute to another, the assassinated West Papuan warrior Kelly Kwalik.

The symbol of the Morning Star is layered with significance in West Papuan history and culture. From the West Papuan island of Biak, located to the north of the mainland, comes one of the colony's most well-known myths—that involving Sampari, "the Morning Star," who was caught stealing palm wine from an old Biak man, Manarmakeri, just before morning (the time when Venus is commonly sighted). In exchange for his release, Sampari initiated Manarmakeri in the rituals for bringing about the "resurrection of the dead and the coming of Koreri" (utopia, heaven on Earth; Kamma 1972, 31). Imbued with this newfound power but rejected by his people because of a skin affliction, Manarmakeri sailed away from his island, his community realizing only too late that Manarmakeri could have offered them Koreri. According to the legend, however, if the followers of the Koreri philosophy live peacefully and faithfully, Manarmakeri will return one day with his "immaculately" conceived son, Yesus, to usher in Koreri. Throughout subsequent periods of Dutch, Japanese, and Indonesian occupation, many West Papuans from Biak and elsewhere have come to believe that Koreri, heaven on Earth, will manifest as a decolonized West Papua and consider the Morning Star to be Koreri's ultimate enabler. Thus, the inhabitants of Biak and nearby Numfor were the early architects of West Papua's independence movement (Sharp 1994, 52). Myths similar to that of Koreri holding nationalist significance for West Papuans exist outside of Biak, but these tend to be less well known beyond their locales (Sharp 1994, 40).

The Morning Star is also an important symbol in Christianity, the religion of the vast majority of West Papua's indigenous population since Dutch colonization. In Revelation 22:16 of the Christian Bible, Jesus calls himself the "bright Morning Star," and in Revelation 2:28, the Bible states that "he who overcomes" and is faithful to Jesus until the end will receive "the morning star." In other words, those loyal to Jesus through the dark night of the soul (often interpreted by West Papuans as Indonesian occupation) will, as dawn approaches, receive Jesus himself and his gifts of freedom, resurrection, and heaven. The similarities between the messianic myths of Christianity and Koreri are striking—one of the reasons perhaps why Christianity has taken root so strongly in West Papua. The same similarities, however, make some West Papuans suspicious of Christianity. Historians do not know the date of the origin of the Koreri myth (Sharp 1994, 46), but the late West Papuan independence activist and follower of Koreri, Markus Wonggor Kaisiepo, claimed that Koreri significantly predates Christianity: "We had our Jesus (Yesus) long before your Jesus.... We believe in God, but we do not believe in the Church because it is only dealing in manipulating people and turning the facts upside down" (quoted in Sharp 1994, 93).

The Morning Star adorns the West Papuan national flag. Its white body lies against a red background adjacent to a set of blue-and-white stripes, the three colors symbolizing, in the Koreri religion, faith, peace, and courage (Sharp 1994, 49). In 1961 the New Guinea Council, a group that included West Papuans sanctioned by the Dutch to prepare for independence, chose the star as the nation's unifying symbol, laying "the indelible imprint of divine power symbolised by Sampari [and] recognised as inspirational in all quarters of the country" (Sharp 1994, 63). This is the same flag that, if raised today, carries a prison sentence of up to fifteen years, so potent is its unifying power among Papuans seeking decolonization from Indonesia. Those whose faith is placed in the decolonizing trajectory of the Morning Star remain "undefeated," according to anthropologist Nonie Sharp (1994, 74). Though their hopes have been "dashed again and again" and though "there is anguish [and] frustration, [there is] never hopelessness or bitterness," for in the Morning Star lies continued hope (Sharp 1994, 74).

While it is the Morning Star, specifically, that is West Papua's national symbol, stars more generally symbolize political potency in West Papua's independence movement. In 1988 the West Papuan lawyer and academic Thomas Wainggai declared the independence of West Melanesia (West Papua), symbolically anchoring West Papua within Melanesia, rather than Asia, by raising a flag featuring fourteen stars—one for each of the other Melanesian states and territories Wainggai believed to be culturally aligned with West Papua. Wainggai was imprisoned for this act, as was his Japanese wife who sewed the fourteen-star movement's flag. Wainggai died in prison in 1996. The Star of David is another significant stellar symbol in the West Papuan decolonization repertoire, frequently embroidered next to the Morning Star flag on West Papuan *noken* (traditional bags) and appearing on calendars and stickers displayed by West Papuans in homes or on belongings. Thus displayed, I theorize in chapter 4 of this book, the Star of David aligns the Morning Star with West Papuan Zionist affinities. Surrounded by what they consider to be an expansionist Muslim enemy, many West Papuans see their land as a Melanesian, Christian "Israel." The Star of David also connects West Papuan decolonization politics with an emerging activist Rastafarian identity in the colony (see chapter 4). And stars are of fundamental cosmological significance to West Papuans, with the appearance of different constellations determining various traditional work and social patterns across the colony (Kamma 1972, 6).

Colonialism in West Papua: A Localized Problem with International Resonances

This book investigates the significance of political unity and disunity in decolonization movements—particularly that of West Papua. It builds on the important insights that authors such as Carmel Budiardjo and Liem Soei Liong (1983), Robin Osborne (1985), Jim Elmslie (2002), Peter King (2004), Otto Ondawame (2010), Eben Kirksey (2012), Jason MacLeod (2015), and others have provided into West Papua's unfolding decolonization movement by connecting the struggle in West Papua with decolonization literature from around the world. In particular, it takes concepts offered by several of modern history's most renowned decolonization thinkers and leaders and applies them in novel ways to the West Papuan context. For example, ideas from key texts by Haunani-Kay Trask, Ngũgĩ wa Thiong'o, Aimé Césaire, Frantz Fanon, Amilcar Cabral, Albert Memmi, and Mahatma Gandhi are brought to bear on the situation in West Papua—ideas emerging from worlds so far away from West Papua that one might wonder at their relevance but which, upon closer inspection, speak to the core of the West Papuan conflict.

Hawaiian activist and academic Trask (1949–2012) worked for Hawaiian sovereignty from the United States in a postcolonial world a century after the United States overthrew (1893) Hawai'i's Queen Lili'uokalani, and Hawai'i was made an American annex (1898). Trask accepted the comparison sometimes made of her advocacy style to that of Malcolm X (Franklin and Lyons 2004, 241) because of her preference for directness over diplomacy, particularly in regard to her fierce promulgation of indigenous Hawaiians' rights and her open labeling of settlers and visitors as intruders.

Like Trask, Kenyan novelist and playwright Ngũgĩ (1938–) has become renowned as a postcolonial thinker, and the two shared a friendship. Having lived through Kenya's struggle for independence from Great Britain (1964), Ngũgĩ became critical of the postindependence dictatorship of Daniel arap Moi, expressing himself using the same tool—writing (books, plays, and poems)—as he did to criticize Western neocolonialism. Ngũgĩ focused on the role language could play in continuing decolonization, eventually writing only in his indigenous language. He believes in international cultural exchange but has argued that one must ensure one's own nation has a stable base first. Ngũgĩ was inspired by Fanon and Marx (Jaggi 2006).

Martinican poet and politician Césaire (1913–2008) was one of the founders of the "negritude" literature and art movement in France in the 1930s championing black culture and identity. He represented Martinique in the French National Assembly. Although in his early years he belonged to the Martinican Communist Party, he later abandoned it, proposing that instead of working toward independence from France, Martinique should focus on self-rule while maintaining links with France at the same time.

Fanon (1925–1961), a Martinican (like Césaire) psychiatrist and author during the Algerian revolutionary war, was a harsh critic of the antiblackness he viewed as underpinning colonialism. He was simultaneously critical of the essentialism inherent in the early negritude/black pride literary movement in Paris but understood that it was being used as an antidote to what he identified as the black inferiority complex. He viewed violence as necessary to revolution, as did his contemporary Amilcar Cabral.

Guinea-Bissauan and Cape Verdean agronomist Cabral (1924–1973) was a skilled guerrilla tactician who developed revolutionary theory based on the practical realities of being an insurgent. Cabral admired aspects of the negritude movement and was influenced by Marx. To an extent that sets him apart from the theorists just mentioned, Cabral was sympathetic toward colonizers (in his case, the Portuguese in Africa), seeing in them a common humanity. For this reason, he believed diplomacy, in addition to violence, could be a valuable decolonization tool.

Tunisian-Jewish essayist and educator Memmi (1920–2020) was a nationalist, a secularist, and an anticolonialist committed to socialism throughout his political life. Like Ngũgĩ, Memmi saw the value in internationalism as well as nationalism and was critical of the postcolonial dictatorships that have taken hold in some African countries. Like Cabral, Memmi sympathized with his oppressor, the postcolonial Arab-Tunisian regime that considered its Jewish population of little value to the new state—Tunisian Arabs had, after all, been colonized themselves. But because he saw that Jews continued to be persecuted in Tunisia, Memmi became a Zionist. Memmi's work was admired by negritude theorists, including Senegal's first president, Leopold Senghor, even though, unlike other negritude activists such as Fanon, Memmi neither rejected so-called Western values such as democracy nor condoned violence as a means to decolonization.

Similarly eschewing violence, Indian independence leader Gandhi (1869–1948) took up nonviolence (*satyagraha*) as a spiritual philosophy and revolutionary strategy. And, like Cabral and Memmi, Gandhi preached love for both the oppressor and the oppressed and viewed national liberation as a step toward the ultimate liberation of humankind from oppression of any type.

Despite the different backgrounds (Hawaiian, Kenyan, Martinican, Guinea-Bissauan and Cape Verdean, Tunisian and Indian) and doctrines (indigenous rights, diplomacy, Zionism, negritude, antiessentialism, guerrillaism, and nonviolence) of these thinkers, there are critical points of similarity in their thought: the need for national independence (all except Césaire believed independence was a necessary component of decolonization) from colonial oppressors so that indigenous dignity might be restored and recognized, and the value of culture to the foundation of indigenous national identity. And, of interest to this book, aspects of these authors' standpoints strike a chord with the revolutionary praxis of West Papuans. Many West Papuans are anti-immigration (like Trask); fearful of the loss of indigenous languages and with them, indigenous identity (like Ngũgĩ); critical of the antiblackness expressed by their colonial occupiers (like Fanon); open to the principles of Western democracy in a future state (like Memmi); and dedicated to a philosophy of pursuing peace by peaceful means (like Gandhi), although not at all costs—West Papuans are proud (like Cabral) of their guerrilla military, which stands, in the Papuan imaginary, as a struggle method of last resort should all other means of pursuing independence fail.

In drawing links between the work of well-known decolonization theorists from around the world and from different historical periods, including the conflict in West Papua, I highlight elements of the Papuan struggle that have international resonances. Such connections have not previously been made. Importantly, they show that although the West Papuan occupation has its own unique dynamics, it is not an isolated case: there are lessons West Papuans can learn from other indigenous peoples' quests for sovereignty and wisdom that other struggles can glean from West Papuans.

Observers frequently describe the pursuit of decolonization in West Papua as hopelessly mired in disunity (McGibbon 2006; Radio New Zealand International 2014; Stott 2011). Here, I present a counter thesis—that West Papuans thrive on the power of hope represented by the Morning Star, and as a result, their decolonization movement is progressing. As the star whose transit tracking was a key reason one of colonial Europe's most significant voyagers, Captain James Cook, set sail into the Pacific, the Morning Star is also the celestial promise that motivates West Papuans as they herald its setting and work toward the dawn of their decolonization. There is no denying that West Papuans are in a position of comparative disadvantage to their powerful occupier, Indonesia. This ethnography of West Papuan decolonization politics demonstrates, however, that West Papuans remain undeterred by the disparity. Instead, they are connected and connecting in increasingly powerful ways, and even their discord has at significant moments manifested, contrary to received wisdom, as a source of strength in the movement. The light of the metaphorical Morning Star—the harbinger of decolonization—is clarifying West Papuans' visions for their future, strengthening their international alignments, forging articulations between diaspora groups, and sharpening West Papuans' strategic insights.

West Papua, a Colony

It is a fundamental premise of this book that West Papua is an Indonesian colony and that its struggle for self-determination is a decolonization struggle. Some will contend that under the international legal doctrine of *uti possidetis juris,* in which the prescribed boundaries of a decolonized territory must match those of the former colony, the territory of West Papua rightfully belongs to Indonesia. This argument depends on the logic that because West Papua and Indonesia were both Dutch colonies, West Papua should have become part of Indonesia when the latter won its independence in 1949 (see Robinson 2010, 171; Saltford 2003, 8). However, as lawyer Jennifer Robinson maintains, this argument obfuscates the debate. The real issue was

> the identification of the pertinent unit of self-determination: was it the entire colony of the Dutch East Indies, including West New Guinea [West Papua]? Or did subsequent events and the practice of the international community with respect to the particular situation existing in West New Guinea recognise West New Guinea as the pertinent unit for self-determination?[2] Arguably, the latter is true: [by acknowledging the need for the 1969 referendum in the first place,] the international community had recognised West New Guinea as the pertinent unit of self-determination. (Robinson 2009, n.p.)

In any case, international relations scholar Akihisa Matsuno challenges the legitimacy of the principle of *uti possidetis juris* in general by citing the example of the January 2011 referendum that foregrounded the creation of the independent state of South Sudan. Noting the similarities to Indonesia's claim on West Papua, Matsuno writes: "There were significant ethnic, linguistic, religious and social differences between North and South [Sudan], and in fact the [previous colonial power until 1956, the] British[,] ruled them as separate entities. The history of Sudan seems to suggest that lack or low level of integration, natural or historical, between areas ruled by the same colonial power can be a reason for the establishing [of] a separate state. This means that colonial boundaries are not as absolute as usually assumed" (2011, 4).

Historian Tracey Banivanua Mar identified West Papua as an archetypal settler colony, invaded by Indonesia in 1963 and subsequently subjected to "the kind of determined policies of transmigration, assimilation, and sustained physical and administrative violence against indigenous Papuans that are common to settler-colonialism" (2008, 584).[3] Haunani Kay Trask described settler colonialism as a concatenation of "genocide, land dispossession, language extinction, family disintegration, [and] cultural exploitation" (1993, 31), all of which, there is evidence to suggest, are present in West Papua. The "obliteration rather than the incorporation of indigenous peoples" is one of settler colonialism's objectives (Trask 1993, 33). This was made strikingly clear in West Papua by the Indonesian general Ali Murtopo, who told a group of West Papuans in 1969 that Indonesia was interested not in West Papuans but only in their land: if they wanted a country of their own, they should locate another Pacific island or ask the Americans to find them a home on the moon (Budiardjo and Liem 1983, 32). In situations of settler colonialism, historian Patrick Wolfe (2006) writes, "Invasion is a structure not an event....To get in the way, all the native has to do is stay at home" (388). This, West Papuans have discovered, is painfully true.

The late West Papuan scholar and diplomat Otto Ondawame also took care to demonstrate that West Papua is not just a victim of neocolonialism but a colony in the conventional sense. He argued: "In the view of the people of West Papua, the current Indonesian political domination is nothing other than traditional colonialism. Geographically, West Papua is located 'overseas,' separated by the 'blue waters' of the Arafura Sea and the Indian Ocean; militarily, West Papua was forcibly annexed by a foreign power, during the brief war of 1962 [when Indonesia invaded West Papua]; and the level of oppression, exploitation and genocide that has been carried out in the territory over the last three decades is further justification for this conclusion" (Ondawame 2010, 5).

Political scientist Stephanie Lawson argues that the world tends to perceive colonial predation as a predominately European phenomenon. This prevents the expansionist actions of non-European actors from being appropriately countered by governing bodies such as the United Nations (Lawson 2017, 151) and permits countries such as Indonesia to engage in colonialism by using, unquestioned, the "soothing rhetoric of development, rehabilitation, stability and security" (Ondawame 2010, 5). Ondawame was adamant that the ongoing conflict between West Papuans and Indonesians for sovereignty in the territory will not dissipate if the prointegrationist, developmentalist solutions proffered in such rhetoric are the only ones advanced in the face of Indonesian colonial hegemony. Instead, "the problem must be seen in a political context and addressed from a West Papuan perspective. It must be analysed in terms of traditional colonialism, not neo-colonialism" (Ondawame 2010, 7). West Papuans "did not politicize their existence[:] that began at the moment of colonization," to use Trask's (1993, 55) words. They do, however, insist on its politicization being acknowledged as front and center in any conflict resolution attempts.

A History of Unity

West Papua's colonial history has been told many times by outsiders who have painted the decolonization movement as a chorus of inharmonious aspirations and demands. Observers variously name ethnic divisions, a lack of leadership, political factionalism, and ideological clashes within the decolonization movement as reasons why West Papuans have not yet achieved independence (see McGibbon 2006, 27–28; Stott 2011, 31).

While there are, without a doubt, many problems that beset West Papua's decolonization movement from without and within,[4] outsiders' concerted focus on West Papuan disunity prevents an accurate understanding of West Papuan decolonization history on three counts. First, as Maori decolonization scholar Linda Tuhiwai Smith observes, such a focus overlooks the conflict that takes place in every political system in the world, concentrating instead on instability as if it were a trait inherent to the Third World: "At the very heart of [Western ideas] of authenticity is a belief that indigenous cultures cannot... be complicated, internally diverse or contradictory [and still functional]. Only the West has that privilege" (1999, 74). Second, the attention paid to West Papuan disunity tends to skirt around the origin of some of the conflict present—the "divide and rule" tactics of Indonesia that form the "basic strategy for dealing with indigenous peoples" in West Papua (99). Such an emphasis feeds into a long-established colonial rhetoric that plays up political clashes as primordial ethnic feuds between indigenous peoples rather than as consequences of imperialism (Ngũgĩ 1981, 1). And third, it blinds observers to the considerable history of unity within the West Papuan movement, a history of West Papuans working in strategic synchronicity and complementarity. This leaves outsiders unable to imagine, and thus support, a future decolonized and functional West Papuan state.

To counter the colonialist narrative of West Papuan disunity and failed decolonization, West Papuans tell their history as a series of anticolonial triumphs interspersed with setbacks but linked by acts of West Papuan unity that, in combination, are gradually leading to the realization of decolonization. As an anticolonial act, this book adopts a West Papuan view of Papuan history, demonstrating its historical and political merit while tracing the hopeful trajectory of this history. Indonesia has attempted to present itself as West Papua's colonial liberator from the Dutch and anticolonial champion in subsequent decades, accusing outsiders who express concern about human rights abuses in West Papua of harboring neocolonial designs. But as the following brief account of West Papuan history will show (and here I borrow

Frantz Fanon's words), West Papuans "allow nobody to come forward as their 'liberator.' They prove themselves to be jealous of their achievements and take care not to place their future, their destiny, and the fate of their homeland into the hands of [Indonesians or others]" (1963, 51–52; on this, see also Pouwer 1999, 163). "No matter the praises sung by the colonizer" about its own efforts to assist the people it is colonizing, writes Trask, "for peoples who suffer the yoke of imperialism[,] it is a total system of foreign power where another culture, people and way of life penetrate, transform, and come to define the colonized society. The results are always destructive" (1993, 52).

The following potted history of the decolonization movement shows how Indonesia seeks to demonstrate that West Papuans depend on the Indonesian state for survival, as it responds to each West Papuan step toward decolonization by placing new obstacles in the way. On occasion, obstacles also materialize as a result of West Papuan internal disunity. Instead of demoralizing West Papuan nationalists, however, these setbacks have often acted as spurs for the decolonization movement, inspiring novel acts of bravery and prompting new partnerships between West Papuans and the international community.

An Overview of West Papuan Decolonization

1961: THE MORNING STAR FLIES (TRIUMPH); 1962: THE NEW YORK AGREEMENT (SETBACK)

This overview begins on December 1, 1961, a day marking the first significant occasion of a nationally oriented West Papuan unity. This date, some have claimed, represents West Papuan independence from the Dutch and the establishment of West Papuan sovereignty (see Webster 2001–2002, 507). While, in fact, West Papuans did not become legally independent on that date, a New Guinea Council with a majority of West Papuan members had been formed in October of that year, and on December 1 the council subsequently celebrated the adoption of national unifying symbols, including the Morning Star flag, a national anthem, and the name of the territory, West Papua (King 2004, 49). For this reason many West Papuans still celebrate December 1 annually as a commemorative day of West Papuan national unity and identity.

But the optimism engendered by the events on that date waned when a deal between the United States, the Netherlands, and Indonesia, known as the New York Agreement, was signed on August 15 the following year. The United States, fearing Indonesia's Communist leanings, undertook to ensure that Indonesia's pursuit of West Papua's coveted territory would not give the Indonesian leader, President Sukarno, reason to forge closer relations with the Soviet Union. Without consulting West Papuans, the three powers agreed that, ostensibly, political power would be transferred from one "colonial power, the Dutch, to a new colonial power, Indonesia" (Ondawame 2010, 53). Thus, following a period of just under nine months' stewardship by the United Nations Temporary Executive Authority (UNTEA), West Papua became an Indonesian administered territory (Saltford 2003, 13). The New York Agreement specified that an act of self-determination would be granted to the West Papuan people some time prior to 1969. "The Agreement contained formulations that permitted the betrayal of this principle," however, stipulating that it be carried out "in accordance with international practice" but failing to detail what this might be (Budiardjo and Liem 1983, 21).

1965: THE BIRTH OF THE OPM (TRIUMPH); 1969: THE ACT OF FREE CHOICE (SETBACK)

Scholar of West Papua Robin Osborne states that the violence and harsh regime of the Indonesians from early on in West Papua "swelled the ranks of the resistance" (1985, 38). In defiance of the Indonesian military and administrative occupation, and also in response to then-Indonesian president Sukarno's declaration that he no longer intended to carry out an act of self-determination for the West Papuans, West Papuans began to stage large-scale rebellions against Indonesian authority (Elmslie 2002, 36). This resistance from the urban centers of Manokwari and Jayapura was formally organized in 1965, gaining momentum in 1968 when law student Jacob Prai set up a post in the jungle, giving birth to the movement that became known by West Papuans as the OPM (Organisasi Papua Merdeka, or Free Papua Movement). The OPM was and still is supported by a wide sector of the population in West Papua and attracted its early recruits, particularly around Jayapura, from Cenderawasih University (Elmslie 2002, 37). The OPM continues to be of considerable symbolic significance to West Papuans, even though its military strength is negligible. A common and celebrated saying among West Papuans is "We are all OPM" (Osborne 1985, 45; see also Blaskett 1993 for a discussion of the OPM's expansive popular support base). The OPM has given a unifying identity to diverse groups of Papuans throughout the West Papuan nation, despite the many internal divisions its structures of command have endured.

As negotiated in the 1962 New York Agreement, the United Nations was to supervise a West Papuan vote (the "Act of Free Choice") on independence by 1969, an agreement that Indonesian president Suharto had to comply with (contra to the wishes of his predecessor) in order to remain a member of the United Nations. Rather than utilizing universal suffrage, however, as was the internationally accepted practice, Indonesia argued that most West Papuans were too primitive to know how to vote in their own best interests (Blay 2007). Instead, 1,025 West Papuans were handpicked by Indonesians, then bribed and coerced into "voting" for integration with Indonesia under the threat of horrific violence (Budiardjo and Liem 1983, 30). West Papuans therefore refer to the Act of Free Choice as the "Act of No Choice." It is widely considered to be a sham, an illegitimate representation of the West Papuan people's political aspirations (Osborne 1985, 45–49; Saltford 2003, 146; Worth 2004). West Papuans' right to self-determination was undermined in the 1969 Act of Free Choice, and the pursuit of its fulfillment continues to drive West Papuan resistance to Indonesia today.

1971: INDEPENDENCE PROCLAMATION (TRIUMPH); 1976: LEADERSHIP SPLIT (SETBACK)

Ever optimistic, the OPM was not expecting defeat in the Act of Free Choice, according to OPM member Rex Rumakiek (Interview, 2010). The resultant disarray among the OPM in the act's aftermath, however, eventually gave way to unification and enhanced strategic planning within the organization when a West Papuan with military expertise, Seth Rumkorem, defected from the Indonesian army to restructure the OPM alongside Jacob Prai. The climax of this new partnership was an OPM declaration of West Papuan independence at the OPM base of Markas Victoria near the Papua New Guinea (PNG) border on July 1, 1971 (for more detail, see chapter 4).

The refreshed and unified OPM was to last only five years before a leadership rift in 1976 between Rumkorem and Prai resulted in the establishment of several OPM factions and the dispersal of OPM leaders, who relocated to other parts of Papua and overseas (Elmslie 2002, 38–48; see chapter 4).

1978: MAMBESAK (TRIUMPH); 1984: ARNOLD AP'S ASSASSINATION (SETBACK)

Physical resistance against Indonesia in West Papua has proved to be ever fraught, but cultural resistance has been an invaluable weapon. An important historical example of this is evident in the work of West Papuan anthropologist and musician Arnold Ap. From 1978, Ap traveled with his performance group Mambesak to collect and perform songs and dances from around West Papua as a method of strengthening pan-Papuan identity. Anthropologist Diana Glazebrook writes, "The bounded nature of the repertoire imagined a certain cultural congruity—an overarching cultural West Papuanness" (2008, 47). Through Mambesak, Ap and his colleague Sam Kapissa contributed to the establishment of a West Papuan consciousness that transcended regional differences. In an attempt to disrupt the powerful united cultural identity coalescing as a result of Mambesak, the Indonesian army assassinated Ap in 1984 (B. Anderson 2006, 178).

2000: THE MORNING STAR FLIES AGAIN (TRIUMPH); 2001: THEYS ELUAY'S ASSASSINATION (SETBACK)

In 1998 the Indonesian president, Suharto, was deposed. The euphoria spreading throughout Indonesia extended to West Papua (the period between

1998 and 2000 became known as the Papuan Spring; Chauvel 2006), as successive presidents B. J. Habibie and then Abdurrahman Wahid made special efforts to listen to West Papuan aspirations. Taking advantage of what they believed was a new dawn of Indonesian democratization, in 1999 a delegation of one hundred esteemed West Papuans, known as Team 100, traveled to meet President Habibie in Jakarta to demand independence. Habibie was shocked at the demand, but the fact that he received the West Papuan team at all showed that, at least temporarily, the political dynamics of the West Papua–Indonesia relationship were shifting (Chauvel 2006).

In 2000 Habibie's successor Wahid declared, in accordance with West Papuan wishes, that West Papua would no longer be known as Irian Jaya but as Papua, decreed that the Morning Star flag could be flown in the province, and contributed significant funds to support a West Papuan Kongres meeting, the outcome of which was a West Papuan political front momentarily united as never before under the Papua Presidium Council (PDP; Elmslie 2002, vi–xiii).

In October 2000, however, West Papuans were informed that their newfound "right" to fly the Morning Star flag had been rescinded by Indonesia's subsequent president, Megawati Sukarnoputri. Then, on November 10, 2001, the charismatic "Chief" Theys Eluay, who had been elected leader of the PDP at the Kongres Wahid had sponsored, was assassinated in Jayapura by Indonesian Special Forces. This turn of events forced the independence movement back underground and temporarily into disorder, weakening its public front.

2001: SPECIAL AUTONOMY LAW PASSED (TRIUMPH); 2006: SPECIAL AUTONOMY FAILS (SETBACK)

Not to be suppressed for long, in 2001 a group of West Papuan academics, politicians, and church leaders submitted an optimistic draft "Special Autonomy" bill to the Indonesian government, aimed at giving the West Papuan body politic wide-ranging political powers. The government passed the bill, albeit an extremely pared back version. Had the bill been sincerely implemented even in its restricted form, military analyst Clinton Fernandes writes, "it would have gone a long way towards rebuilding trust between Jakarta" and West Papuans (2006, 101). Papuans would have had representation and considerable political power in an all-Papuan upper house, control over all administrative divisions of West Papua, jurisdiction over in-migration, health and education benefits, and a greater share of resource revenue (Fernandes 2006, 101–102).

But the Indonesian government has not taken the Special Autonomy Law seriously. Never properly implemented, and at times blatantly contravened, it is considered a monumental failure by West Papuans. In 2003 the Indonesian government seriously undermined the Special Autonomy Law by illegally dividing West Papua into the two provinces of Papua and Papua Barat (a territory-splitting process known as *pemekaran*). *Pemekaran*, historian Richard Chauvel points out, provides administrative opportunities and jobs for migrants and military personnel (2004, 4) and as such is an attempt to "break the symbolic nexus between the name Papua... and Papuan nationalism" (2008, n.p.). What few development opportunities Special Autonomy has delivered in West Papua rarely benefit indigenous West Papuans. This brings to mind the following observation by Albert Memmi: "It is... a fact that the institutions of the colony do not operate directly for [the colonized]. The educational system is directed to him only haphazardly. The roads are open to him only because they are not pure offerings" (1965, 137). Equally, in Mohawk (Native American) educator and activist Taiaiake Alfred's words, to "the extent that self-government, land claims, and economic development agreements have been successfully negotiated and implemented, there is no evidence that they have done anything to make but a very small minority of our people happier and healthier" (2005, 30). In Jayapura in 2006, West Papuans took to the streets to protest the law's spectacular failure, presenting a coffin marked "Special Autonomy" to the local government.

2014: FORMATION OF THE UNITED LIBERATION MOVEMENT FOR WEST PAPUA (TRIUMPH)

Following the failure of Special Autonomy, West Papuan political leaders have been involved in organizing various umbrella groups and interim governments to represent the interests of West Papuans seeking independence. Three of the most important of these groups, the West Papua National Coalition for Liberation (WPNCL), the Federal Republic of West Papua, and the West Papua National Parliament, joined forces in 2014 to form the United Liberation Movement for West Papua (ULMWP). The ULMWP is recognized in the region and around the world as West Papua's most representative and unified political movement to date, and it seeks a referendum on West Papuan independence and a revisiting of the 1969 Act of Free Choice by the United Nations. In recognition of the legitimacy the ULMWP enjoys within West Papua, in 2015 the Melanesian region's intergovernmental organization, the Melanesian Spearhead Group (MSG), granted observer status to the ULMWP, and West Papuans attracted support for their cause from a record seven Pacific island countries at the 2016 United Nations General Assembly meeting.

This short history of West Papuan resistance to Indonesian occupation has demonstrated that West Papuans are leading their own decolonization. Decolonization is a process rather than an event, dawning because of West Papuan determination regardless of the imminence, or otherwise, of a definitive "act" of self-determination such as a referendum. As shown, each time Indonesia attempts to interrupt West Papuans' decolonizing progress,

West Papuans reunite and persevere. This historical account I have presented intentionally culminates in West Papuans' latest political triumph—the formation of the widely supported ULMWP. Of course, Indonesia is working to discredit the ULMWP in the eyes of the international community, but their efforts so far have not diminished the efficacy of the ULWMP, as will be seen in later chapters. Finishing this section with an example of West Papuan agency and strength rather than Indonesian intervention underscores how West Papuans view their history and future: as strong, hopeful, and forged in unity.

Theorizing Unity

I have long been bothered by the essentialism and injustice of claims that West Papuans' unfinished decolonization is the result, at least in part, of innate Melanesian social and cultural disunity (see McGibbon 2006, 27–28; Sidik 2018; Stott 2011, 8). Apart from their racialist overtones, such claims underplay the enormous power differential between West Papua and Indonesia, the latter of which is able to incite disunity in the former, according to many Papuans, through intimidation and other "divide and rule" tactics (see Elmslie, Webb-Gannon, and King 2011) that have little to do with inherent cultural dysfunction. Fanon described the sorts of internecine clashes that capture the attention of many observers of colonialism as "colonized subject[s] releas[ing their] muscular tension . . . through very real collective self-destruction (1963, 17). "Such behaviour," Fanon contends, "represents [to observers] a death wish in the face of danger, a suicidal conduct which reinforces the colonist's existence and domination and reassures him that such men are not rational" (1963, 17–18), perpetuating culturalist stereotypes.

As in many political movements, there exist structural, political, and personal factors that divide West Papuans, including ideology, class, generational belonging, place of origin, and religion. But in West Papua, as this book will show, these factors have far less impact on the cohesiveness of the movement than does Indonesian colonialism, which, as Fanon observed, "undertakes to break [the] will to unify by taking advantage of every weak link in the movement" (1963, 107; see also Memmi 1965, 115). As a result, West Papuans attempt to fortify their weakest links by strengthening the ways in which unity works in their movement. The concept of unity has distinctive cultural, cosmological, and pragmatic significance to West Papuans as Melanesian peoples. Appreciating and striving toward what many West Papuans see as a "Melanesian" type of unity helps them ride out the bumps and even take advantage of the opportunities that arise during periods of disunity. From a pragmatic point of view, Papua New Guinean political leader John Tekwie (who also claims West Papuan descent) speaks of unity among West Papuans thus:

> Of course technically, there is never unity in a real democracy due to the principle of freedom of speech, freedom of association and freedom of religion, being the three most guarded universal pillars of governance in democratic systems of governments all over the world. However, the unity we speak of is based on collective agreement and undertaking of groups, tribes, clans and solidarity NGOs. Until we reach full independence, our humble principle should be to work with all pro-independence groups on the basis of respect and understanding. Rubbishing one and pitting one against another only opens doors for the enemy to launch his divide and rule strategy. (Pers. comm., 2010)

A key reason West Papuans value the idea of unity relates to the Melanesian region's extreme ethnolinguistic diversity. Melanesia is the "most linguistically complex and diverse region on earth" (Moore 2003, 29). This in itself is a unifier for the region, according to scholars of Melanesian history and culture. Historian Clive Moore writes that "although the [New Guinea] region's linguistic complexity is awesome... New Guinea and adjacent islands have seen constant changes over tens of thousands of years as different language groups replaced each other, intermingled, or engaged in regular contact, and because of this, Melanesia's small-scale societies possessed cultural mechanisms that enabled them to cope with change and diversity" (2003, 41).

The late Pacific scholar Epeli Hau'ofa points to the interlocking systems of exchange and travel that unite Melanesia: "Melanesia is supposedly the most fragmented world of all: tiny communities isolated by terrain and at least one thousand languages. The truth is that large regions of Melanesia were integrated by trading and cultural exchange systems that were even more complex than those of Polynesia and Micronesia" (2008, 33). The Summer Institute of Linguistics Ethnologue website lists a remarkable 276 languages for "Indonesia (Papua)" and provides an inventory of the cultural groups and areas in which these languages are spoken (Lewis 2009). While political wisdom might suggest that this extreme cultural and linguistic heterogeneity could lead to conflict between groups in West Papua, the late New Caledonian independence leader Jean-Marie Tjibaou has suggested instead that peoples of the Pacific, with their spectacular diversity, are "condemned to solidarity with each other" (2005, 105). And Papua New Guinean intellectual Bernard Narokobi has commented: "It is the simplistic imperialist who seeks uniformity as a technique to command obedience while portraying Papua New Guinea [or, in the context of this book, West Papua] as a [place] of division, of disunity, of [hundreds of] languages and thousands of cultures. More and more as I travel throughout these rich and beautiful lands of ours... I am convinced Melanesians are guided by a common cultural and spiritual unity. Though diverse in many cultural practices, including languages, still we are united, and are different from Asians or Europeans" (1983, 7).

The significant influence of Christianity in Melanesia, with its valorization of unity, may also have helped situate unity as a key West Papuan value. Anthropologists and historians have noted Christianity's role in unifying Melanesians by reducing internecine warfare in some areas (see, for example, Rodman and Cooper 1979). Historian Bronwen Douglas argues that it is important not to "underrate the ideological importance of Christianity in nation making in Melanesia" (2002, 8). It is "arguably the key national symbol in these states," despite the fact that "anthropology's influential literatures on the 'politics of tradition' or nation making often privileged custom over Christianity, presumably on the grounds of authenticity" (Douglas 2007, 161).

The concept of the "Melanesian way" (which, among other ideas, promotes freedom for West Papua) was popularized after PNG's independence by Bernard Narokobi and ultimately hinges on an emphasis of Melanesian unity (Otto 1997, 33). Narokobi defines the Melanesian way as a cohesive "total cosmic vision of life" (Narokobi et al. 1980, 20). Jean-Marie Tjibaou also articulated a unifying Melanesian way, particularly in relation to understanding the Melanesian person in society:

> Melanesians . . . are never . . . I am never *I. I* is linked to the individual. I am always someone *by reference to.* By reference to my fathers, by reference to my uncles. . . . That is important. That is important because the relationship which exists at the level of the individual person exists also in society. People exist only *by reference to.* Always. In that context, I would say that the successful man is the one who tends the connections on each side well. With the fathers and with the uncles. The maternal uncles and the mothers. (2005, 79; italics in original)

The Melanesian way is a holistic approach to life (Otto 1997, 46) rather than any set of specific customs. Narokobi holds that "we are a united people because of our common vision" (Narokobi et al. 1980, 16). According to anthropologist Ton Otto, "Diversity is only the surface phenomenon of a deeper underlying unity" in Melanesia (1997, 46).

Unity is central to the idea of the "Melanesian solidarity" that has frequently been invoked by West Papuans to engender support in the region for their independence and played out formally in the creation of cultural, economic, political, and religious institutions and affiliations. For example, the PNG political organization Melsol, formed in 1985, has focused on "agitat[ing] on [the University of Papua New Guinea] campus for solidarity with the struggles of the Melanesian people in Kanaky and West Papua and liberation struggles [elsewhere] in the Pacific as well as for social justice in PNG" (Dixon 1996). And Melanesian solidarity was behind the 1986 foundation of the MSG, a "sub-regional political and economic alliance" (Pacific Institute of Public Policy 2008) comprising PNG, the Solomon Islands, Fiji, Vanuatu, and New Caledonia's Front de Liberation Nationale Kanak et Socialiste (FLNKS; with Indonesia being granted associate membership status and West Papua, observer status, in 2015). The MSG was formed, initially, to lobby for New Caledonia's independence.

Notably, none of these Melanesian ways of valuing unity—as an indigenous, Christian, strategic, and decolonizing force—resembles the emphasis placed on unity by the Indonesian state. While "unity in diversity" is Indonesia's national motto, cultural and political diversity is permitted only when tightly monitored by the Indonesian state. Unity implies forced political affiliation with the state rather than a loose association between nations within the state. Alfred captures the paradox of Indonesia's glorification of unity, even though he is writing about postcoloniality in North America: "[Such an approach to the concept is] rooted in a simplistic liberal ideology that has as one of its core premises that unity requires homogeneity: we can all get along only if we are all made to be the same. Hence, the rejection of pluralistic notions of relationship" (2005, 111–112).

In contrast to forced Indonesian unity, an indigenous cosmology unites indigenous West Papuans. Australian Aboriginal academic Mick Dodson writes that indigenous peoples everywhere "are united by common territories, cultures, traditions, histories, languages, institutions and beliefs. We share a sense of kinship and identity, a consciousness as distinct peoples and a political will to exist as distinct peoples" (quoted in Tuhiwai Smith 1999, 115). West Papuans are also united in their understanding that a loose unity of sorts, but no more, is strategically important for their struggle. In Cabral's words, "Unity is [a] means, not an end... and as with all means a little goes a long way.... A certain degree of unity is enough" (1979, 31).

Because of the culturally specific ways in which West Papuans value unity, there is room for disunity when it takes the form of diversity and respectful disagreement. This book will demonstrate that when differences are given room to breathe in the struggle—put to work in diverse ways for the same goal—disunity can lead to new unities. This concept of "extended unities," according to West Papua analyst Nonie Sharp, or of "diversities-in-unity," "is antithetical to the concept of 'a homogeneous cultural entity'" and allows "culturally diverse communities [to] com[e] into wider association" (1994, 43).

Argument and Overview

For more than five decades, West Papuans have struggled to find a way through the long night of Indonesian colonization. While commentators on the fight for decolonization have focused on the lack of unity among West Papuan leaders of the movement, few have recognized that its internal contentious politics, marked with the peaks and troughs of unity and disunity, have propelled the effort forward against overwhelming odds. Contrary to received wisdom, this book argues that what holds West Papuans together is greater than what divides them. It also demonstrates, counterintuitively, that the issues and matters that have proven divisive for West Papuans have, at key moments, buttressed the movement. Over the past five years, defying all expectations, the issue of decolonization in West Papua has gained unprecedented global attention. Currently, West Papuan leaders are more effectively organized than at any previous time. The Morning Star, the supreme symbol of freedom to West Papuans, glimmers on the horizon, heralding, West Papuans hope, the imminent arrival of peace and justice in their land.

This book takes West Papua's Morning Star as its organizing metaphor and an analogy for the decolonization movement itself. At the center of the star is the unifying goal of the decolonization of West Papua, which, West Papuans say, binds them together spiritually and politically. The points of the star represent five key issues that currently occupy West Papuans in their pursuit of decolonization. Each chapter works through one of these issues, showing how increased unity on particular issues—with the lessons learned from moments of disunity—are leading West Papuans ever closer to decolonization, just as dawn approaches when the Morning Star appears. The five points include the following: (1) cherishing a common understanding of what the decolonization of West Papua means; (2) developing a vision for a decolonized West Papua; (3) performing West Papuan culture at home and in diaspora, thus enacting solidarity and resistance; (4) creating new and effective political decolonization strategies; and (5) shoring up solidarity with black and indigenous peoples in the Pacific and beyond.

Each star point tapers from a wide base (West Papuans' majority consensus views) to a sharp tip (dissenting perspectives). Most of the points produce difference—even disunity—yet they unite, in toto, to form the Morning Star pentagram, a figure of symmetry and illumination. Considering each of the five issues in turn, the book seeks a nuanced understanding of the cultural and political dynamics of unity and disunity that have forged West Papuans' path from the dimness of Indonesian occupation to the radiance of decolonization that emanates from the Morning Star as it hovers on the horizon of change. In so doing, it asks three broad questions: (1) What effect has the lack of unity had on the struggle for decolonization in West Papua? (2) How important is unity to the ongoing struggle? and (3) How does West Papua's struggle fit within current discussions of decolonization and nation building more widely?

Chapter 1 explores the West Papuan vision of *merdeka,* or a peaceful, just, and necessarily politically independent Papua, which is perhaps the most powerful force unifying indigenous West Papuans. It explores the origins of this suprauniting vision, providing examples of how *merdeka* is envisaged by West Papuans as the best outcome of their struggle for decolonization. It critiques the contested meanings of the term among West Papuans and foreigners but demonstrates that considerable unity exists among West Papuan leaders regarding its constituent parts, as well as in the belief that *merdeka* cannot prevail in Papua without political independence from Indonesia. Holding fast to this common goal has sustained West Papuans through the darkest nights of their dispossession.

Chapter 2 examines West Papuan perceptions of a genocide campaign enacted against them. Without the dawn of decolonization, Papuans believe, the shadow of oppression that currently shrouds the occupation will allow Indonesia to render the Papuan people absolutely powerless—an abject minority. It also explores the foundations of their unswerving confidence in ultimately achieving independence. Looking at how fears and hopes for the future create divisions and alliances within the West Papuan leadership, this chapter assesses the consensus surrounding various proposals offered by Papuan leaders for postcolonial governance.

Chapter 3 considers how the expression of "West Papuan-ness" has been critical to establishing indigenous pride in place and culture, which has deeply involved those in dispersal. Through the expression of culture, dissent is temporarily overcome—that is, between those "inside" and those who have left West Papua, as well as among diaspora groups themselves. Amid fear that their distinctive cultures are being annihilated, this chapter demonstrates how West Papuans wield the performance of culture as a "weapon" to counter cultural genocide and how culture functions as a point of indigenous articulation between West Papuans at home and abroad.

Chapter 4 analyzes West Papua's primary resistance strategies since 1962 from the perspectives of three generations of decolonization leaders. Broadly, these include polycentric networks of guerrilla warfare, peaceful dialogue, capacity building through the Special Autonomy Law, and international advocacy for a referendum. The chapter identifies major factions formed within the struggle and considers opportunities afforded them under conditions of globalization. It assesses the growing strategic consensus in the movement and argues that factionalism and generational change have led to the broadening of the battleground from West Papua into the Pacific and beyond. With increased unity, this expanded scope for action signals positive change.

With the indigenous turn in global politics, Melanesian and Pacific regionalisms are experiencing a renaissance, articulating with, in particular, a resurgence of global black power campaigns such as Black Lives Matter. West Papuan decolonization, chapter 5 argues, is at the heart of these Pacific movements, providing the focal point for what some scholars now refer to as the "Black Pacific." Through its black and indigenous alignments in the Pacific and elsewhere, West Papua is also making waves at the United Nations. Connected like never before, West Papuans are more united than ever. This chapter examines the impact of their engagement with revivalist black power politics and the "indigenous moment" on unification within their decolonization movement.

The book concludes by arguing that, globally, politics are unpredictable, as East Timor's unexpected independence from Indonesia in 2002 demonstrated. As a result, West Papuan political leaders, no matter how beleaguered, are ever hopeful. And if independence and more comprehensive decolonization do lie ahead, West Papuans are ready to take on the challenge. The conclusion also discusses in detail the significance of West Papuan decolonization efforts to follow a Melanesian way, a flexible ideology that has guided in various ways the preceding decolonization struggles in the region, as well as the ongoing decolonization movement in New Caledonia. Finally, it raises questions to be taken up in further research, including whether a postcolonial West Papua might become a "failed state" and what impact continuing West Papuan colonization might have on the region.

More than seventy West Papuan decolonization leaders in West Papua, PNG, Australia, Vanuatu, the Netherlands, Sweden, and the United Kingdom took part in interviews that informed this book, entrusting me with their stories on the premise that I would provide an academic platform for amplification. As a non-indigenous researcher attempting to work in solidarity with indigenous West Papuans, it is my intention that this book contribute to informing those who are still unaware of an almost forgotten people's quest for sovereignty. I hope it will relieve some of the burden that currently falls on the shoulders of West Papuans, who fight to near exhaustion in order to create awareness of their struggle. Another aim of the book is for West Papuans to learn, some perhaps for the first time, about other decolonization initiatives being led by other West Papuans in diverse parts of the world. As a decolonization and an academic undertaking, this book is situated, to borrow a phrase from Nicholas Thomas, "between [a] kind of public anger and a cooler scholarly project, the continuing reinterpretation of colonial histories and representations" (1994, 2). Albert Memmi recognized "what help to fighting [people] the simple, ordered description of their misery and humiliation could be...how explosive the objective revelation to the colonized and the colonizer of an essentially explosive condition could be" (1965, x). It is my hope that this "simple, ordered description" of West Papuans' struggle and unflagging agency contributes to dissolving the injustices they continue to suffer.

1

WISH UPON A STAR

Merdeka *as West Papuans' Decolonization Hope*

"Papua!" shouts the man dressed in a *koteka* (traditional penis gourd), standing on a remote, misty mountaintop in West Papua's highlands. *"Merdeka!"* call the group of Papuan freedom fighters in enthusiastic unison as they—old and young—stand gathered around him. The repeated call and response of "Papua, *merdeka*" builds in a rousing rhythmic chant.

This powerful scene of West Papuan solidarity and determination of spirit concludes UK filmmaker Dominic Brown's documentary on the independence movement in West Papua, *Forgotten Bird of Paradise* (2009). The Papuan resistance fighters he had embarked on a difficult trek to meet, resplendent in beads and pig tusk necklaces, army camouflage, and modern accessories, including mirrored sunglasses, had been forced to flee their villages by Indonesian armed forces. In hiding, they worked on strategies for achieving independence, practiced combat drills, recited with passion their allegiance to an anticipated independent West Papuan state, and participated in elaborate ceremonies in which the Morning Star flag was raised high (Brown 2009).

Several hundred kilometers from this scene, in West Papua's largest city, Jayapura, footage bearing witness to thousands of urban West Papuans taking to the streets in June 2010 was recorded anonymously and uploaded to YouTube (Westpapuambaham 2010). The leader of the protest continuously booms "Papua!" through a distorting megaphone; the charging crowds, painted in the red, blue, and white of the West Papuan Morning Star flag and wearing feathers and traditional jewelry, shout back "*merdeka!*" This demonstration marked the lead-up to what at that time were the biggest popular protests in West Papua's history, calling for a referendum on West Papua's political status. And in 2017, the Vanuatu Free West Papua Association posted a video to YouTube showing diaspora West Papuan leaders and hundreds of Ni-Vanuatu and other Melanesian supporters proudly carrying the Morning Star flag and signs bearing the word *merdeka* through the streets of Port Vila, Vanuatu, amid shouts of "Free West Papua!" (West Papua Unification Vanuatu 2017).

The vision for "Papua *merdeka,*" or a decolonized West Papua, is perhaps the most powerful force unifying indigenous West Papuans, whether they live in rural locations, cities, or the diaspora (Golden 2000, 33). It is a vision powered by a West Papuan disposition of fierce hope. This chapter explores the origins of this supra-uniting goal and its roots of radical hope, showing how *merdeka* is envisaged by West Papuans as complete decolonization. It critiques the contested meanings of the term among foreigners but reveals considerable unity among West Papuan leaders regarding its components, as well as in the near-universal belief that *merdeka* cannot prevail in Papua without political independence from Indonesia. Holding fast to this common ambition has sustained West Papuans through the duration of their dispossession.

Merdeka: *The Etymology and History of the Term*

The Malay word *merdeka,* meaning "freedom," derives from a Portuguese version of the Dutch term *mardijker. Mardijker,* in turn, is a derivation of *maharddhika,* a Sanskrit word meaning "wealth, wisdom or competence" (Junker 1999, 126). The Sanskrit term was already in use in Javanese texts from the tenth century (Reid 1998, 143). *Mardijker* referred to former Spanish or Portuguese slaves from India, some of whom the Dutch brought to live in the Malay Archipelago (Ganap 2006, 4). It is from *mardijker* that the term *merdeka* acquired its association with freedom (Reid 1998, 143).

The word *merdeka* has a considerable history of political usage, internally uniting successive nationalist movements in the Malay Archipelago. The city-state that became modern-day Singapore was under British colonial rule from 1824. British Singapore capitulated to the Japanese during World War II, but the British resumed colonial administration in 1945. The administration was challenged in 1956 by a proindependence Singaporean, David Marshall, in what were known as the Merdeka Talks. A simultaneously circulating petition demanding independence and bearing the header "We want *merdeka* now!" was signed by 167,000 Singaporeans. The Merdeka

Talks paved the way for self-government in 1959 and political independence from Britain in 1963 (Singapore Press Holdings 2010).

In Malaysia, the concept of *merdeka* is of such significance that the country calls its national independence day Hari (day) Merdeka. August 31, 1957, marked the official independence of the Federation of Malaya from British colonial rule, which was announced at Stadium Merdeka, in Kuala Lumpur. The current composition of the state of Malaysia, however, was not formed at the point of independence from British colonialism. Rather, because of objections by Indonesia, which considered two of the Malayan states to be Indonesian, a United Nations organized referendum was held to determine the political will of the people in those territories. After the concerned populations voted for integration with the independent Malayan Federation, the Malayan Federation was renamed the Federation of Malaysia on September 16, 1963. Significantly, though, it is Merdeka Day, the day of political independence, rather than the day of federation, that is celebrated as Malaysia's national day (Hirschman 1979, 68; Sopiee 1973).

Historian Anthony Reid reviews the various meanings of *merdeka* throughout Indonesian history. *Merdeka* has been used to refer to an individual's legal status (slave or free), an old, wise person freed from work responsibilities, or a village exempt from tax (Reid 1998, 143). Among the Bugis people in the 1700s, *merdeka* referred to individual freedom and entrepreneurship. From the early twentieth century through the present time, Indonesians have used it to connote freedom from Dutch colonialism. *Merdeka* now holds explicit political connotations, while other Malay words are used for freedom more generally (*kebebasan*, for example; Reid 1998, 143).

From the 1920s onward, a number of newspapers, journals, and publishing houses in Indonesia adopted the word *merdeka* in their titles. *Merdeka* began to acquire a close association with a nationalist Indonesian identity. In Reid's words, from 1925 onward, "Nationalists linked the new word Indonesia to the old word *merdeka*, defining the latter above all as independence. The politically repressive policies pursued by colonial governments after 1926 tended to confirm the idea that this was the one freedom that had to be won before anything else could change" (1998, 155).

During Indonesia's political revolution from 1945 to 1949, *merdeka* was "not just a political program but a felt reality," and it "became the battlecry with which the citizenry was summoned to support the cause, the salute with which revolutionaries would greet each other, the cry of solidarity at every mass rally, and the signature at the end of every Republican document" (Reid 1998, 155). For Indonesian nationalists of the twentieth century, *merdeka* meant decolonization from the Dutch, including political independence.

The Free Aceh Movement, known locally as Gerakan Aceh Merdeka (GAM), was formed in 1976 under the leadership of Hassan di Tiro to pursue independence from Indonesia. The *merdeka* in GAM's name undoubtedly referred to political independence. The Acehnese people's staunch adherence to Islam conflicted with the "secular" ideology of the Indonesian state, and the state's resource exploitation of the rich province and widespread military violence further alienated the Acehnese from centralized Indonesian governance (Aspinall 2006, 149; Schulze 2003, 242). With the aid of Libyan government military training assistance, Malaysian and European amnesty arrangements, and financial contributions from the wealthy Acehnese diaspora, GAM survived a series of broken cease-fire and false-start peace agreements with the Indonesian government and became a force to be reckoned with (Schulze 2003).

International attention turned to Aceh following the devastation of the region in the December 2004 Indian Ocean tsunami. This attention facilitated the conditions for the brokering of the 2005 Helsinki Peace Agreement between the Acehnese leadership and the Indonesian government. Up until this point, GAM had been uncompromising in its insistence on political independence from Indonesia (Aspinall 2005). According to historian Kirsten Schulze, GAM's Acehnese nationalism had always focused on a distinct Acehnese identity that was anti-Javanese and anticolonial, the contention that Aceh had been an authentic nation-state for two centuries until colonized by the Dutch and then Indonesia, and the desire to take back the nation-state from Indonesia and administer it in line with the principles of Islamic statecraft (2003, 246–248). The 2005 peace deal, however, has given the province significant autonomy and GAM members a role in the provincial government, and this seems to have quelled Acehnese independence aspirations. Only time will tell how sustainable the autonomy agreement in Aceh is and whether calls for *merdeka* will reemerge, given that the long-sought-after goal of political independence has not yet been fulfilled.

In pivotal moments in each of the *merdeka* movements in Singapore, Malaysia, Indonesia, and Aceh, the concept of *merdeka* superseded its original, broader brushstroke connotations of freedom and assumed the weighted and particular meaning of political independence. In contrast to a handful of scholars who, for realpolitik reasons, argue either that West Papuans do not or should not insist on political independence when they call for *merdeka* (a subsequent part of this chapter engages with such views), this history demonstrates that in previous decolonization movements in the surrounding region, invocations to *merdeka* were appeals for independence. Why then, this chapter asks, would West Papuan conceptions of *merdeka* preclude the central meaning of the mantra?

Key Merdeka *Moments in West Papua*

West Papua's history of decolonization efforts can be set out in a series of what I identify here as "*merdeka* moments," significant milestones, declarations, and protests through which West Papuans have appealed to the concept of *merdeka* in their long fight for freedom. Missionary anthropologist F. C. Kamma identified West Papua's early religious-political movements, often described as cargo cults or millenarian movements, as the foundation of the territory's nationalism (1972, 185). This assertion is supported by a rich set of earlier literature describing Melanesian millenarian movements as "'proto-national' formations of a transitional kind" (Worsley 1957, 263) and as the "forerunners of Melanesian nationalism" (Guiart 1951). The Koreri millenarian movement of the 1930s and 1940s in Biak is arguably the first significant West Papuan "*merdeka* event," emerging out of the "ancient [Biak] legend which predicted that the Lord, Manseren Mangundi, would return one day to free [the West Papuan] people" (Osborne 1985, 10).

In 1939 a Biak woman by the name of Angganita Menufandu claimed to have received miraculous healing from Lord Manseren from a serious affliction. Following her rehabilitation, she became a prophet of Koreri, preaching that discipleship to Manseren involved active resistance to Dutch colonialism. She was subsequently arrested for leading related uprisings that involved the performance of traditional songs and dances.

Angganita's successor in the movement, Stephanus Simiopiaref, followed in her path, resisting Japanese occupation during World War II. He was subsequently killed (Osborne 1985, 12), but the anticolonial Koreri movement survived. Nonie Sharp describes Koreri as being "about beginnings, about genealogy, about endings in the sense of coming together in the process of becoming . . . and [about] people who are moving through a darkness toward the full light of the Sun" (1994, 23). Koreri brings Biak and other West Papuans together, as a people, in hope.

Several other *merdeka* moments in West Papua's colonial history compare in significance to the Koreri-inspired uprisings of Angganita Menufandu and Stephanus Simiopiaref. "The day the Morning Star flag flew for the first time . . . alongside the Dutch flag; and the day the new anthem Hai Tanahku Papua, was sung" (King 2004, 49)—December 1, 1961—was one of these. The formation of the Organisasi Papua Merdeka (OPM) in 1965 was another. Notably, the name of this first pan–West Papuan anticolonial organization included the term *merdeka,* indicating that along with many of the decolonizing populations of the Malay Archipelago, West Papuans, too, found the word and concept representative of their desire for political freedom. The July 1, 1971, *merdeka* moment when the OPM issued a *proklamasi kemerdekaan* (independence proclamation) from its headquarters at Markas Victoria along the West Papua–Papua New Guinea (PNG) border, declaring the land and people of West Papua "free and independent," was energizing for the decolonization movement. And, commencing at the beginning of this century, the so-called Papuan Spring triggered by the fall of Suharto generated a new optimism among the West Papuan population that *merdeka* was imminent. Although the events of the Papuan Spring did not result in the West Papuans' desired political independence—indeed, in the years following the spring, Indonesia intensified its oppression of West Papuans—they fueled the hope that change was possible in West Papua and provided a glimpse of what *merdeka* might entail.

That the yearning for *merdeka,* with its inherent implications of political independence, was in the hearts of many West Papuans was made abundantly clear to me when I visited the territory in 2008. All over West Papua, from the very elderly man who touched my elbow outside of the police station in Jayapura and whispered, eyes clouded by cataracts and tears, "Papua *merdeka*"; to my young female friend who, despite her fear of the Indonesian military, was desperate to connect me with active members of the independence movement; to the dreadlocked and imposingly built Papuan resistance army soldier who approached me at a festival in Wamena, stared meaningfully into my eyes, and declared, "Today it rains but tomorrow the sun will shine," the desire for *merdeka* was palpable.

Since 2010 a second "Papuan Spring" has gradually emerged. Thousands (estimates have ranged up to fifty thousand; Radio New Zealand International 2010) of West Papuans regularly protest across West Papua for a referendum on independence. The Papuan People's Consultative Assembly (MRP) convened in 2010 as part of the upsurge of *merdeka* sentiment in Jayapura, demanding a referendum "directed towards political independence" and "that the Government of the Republic of Indonesia recogni[ze] the restoration of the sovereignty of people of West Papua which was proclaimed on 1st December 1961" (Papuan People's Consultative Assembly and Indigenous People of Papua 2010). The United Liberation Movement for West Papua (ULMWP) was formed in 2015 from representatives of the three main independence-seeking bodies in West Papua and diaspora, attracting the backing of many countries within the African, Caribbean, and Pacific Group of States (ACP). And in what is possibly the West Papuans' boldest *merdeka* initiative to date, the ULMWP delivered to the United Nations Special Committee on Decolonization on September 27, 2017, a petition of approximately 1.8 million signatures gathered across West Papua (at great risk to those who signed) in support of an independence referendum.

Merdeka: *Peace, Justice, and Contested Meanings*

"Some have argued," writes Chauvel, "that merdeka, the slogan of [West Papua's] nationalist movement, means not just political independence but freedom, and freedom has been defined variously as freedom from poverty, ignorance, political repression and abuse of human rights" (2005, 4). While this might be true, Chauvel goes on to raise two questions that in his reckoning stem from this contention and that are unsettling from a West Papua decolonization perspective. The first is whether "the freedoms to which Papuans aspire could perhaps be achieved within the Indonesian state," and the second is "whether these freedoms would be realized even if Papuans succeeded in establishing an independent nation state" (Chauvel 2005, 4).

To attend to Chauvel's first question, an examination of history indicates that it is highly unlikely that "freedom from poverty, ignorance, political repression and abuse of human rights" for West Papuans could be achieved under Indonesian rule. It is clear from past and current accounts of West Papuans' treatment under Indonesian occupation that Indonesia has never had and currently does not have the political will or capacity to guarantee these freedoms for West Papuans. This is despite the latter's attempts at various times to work collaboratively with the Indonesian state—for example, by requesting dialogue with the Indonesian government and proposing what respected West Papuan leaders considered to be a workable Special Autonomy Law of 2001 (this was a very different version to what Indonesia eventually agreed to and bears almost no relation to the few pieces of legislation actually enacted; see chapter 4). In 2015 and 2016, under the presidency of Joko Widodo, who is nominally committed to a wide range of improvements for West Papua, the extent of police crackdowns on peaceful dissent has been unprecedented. More than 6,400 people were arrested for political activism, local journalists continued to face harassment from security forces, foreign journalists were denied entry to West Papua, and preventable disease and malnutrition had devastating effects throughout West Papua (International Coalition for Papua 2017, 1–2).

Chauvel's second question—whether some of the freedoms associated with *merdeka* "would be realized" even if Papuans do attain a sovereign state—skirts the point of self-determination—that is, that a people have a right to choose their own political future regardless of outsiders' conjecture about how that future might unfold. Self-determination is one of the fundamental universal human rights that has been denied West Papuans, the pursuit of which has driven their decolonization struggle since 1962. This second question is perhaps not even appropriate for a non–West Papuan to ask until West Papuans' right to self-determination has been implemented. Chauvel, and others who pose similar questions (see, for example, Aspinall 2006; McGibbon 2006; Stott 2011), is without a doubt concerned about facilitating "freedom from . . . abuse of human rights" in West Papua (2005, 4). But the primary struggle in West Papua is for decolonization, and the highest-order freedom and human right in such a struggle is that of self-determination. Non-Papuans' concerns about other freedoms and rights in West Papua can be assessed and addressed once the latter's right to self-determination has been granted.

The other freedoms mentioned by Chauvel (freedom from poverty, ignorance, and political repression) are secondary to self-determination in the decolonization struggle—not in importance, necessarily, but in order of goals to pursue. Speculating about whether West Papuans are capable of implementing a robust human rights framework prior to the implementation of their own right to self-determination is premature, while proposing a discourse of abstract freedoms to be sought within the context of prohibitive colonial conditions is facile (Lowe 2015). The first step to rectifying the abuse of West Papuans' human rights—and such rectification is one of the components of *merdeka* that Chauvel outlined above—would be, according to the West Papuans whose views I examine for this chapter, to facilitate a fair act of self-determination that would open up the possibility of West Papuan political independence.

Chauvel is not alone in his reticence to acknowledge independence as integral to West Papuan decolonization. In an article alleging that supporters of West Papua's decolonization movement are participating in "selective outrage," political scientist Edward Aspinall contends: "Even imagining that a peaceful act of self-determination was possible in the foreseeable future, there is no guarantee that peace would necessarily follow. Acts of self-determination can create new problems even while they solve other ones" (2006, 124). In a report for the Lowy Institute on "the pitfalls" the conflict in West Papua poses for the Australia-Indonesia relationship, Rod McGibbon writes: "A challenge to Indonesian authority [by the Australian government] in Papua would almost certainly expose the deep divisions within Papuan society, divisions that could erupt into open conflict that would be exceedingly difficult for any outside force to put a lid on. In fact the combination of conditions present in contemporary Papua including deep-seated social divisions, low levels of education and a rich natural resource base make Papua a prime candidate to become a conflict-ridden failed state if it were to attain independence" (2006, 112–113).

David Adam Stott's 2011 article "Would an Independent West Papua Be a Failing State?," although rather more circumspect in its conclusions, addresses a similar point to McGibbon. Referring to what he views as the "inherently unstable" basis of democracy in the Solomon Islands, in East Timor, and in PNG, Stott claims that "grafting liberal democratic political systems onto traditional authoritarian arrangements of hierarchy and leadership" does not work (2011, 7). This is a flawed reading of modern and traditional political systems in these three states, however. PNG, for example, boasts a constitution that was highly consultative in its drafting, and a variety of political traditions exist throughout Melanesia that are considerably less hierarchical than in other regions of the world (May 2004).

Of course, independence is always relative (Cabral 1979, 79) and cannot alone guarantee complete decolonization nor the realization of human rights in West Papua. Cognizant of this, many West Papuans are careful to describe *merdeka* as consisting of much more than independence—the latter is viewed as the initial enabler of an entire *merdeka* "complex." But many Papua observers, including those just cited, appear to agree that even this nuanced view of *merdeka* is too radical. There is a discernible sense, among many scholars of politics, of it being "vaguely embarrassing to talk about revolution" (Kohn and McBride 2011, 58), "that the central idea of liberation through collective self-determination has been pushed to the periphery in current discussions of democracy" (Kohn and McBride 2011, 58), that "in the modern era, gloom appears a more sophisticated stance than cheerfulness" (Eagleton 2015, 41), and indeed, that "the left... feels ill at ease before nationalism" (Memmi 1965, 29). The problem with this make-no-waves scholarly stance is that it contributes to colonial alienation. When applied to West Papua, it enables outsiders to deliberately disassociate various components of the indigenous West Papuan concept of *merdeka* from each other to work out, on West Papuans' behalf, which components West Papuans should sacrifice (see Ngũgĩ 1981, 28) in order to appease Indonesia.

The right to self-determination is spelled out in the United Nations General Assembly's 1960 Declaration on the Granting of Independence to Colonial Countries and Peoples Resolution 1514. It states that "the subjection of peoples to alien subjugation, domination and exploitation constitutes a denial of fundamental human rights, is contrary to the United Nations Charter, and is an impediment to the promotion of world peace and cooperation, and... steps should be taken to transfer, unconditionally, all powers to the trust and non-self-governing territories so that they might enjoy complete freedom and independence" (United Nations General Assembly 1960).

Additionally, the International Covenant on Civil and Political Rights (ICCPR; United Nations General Assembly 1966a) and the International Covenant on Economic, Social and Cultural Rights (ICESCR; United Nations General Assembly 1966b) both declare that "all peoples have the right of self-determination. By virtue of that right they may freely determine their political status and freely pursue their economic, social and cultural development." The International Court of Justice has found that the principle of self-determination takes precedence over "states' historical claims to territorial integrity" (Trask 1993, 39). It would appear, however, that in academic arguments such as the examples cited above, realpolitik concerns such as amicable diplomatic, security, or trade relationships with the Indonesian state (rather than with groups that currently make up Indonesia's body politic), or avoiding the prospect of a "failing state," take precedence, for some observers, over human rights concerns (King 2004, 141).

Regardless of what arguments against a *merdeka* inclusive of political independence analysts of the West Papuan *merdeka* movement put forward—arguments Taiaiake Alfred might call "hypocritical and pacifying moralities" (2005, 32)—it is clear from my research with West Papuan communities that the majority of West Papuans are in favor of independence.

International human rights lawyer Jennifer Robinson notes that even at the time the United Nations sanctioned the Act of Free Choice, "UN officials admitted in private that 95% of Papuans supported independence" and that the "process of consultation did not allow a genuinely free choice to be made" (2010, 173). That political independence cannot be separated from the goal of *merdeka* is one of the strongest views currently uniting West Papuans.

Scholars other than those discussed above have reflected on the meanings of *merdeka,* many drawing on its roots in West Papuan "millenarian" or "utopian" discourses, including Koreri. Anthropologist Danilyn Rutherford, for example, observed Koreri inspiration in the actions of a group that gathered on July 6, 1998, in downtown Biak around a Morning Star flag to demonstrate for a political referendum on West Papuan independence (1999, 42). When Indonesian troops opened fire on the demonstrators, killing and injuring many, the tragedy became known as the Biak Massacre. The leader of the flag raising, Filip Karma, had previously read out an "oath of allegiance" to the sovereign nation of West Papua. Appealing to "God, the Father, Son and Holy Ghost" (the three of whom together, according to Rutherford [1999, 45], constitute Manarmakeri in Koreri theology), Karma vowed not to leave the flag. He received gunshot wounds to his legs, however, and was forced to capitulate. In a similar fashion to the followers of Angganita Manufandu's Koreri movement, Karma's "disciples" at the flag raising in Biak spent the days before the massacre dancing around the Morning Star flag, singing and acting out traditional performances, praying regularly, and even "baptizing" the ground around the flag (Rutherford 1999, 56). When their actions failed to result in an independent, decolonized West Papua, some in Biak interpreted the delay as divinely orchestrated, suggesting that *merdeka* had merely been postponed so that "more people would hear about the cause" (Rutherford 1999, 56–57).

Anthropologist Eben Kirksey and J. A. D. Roemajauw, a member of the former West Papuan performance group Mambesak, cite correspondence with the late West Papuan activist Viktor Kaisiepo, who lived in exile in the Netherlands, when they define *merdeka* as "variously a desire for divine salvation, equitable development, environmental sustainability and political independence" (2010, 191). Anthropologist Brigham Golden's definition differs from that of Kirksey and Roemajauw, however, when he contends that *merdeka* is "supra-political in Papua, fundamentally transcend[ing] the political concept of 'independence'" more closely linked with "a liberation theology, an ideology of moral salvation in which a Christian desire for a world of human dignity and divine justice is finally manifest in Papua" (2000, 33).

Anthropologist Jaap Timmer argues that *merdeka* is located within Papuan "ontological ideas about sovereignty and dignity (harga diri)" and is "a response to decades-long denial of the people's competence in learning and performing in modern colonial and postcolonial contexts" (2005, 4).

Timmer concludes, however, that "the idea of having one's own state, right now and for all times, is seldom on the minds of most Papuans, as it is a construct far from the more intrusive largely individual and communal concern with sovereignty and harga diri" (4).[1] The data he provides to support this point appear to be drawn largely from his research with one particular people in West Papua, the Imyan, although his contention does highlight that the definitional delimitations of *merdeka* are far from clear-cut and that ideas of statehood and its importance may vary according to ethnic group and location (3–4). Nevertheless, political independence is still a popularly held goal within the *merdeka* vision shared across West Papua and its diaspora, as conceded by the geographically comprehensive research of the usually conservative International Crisis Group that concludes there is "widespread, straightforward and uncompromising support for independence at the village and provincial town level of Papuan society" (2001, 14).[2]

"Both the apparent contradictions of independence without *merdeka* and *merdeka* without independence are possible," contends Golden, and "Jakarta's goal should be the latter." He notes, however, that this would be a possibility only if Jakarta addresses the "*moral* concerns of Papua *merdeka*" (2000, 33; my emphasis). Given that human rights are both acutely moral and political and therefore West Papua has a moral right to political self-determination, there is no possibility of *merdeka* being realized without at least an act of self-determination occurring. It is difficult to imagine West Papuans accepting a Jakarta interpretation of *merdeka* that does not offer independence as an option.

By contrast, *merdeka,* as alluded to by the West Papuans I have interviewed, expresses metaphysical qualities that are inseparable from its material and political manifestations. *Merdeka* is a concept that implies unity—the unity of transcendental freedom and physical and political freedom on earth. It cannot support the dualism suggested in Timmer's and Golden's analyses. As anthropologist Stuart Kirsch argues, "The Christian association of *merdeka* with independence draws on the prevailing assumption that both self-determination and territorialized nations are manifestations of divine will" (2010, 14). However, that *merdeka* is not just a Christian-influenced ideal is evidenced by the political support it receives from Muslim Papuan leaders. For example, Thaha Al Hamid, the Muslim secretary-general of the independence organization known as the Papuan Presidium Council, openly demanded *merdeka* with independence at a protest on December 1, 2008, using a flier to call upon the international community to recognize "the existence of the West Papuan state and its sovereignty declared on December 1, 1961" (Unpublished data).

Merdeka in its fullness, as the amalgamation of what Kirksey, Roemajauw, Golden, Timmer, and Kirsch have set out, is very similar to the ways in which theorists and activists from around the world describe decolonization—"an ethical and political vision" (Alfred 2005, 20; italics removed) seeking, through praxis (Waziyatawin and Yellow Bird 2012, 2), a "restored spiritual foundation" (Alfred 2005, 22) from which to "revolt against the unequal distribution of power in the world" (Kohn and McBride 2011, 3). Decolonization is "the dream of self-rule" (Kohn and McBride 2011, 3) through which the previously colonized can set about revitalizing and restoring "societies drained of their essence, cultures trampled underfoot, institutions undermined, lands confiscated, religions smashed, magnificent artistic creations destroyed, [and] extraordinary possibilities wiped out" (Césaire 1972, 43). Aimé Césaire, the decolonization theorist from Martinique, was adamant, in his early years of activism, that decolonization required revolution—a clean-slate political beginning incorporating the best characteristics of precolonial society:

> For us, the problem is not to make a utopian and sterile attempt to repeat the past, but to go beyond. It is not a dead society that we want to revive. We leave that to those who go in for exoticism. Nor is it the present colonial society that we wish to prolong, the most putrid carrion that ever rotted under the sun. It is a new society that we must create, with the help of all our brother slaves, a society rich with all the productive power of modern times, warm with all the fraternity of olden days. (1972, 53)

Decolonization, from the perspectives of these thinkers, requires that a break be made with the occupying power so that what was once good in the colonized society and might be good once again can be determined, in unity, by the colonized population. Until West Papuans' right to self-determination has been fulfilled, decolonization, and therefore *merdeka*, will not be realized.

Merdeka: *West Papuan Aspirations*

Meanings of *merdeka* (decolonization) communicated to me by West Papuans resonate with many of the needs defined in political theorist John Burton's "human needs theory." Some "relate to growth and development," while others are as "obvious [as] biological needs of food and shelter" (Burton 1990, 36). The decolonization process is one of ensuring the fulfillment of various human needs; indeed, West Papuans would argue that decolonization itself, via a process of self-determination, is a human need (on this point in the Hawaiian context, see Trask 1993, 132). Burton writes that "human needs in individuals and identity groups who are engaged in ethnic and identity [and, I argue in this case, also decolonization] struggles are of this fundamental character... and will be pursued by all means available" (1990, 36). Further, he argues that the "needs [of which *merdeka* is composed]... are inherent drives for survival and development, including identity and recognition. It is not within the free decision making of the individual to trade them" (39–40).

Burton supports his theory, writing, "The issue whether behaviour is determined genetically, environmentally or both, is not a profitable one for us to engage in at this state of knowledge. The fact that there are behaviours that cannot be controlled to fit requirements of particular societies [for example, West Papuans' relentless struggle for self-determination despite Indonesia's insistence on its own current territorial integrity] is our concern, rather than the evolutionary explanation of this phenomenon" (1990, 37). Needs in the West Papuan context encompass West Papuans' need to exercise power and control over their lives through political and social planning; the need for justice—an end to impunity for those meting out violence, as well as recognition of West Papua's still unfulfilled right to self-determination; the need to survive and ensure the fulfillment of basic rights such as employment, health care, education, security, and freedom from violence and fear; and the need to protect the natural environment and resources as well as religious, cultural, and spiritual freedoms.

POLITICAL FREEDOM AND DIGNITY

The most popularly invoked dimension of *merdeka* is that previously discussed, political freedom, which West Papuans usually expressed in terms of political independence or sovereign statehood and linked to the concept of righting past political wrongs such as the Act of Free Choice. When the desire for independence was articulated explicitly by West Papuans, as it often was, it was frequently spoken of as nonnegotiable. For example, Jacob Prai, a founder of the OPM now exiled in Malmö, Sweden, told me of the time he was jailed in PNG and faced the choice of either amnesty in Sweden or repatriation to West Papua, the latter on the condition he would give up the struggle for independence. Prai responded: "It is better for me to die than go back and... [not] struggle" (Interview, 2008). Albert Memmi (1965) wrote something similar—under conditions of colonialism, eventually the choice is "either to revolt or to be calcified" (98). Prohibited from choosing the first (revolt) and unwilling to be consumed by "calcification," Prai took up activism in Sweden.

West Papuan activist in The Hague, Netherlands, and the son of Arnold Ap, Oridek Ap explained: "When I talk about *merdeka*, when most Papuans talk about *merdeka*, they mean independence. *Merdeka* is a word, an Indonesian word, but what we mean by *merdeka* is independence.... We want to have the opportunity to solve our own problems.... That is what we want, *merdeka*" (Interview, 2008). Benny Wenda, a West Papuan refugee (and leader of the ULMWP) from the highlands of Wamena, West Papua, and currently living in Oxford, England, agrees with Ap and denies assertions that the freedom Papuans want is primarily metaphysical or spiritual. To make his point, he refers to the Indonesian struggle for *merdeka* during the Dutch East Indies' decolonization process. "This is always my question," Wenda states. "If [Indonesians just] wanted freedom spiritually, why [did] they fight against the Dutch?" (Interview, 2008). The late Zachi Sawor, a West Papuan refugee who lived in Ede in the Netherlands, similarly explained that "*merdeka* is independence.... Independence is to raise everything yourself, like Australia and the Netherlands.... And, until now, Indonesia [is] the boss of the country, so the Papuans do nothing... there is no independence at all" (Interview, 2008). It is clear that *merdeka* is envisaged by many West Papuans as total, including political, decolonization. This is in contrast to those foreign interpretations that highlight only a few of the freedoms *merdeka* entails and that, by neglecting what West Papuans consider its foundation—political independence—provide academic legitimacy to Indonesian colonialism.

The right to self-determination is inherently important to West Papuans, not just because it is a first step in enabling the other benefits of *merdeka* but because it also represents West Papuan dignity and identity (which is Timmer's point earlier in this chapter). This is echoed in the words of the late Andy Ajamiseba, a former member of the Papuan band the Black Brothers who resided in Port Vila, Vanuatu. He was originally from the Wandamen region of West Papua and in his later years became a leader in the ULMWP. Speaking of the relationship between independence and Papuan identity and dignity, Ajamiseba told me: "The issue here is that [of] identification of ourselves, our identity is—we are not Indonesian. Maybe when we become independent, the situation may be [that] our economy is not as good as [it was] under Indonesia, we have to crawl out, but you know we want to be ourselves... I am a Papuan.... So, in all due respect to the Indonesians... we are two different people: we are not Indonesians; they are not Papuans" (Interview, 2008).

Of course, West Papuans are hopeful that their most basic human rights and needs will be met, but self-determination is of a higher ideological order. In Trask's view, "Ideologically, 'rights' talk is part of the larger, greatly obscured historical reality of... colonialism.... The language of 'civil rights' operates to legitimize [colonial] control" (1993, 112–113). As Ajamiseba points out, self-determination is about more than basic rights. It is about identity, the ability to determine the world in keeping with the parameters considered important to one's group or nation.

Self-determination is also about dignity, an assertion of common humanity with the colonizers and the power operators elsewhere in the world that perpetuate colonialism (Tuhiwai Smith 1999, 26). Fanon observed that in Africa, people "quickly realized that dignity and sovereignty were exact equivalents [and that] in fact a free people living in dignity is a sovereign people" (1963, 139), and he commented that independence brought to colonized peoples in Africa a "moral reparation [that] recognized their dignity" (40; on decolonization and dignity, see also Cabral 1979, 27). Native American decolonization scholars Waziyatawin and Michael Yellow Bird contend that decolonization "ultimately requires the overturning of the colonial structure. It is not about tweaking the existing colonial system to make it more Indigenous-friendly or a little less oppressive. The existing system is fundamentally and irreparably flawed" (2012, 4). Surface reforms in the colonial context—of which Special Autonomy might be considered one—are, to the mind of the colonized, "offered because they are useless to our survival as [indigenous people]" (Alfred 2005, 37). For decolonization to occur, a compromise, such as *merdeka* without independence, is not possible. To paraphrase Memmi, "The liquidation of colonization [through the phase of political independence] is nothing but a prelude to complete liberation, to self-recovery" (1965, 151), to *merdeka*.

MERDEKA AS SECURITY AND FUNDAMENTAL WELFARE

At the most basic level, *merdeka* is used as a term by West Papuans, at home and abroad, to indicate survival—the kind of survival indigenous peoples have been fighting for, according to Linda Tuhiwai Smith, for at least five hundred years, in the context of "the effects of a sustained war with the colonizers, from the devastation of diseases, from the dislocation from lands and territories, from the oppressions of living under unjust regimes; survival at a sheer basic physical level and as peoples with our own distinctive languages and cultures" (1999, 107). *Merdek*a as survival refers to a sense of physical security and to having access to the fundamentals of "the good" society, and Papuans in West Papua currently feel a lack of security. According to a customary leader of the Marind tribe who spoke to me in Merauke in 2008, people in Merauke are "scared to even talk about *merdeka*" because of the repercussions should the wrong person overhear (Interviewee C, 2008). Otto Ondawame similarly remarked, "If you live under [the] Indonesian colonial system... [you] cannot feel safe.... Many West Papuans believe that only with independence they can create peace in West Papua" (Interview, 2009). United States–based West Papuan refugee Herman Wainggai has emphasized that to counter the current lack of peace and security in West Papua, *merdeka* should be pursued peacefully and democratically: "We want to solve the problem in West Papua by peace—using peaceful means.... I always challenge [the] Indonesian government.... Arresting people, kidnapping people, killing people, raping people, that's not [the] best solution. You can't stop Papuan people from talking about *merdeka*" (Interview, 2009).

As a fundamental element of *merdeka,* security for West Papuans has been ever elusive under Indonesian occupation. Not surprisingly, this has fueled the desire for independence. Markus Haluk, a key member of the ULMWP communications team in Jayapura, West Papua, explains, "Take for example the case of Theys Eluay [the charismatic West Papuan leader who was assassinated by Indonesian Special Forces]: those who killed him were released. The killers have since been promoted.... Other forms of killing are through poisoning of food or drink... water and crops.... The solution to saving the Papuans is independence" (Interview, 2008).

The late priest and West Papuan intellectual Neles Tebay, who was based in Jayapura and was not ordinarily an outspoken advocate of political independence, nevertheless understood Haluk's perspective: "I think the human rights violations committed by Indonesian security apparatus against Indigenous Papuans have been one of the reasons [Papuans have]... strengthen[ed] their demand for independence.... When many people are treated badly, we have reason to join them, just to escape from this" (Interview, 2008).

Benny Wenda also speaks of his hopes for *merdeka* in terms of West Papuans enjoying the basic freedoms of everyday living. He asks, in terms hauntingly similar to those used by Césaire when the latter described the globally colonized "millions of men torn from their gods, their land, their habits, their life—from life, from the dance, from wisdom" (1972, 43): "When [will my people] be free like other people... to go hunting or gardening, [to] enjoy these [activities] with their families and [to] grow their own vegetables?... I want to see them dancing with no military surrounding them.... One day I want to see my people go free, smiling, dancing" (2008).

Frantz Fanon stated that "the colonized world is divided in two. The dividing line, the border, is represented by the barracks and the police stations" (1963, 3). The realities of West Papuan village life, in which the colonized world is spliced with that of the occupier's world (depicted in the images of Indonesian military houses and statues situated among residences, as shown in figures 1 and 2), are such that West Papuans are prevented through surveillance and the incitement of fear from enjoying the freedoms Benny Wenda describes above. The images recall Fanon's declaration that "every statue of... these conquistadors ensconced on colonial soil, is a constant reminder of one and the same thing: 'We are here by the force of the bayonet'" (1963, 43). *Merdeka* is a dream for psychological as well as physical welfare, in which the military and its symbols are no longer present and able to strike fear into the colonized.

Ongoing Indonesian colonialism has led to fears among West Papuans of "fatal impact." The extreme state neglect of West Papuans enhances the desire for *merdeka* with independence, a group of OPM fighters in Merauke, West Papua, told me: "Women have to sell vegetables by the side of the road and scrap metal to buy food.... There is no change, and if [we] wait longer, maybe we'll be dead. All Papuans, small and grown, men and women, want *merdeka!*" The anthropologist and reverend Benny Giay of the Kingmi (Indigenous) Church of West Papua endorses *merdeka* in the form of the

FIGURE 1. Military houses are ensconced between Papuan houses in villages such as this one, Rawa Biru in Merauke, to monitor West Papuans. Photograph by Camellia Webb-Gannon.

FIGURE 2. This statue of an Indonesian soldier in Merauke, West Papua, contributes to an atmosphere of intimidation. Photograph by Camellia Webb-Gannon.

right to political self-determination, hoping that it will lead to improved welfare for West Papuans: "We... strongly support it in our church.... Freedom is from God and, once you deny one's freedom then you are in trouble. God is not happy.... God is being hurt when Papuans are not being given... access to education, to health, nutrition, culture. And God is angry at... [the] church when we sit here silent" (Interview, 2008).

CULTURAL, RELIGIOUS, AND ENVIRONMENTAL FREEDOM

Besides the freedom to determine one's own political future and the basic freedoms necessary for survival identified above, *merdeka* also refers to cultural and spiritual freedom. And highly significant to these two freedoms is West Papuans' connection to their lands and waters and the resources these yield. Cultural dimensions of *merdeka*, such as appropriate development and enjoyment of the West Papuan natural environment, situate *merdeka* as a vision for cultural decolonization, a necessary antidote to the cultural-environmental dispossession West Papuans are experiencing. Forkorus Yaboisembut, head of the Dewan Adat Papua (DAP; Papuan Customary Council), declared to me that there might be "a future for the Papuans if they do not disappear. Their culture, land and resources must be preserved. Government must... issue policies on land that must not be sold. Mining must be controlled and schools established for cultural education and democratic structures" (Interview, 2008). But because "the Indonesian government regards all these as separatist activities," Yaboisembut explains, "West Papua must be independent first.... We are not able to [implement cultural policies] under the Indonesian system. We have tried but it is impossible" (Interview, 2008). To Yaboisembut, *merdeka* is about having the freedom to live in accordance with an indigenous lifestyle.

Indigenous peoples, in the words of Zapoteca (Mexican) activist Isabel Altamirano, have "a strong relationship with their land and territories; they see them as the social space where they recreate themselves, so land and territory are not only commodities. To indigenous people, religion and culture are linked to their natural contexts" (quoted in Alfred 2005, 142). At present, the possibility of living a lifestyle that accommodates such a relationship is still a dream for West Papuans. However, as Altamirano contends: "To be indigenous is to use our dreams, not as a way of thinking about what we are not, but as a way to interpret our reality, our circumstances. To be indigenous is to have a sense of community as a whole, a sense of exchanging and talking until we all have a similar vision of where we are going" (quoted in Alfred 2005, 143). In articulating their dream of and hope for *merdeka*, West Papuans continue to develop a sense of national community and participate in acts of survivance (Byrd 2011, xvi), united in their commitment to survive as a people, in their commitment to resist colonialism, and in their commitment to continue hoping for cultural freedom through *merdeka*.

Many descriptions of *merdeka* include reference to religion, and the lack of *merdeka* is at times a source of interreligious tension in West Papua. Benny Giay describes "a kind of a horizontal conflict between Muslims in Papua and [Christian] churches who are perceived as supporters of independence.... Indonesian Muslims [have been warned that they] should not pay attention to what churches say on human rights issues, because [churches] are all OPM anyway" (Interview, 2008). While it is not the case that all churches support independence (many take a neutral stand on the question, preferring to focus on "human rights" if they engage with West Papuan politics at all), many West Papuans pursuing *merdeka* do believe that it is a God-given right and that God will eventually facilitate its manifestation (see chapter 2). One ordained church minister in Port Moresby, PNG, a former member of the OPM, invoked God to justify his decision to fight for *merdeka:* "West Papua has been given by God, and West Papuans have sole right on that soil. And we... never invited Indonesians to come. We were not part of the New York Agreement.... Even our leaders were not consulted. So that's the reason why we took up arms against Indonesian rule" (Interviewee A, 2009).

Sonny Karubaba, a Papuan from Jayapura who founded the University of Papua New Guinea's (UPNG) West Papua Student Association and who now works for PNG national radio broadcasting, attempted to help me understand the centrality of the West Papuan environment to ideas of *merdeka.* Karubaba is a refugee, living in a settlement with over one hundred other Papuans in Hohola, Port Moresby. He believes that "we are here [in PNG] as passengers on just a temporary basis. We have a home [in West Papua], we have mountains and valleys that we can travel, we have big rivers that we can enjoy. And we have our traditional practices, sing sings [celebrations], and our own land to see and enjoy.... It's just that other people are colonizing us, so we are not enjoying what we are supposed to enjoy" (Interview, 2009). Many West Papuans live like Karubaba, as refugees or in self-chosen exile in PNG or further afield in Australia, Europe, the United States, and Vanuatu. But many others are internally displaced inside West Papua, having sold their land for virtually nothing to Indonesian and foreign corporations; having been compulsorily removed from homelands (such as the Amungme people forced out of their highlands home by the Freeport McMoRan mine, which "decapitated" their sacred mountain home—their tribal "mother"); having been chased from their gardens and villages by rampaging Indonesian troops; or having been displaced as a result of the massive transmigration to West Papua from Indonesia. Like Native Americans whose "sacred lands remain as permanent fixtures in their cultural or religious understanding" (Deloria Jr. 2003, 66), the natural environment circumscribes West Papuan identities (Barber and Moiwend 2011).

To decolonization scholar Haunani Kay Trask, colonized peoples "share many more similarities than differences. We have a common heritage as aboriginal peoples, that is, as First Nations of the world. We are all land-based people, and for some of us, also sea-based people, who are attuned to the rhythms of our homelands in a way that assumes both protection of, and an intimate belonging to, our ancestral places. We have all been colonized by imperialist powers more or less resistant to our human needs for self-determination and self-government" (1993, 132). *Merdeka,* as expressed in Karubaba's vision above, would involve the decolonization process of returning the mountains and valleys and rivers in West Papua to their indigenous custodians (see Cabral 1979 and Tuhiwai Smith 1999, 155, on this process) and acknowledging that West Papuans have rights, culture, and community linked to land that are "collective and inherent to their indigeneity [as well as] autonomous from the Settler society" (Alfred 2005, 113; see also Waziyatawin and Yellow Bird 2012, 1).

United in Hope

Sustaining the vision of *merdeka,* a vision that unites West Papuan nationalists, requires hope. One might ask how, in the face of such overwhelming odds, West Papuans are able to persevere? Hope exists because the future is not predetermined—a West Papuan future involving *merdeka* is not probable, but it is possible (and hope is founded on the possible more than the probable). A situation need not look positive in order to engender hope; indeed, as literary philosopher Terry Eagleton, who has written a wide-ranging treatise on hope, points out, it is better if one does not need to have hope, as such need indicates that one's situation has already fallen short of one's desires (2015, 5). Indeed, noted philosopher of hope Ernst Bloch writes that "misery, once it realizes its causes, becomes the revolutionary lever itself" (1995, 1358), triggering hope. Hope is not a feeling or an experience but rather a disposition that must be learned (Eagleton 2015, 58); one that West Papuans are learning through the difficult work that the daily collective commitment to decolonization requires. Worldviews can be inflected with optimism or pessimism (Eagleton 2015, 6). Hopefulness appears to be an important element of the West Papuan political worldview that, over the course of West Papua's colonial history, has been shaped by Christian teachings as well as endogenous, messianic, anti-imperialist struggles. A West Papuan activist worried about the future eloquently expressed this disposition: "It is like Angganitha [the Koreri prophet] said, you can put me in the jail, you can kill me, but one time the Papuans will rise up. Because we have a hope. The Papuans have a hope" (quoted in MacLeod 2009, 82). The sources of West Papuans' hope that *merdeka* will be achieved are multiple. Participating in the decolonization struggle itself produces hope. The very act of struggling as a method of moving through a world in conflict is a hopeful one because of the unknown nature of the outcome. Struggling for a future good, according to the thirteenth-century theologian Thomas Aquinas, helps one concentrate on solving a problem, which, in self-fulfilling fashion, can increase the likelihood of a positive outcome (Eagleton 2015, 84).

Bloch contends that "it is hope alone that allows us to gain the inspiring and consoling understanding of the world to which it leads" (1995, 1367). Hope offers tools to imagine a radical future that sits outside the current realm of probability, a future that cannot rely on the past or the present to provide precedent or insight. In his 2008 book *Radical Hope,* Jonathan Lear tells the story of Plenty Coups, the last great chief of the Native American Crow tribe. The tribe's population and way of life face imminent and total demise. Plenty Coups wrestles with and succeeds in recognizing that "things are going to change in ways beyond which we can currently imagine" but that "we must do what we can to open our imaginations up to a radically different set of future possibilities" (Lear 2008, 93). He draws hope from that recognition. He hopes that somehow the Crow tribe will find a way to regenerate itself from the ashes. In Lear's words, radical hope "anticipates a good for which those who have the hope as yet lack the appropriate concepts with which to understand it" (2008, 103). As was the case for the Crow for whom Plenty Coups held out radical hope, the West Papuan body politic does not yet have a complete plan for an ideal future—rather, political leaders have a vision of various of its major components. Critics cast West Papuan nationalists as naive for thinking they can escape the struggles facing neighboring, independent Melanesian nation-states; for hoping that independence in West Papua might lead to a state of *merdeka;* for not knowing exactly how they will avoid the pitfalls associated with achieving statehood in a world system rigged against less powerful players.

But what is radical and hope enabling is that, despite the oppression they face, West Papuans have a vision at all. Hope and vision exist in a symbiotic relationship. Hope is future oriented, involving an "imaginative articulation of present and future" (Eagleton 2015, 61; see also Lear 2008, 91). For Césaire, political freedom "is about imagining alternatives" and being able to "see, feel, and then understand that other worlds are possible before one can begin to create them," according to Kohn and McBride (2011, 31). Political freedom depends on radical hope before concrete solutions are apparent. Through rehearsing the vision and focusing on its potentiality, hope becomes "performative as well as optative" and "may help to usher [the object of hope] in" (Eagleton 2015, 84). The potentiality of a vision is what, for Eagleton, "articulates the present with the future, and thus lays down the material infrastructure of hope" (2015, 52).

West Papuans' hopeful political disposition has been influenced both by Christianity, due to Dutch missionization, and (to the extent that Marxism is anti-imperialist) by a Marxist-derived ideology (see chapter 2). Revolution is important in Marxist and Christian thought. A complete rupture from history is hoped for, even expected, with the end of capitalism and the Second Coming of Christ representing the ultimate outcome of each belief set, respectively. Hope for a revolution of sorts characterizes each doctrine. Each holds hope for the "future precisely because [each] seeks to confront the present at its most rebarbative" (Eagleton 2015, 7). For eschatologically oriented West Papuans, hope is no stranger. In another sense, the hope engendered by Christianity expresses itself, theologian Karl Rahner contends, as "a radical abandonment of the self, a commitment to what one acknowledges to be beyond one's control and calculation" (Eagleton 2015, 68). Individual West Papuans exhibit this kind of hope in acts of fierce courage, such as when they have been arrested for peacefully protesting and yet continue to shout for *merdeka* from the backs of police trucks, under the spray of water cannons, and even in prison (Wright and Karmini 2016). In the face of overwhelming danger to their person, reports abound of West Papuans throwing caution to the wind to cry out, in radical hope, for freedom.

Hope is also a central feature of the Biak region's Koreri movements (Sharp 1994, 6). Followers of Koreri have lived in hope that their rituals and practice of peaceful living will lead to the manifestation of heaven on Earth—*merdeka.* And finally, hope is a product of West Papuans' collective memories of their past and of their yearning to see "history straightened" (King 2004, 85). The litany of wrongs inflicted on West Papuans over the course of their colonial history is often recited across West Papua and by Papuans in the diaspora as a cultural liturgy, a verbal outpouring of grief for the collective past that some theological scholars describe as the people's *memoria passionis.* The concept of *memoria passionis* draws on previous work by German liberation theologian Johannes Baptist Metz that emphasizes the "danger of memory," particularly in relation to the Jewish Holocaust and the importance of Christian solidarity with the oppressed. Perhaps the appeal to West Papuans of the concept, which has been circulating in the territory since 1999, relates to their own experience of genocide/holocaust and belief that God is on their side, which is the side of the less powerful (see Glazebrook 2004; Hernawan 2018). In Eagleton's words, "It is not dreams of liberated grandchildren that spur men and women to revolt, but memories of oppressed ancestors. It is the past that furnishes us with the resources of hope, not just the speculative possibility of a rather more gratifying future" (2015, 32). The deep desire to see the past put right and justice served in a future *merdeka* inspires hope in West Papuans.

Independence Problematized

As important as West Papuans consider independence to be, it is worth reiterating that they do not necessarily envisage it as the end point of *merdeka.* Rather, it is seen as an imperative step toward *merdeka*'s realization, the fulfillment of holistic emancipation-focused hopes for decolonization. In the words of Michael Kareth, a West Papuan refugee living in the Netherlands and leader of the independence-focused West Papua National Congress, the "importance of independence is the *first* thing—we need to be free from any type of colonialist system" (Interview, 2008). Markus Haluk has identified three fundamental elements of *merdeka:* "First, politics. Our independence on [the] first of December 1961 was destroyed by Sukarno. Second, human rights issues. And third, development: delivering services in education, health and infrastructure to Papuan people" (Interview, 2008). His words confirm that *merdeka* includes, rather than consists solely of, political independence. Political independence is not enough on its own to produce *merdeka* in West Papua.

The late Viktor Kaisiepo, a West Papuan cultural and political leader who was based in the Netherlands, reflected critically and at length on the idea of West Papuan independence and its limitations in what he believed is an interdependent world: "Of course I'm fighting for independence. When I was younger I believed independence [was] the solution. But in a globalized world, I don't think independence is the [entire] solution because we have entered into a world that we call interdependence. I can't live without them [Indonesians], and they can't live without me. Both of us cannot live without the resources. . . . I don't believe in West Papuan independence if it's not open to outer influences because [West Papua has] already been globalized" (Interview, 2008).

Kaisiepo understood that independence, in and of itself, potentially means little for a postcolonial country in an exploitative global structure. Even with the eradication of formal colonialism, economic imperialism can be paralyzing (see Ngũgĩ 1981, 2). Yet he was also critical of Indonesia's insistence upon its own sovereignty and its refusal to realize the benefits of pooling sovereignty for the regional common good. Kaisiepo envisioned sovereignty for West Papua in a similar way to that imagined by the assassinated Kanaky independence leader Jean-Marie Tjibaou for New Caledonia: "Sovereignty . . . gives us the right and the power to negotiate interdependencies. For a small country like ours, independence means reckoning with interdependencies as well" (2005, 179).

While the majority of West Papuans today support independence as an integral component of *merdeka,* this chapter would be incomplete if it did not acknowledge conflicting West Papuan viewpoints. Various West Papuan refugees in Port Moresby in 2009 told me that most West Papuans desired "full independence" but that "some [were] influenced by [the] Indonesian government." Their reference may have been to deceased former West Papuan independence activist Franzalbert Joku's group, IGSSARPRI (Independent Group Supporting the Special Autonomous Region of Papua within the Republic of Indonesia), which (at least until Joku's death in 2019) received funds from the

Indonesian government and advocated Special Autonomy and the repatriation of West Papuan refugees from PNG to West Papua (Vatsikopoulos 2007).

At a 2007 conference hosted by Australian advocacy group Indonesian Solidarity and the West Papua Project think tank at the University of Sydney, Joku presented his views concerning what West Papua's future is likely to entail: "Papua's status as an autonomous region [rather than independent state] is a *fait accompli,* and having searched the globe in search of answers, the independence campaign has come to a dead-end road.... That's why I say the international system does not support the struggle for an independent nation state of Papua. All Papuans today have a duty to themselves and future generations to rededicating ourselves to working for a new peaceful and prosperous Papua within an equally new and rapidly democratizing Indonesia to take our rightful place in the world of tomorrow" (2007). Joku's apparent pragmatism reflects a realpolitik position calling for political compromise. He went on to argue that Special Autonomy is a "bottom up process... as opposed to perceptions among Papuans abroad and... supporters that it is something shoved down the throat of Papuans by politicians in Jakarta" and to contend that it is "a golden political opportunity for Papuans to manage their own affairs while enabling the central government in Jakarta to preserve their country's sovereignty and national unity" (Joku 2007). Yet he did not go so far as to claim that Special Autonomy achieves what West Papuan people want it to—that is, *merdeka*—or even what it is mandated to do.

In relinquishing the quest for independence, it is possible to speculate that Joku was giving up on *merdeka,* and with it, decolonization. He listed the capabilities the Special Autonomy Law does not allow—a wide-ranging list of limitations to self-rule that prohibits West Papuan governance in political and security affairs; diplomatic and foreign relations with other countries in the pursuit of trade, investment, cultural, and educational objectives; judicial and justice administration; education; and fiscal and monetary policies (Joku 2007). Yet, paradoxically, he entreated that

> Papuans should have every reason to now, I believe, firmly embrace the Special Autonomy Law, however diluted, imperfect or incomplete... [it] may be in [its] present form. Politics is the art of compromise, and political compromise through regional autonomy is an important cornerstone in conflict management and resolution. I... do not see any other option on the table although there are various aspirations expressed.... Realistically there is no other option on the table right now that we can legitimately discuss and pursue... as an achievable goal. (Joku 2007)

Kenyan writer and decolonization theorist Ngũgĩ wa Thiong'o writes of one of the more pernicious effects of colonialism: "It even plants serious doubts about the moral rightness of struggle. Possibilities of triumph or victory are seen as remote, ridiculous dreams" (1981, 3). It is not possible to know exactly why Joku "switched sides": some colonized "people are bought, some are crushed between impossible demands, others are squeezed until they become but images of their former selves" (Trask 1993, 138). But that Joku was convinced to work with Indonesia under any circumstance after his long-standing staunch opposition to West Papua's colonizer supports the accuracy of Ngũgĩ's observation.

In an appeal to Papuans to accept Special Autonomy rather than pursue independence, and using a similar language of defeatist pragmatics, former West Papuan activist Nick Messet (who is deputy chairperson of IGSSARPRI) provided testimony in September 2010 at a hearing of the US Congress on Indonesia's crimes against humanity: "After many years of struggle and hardship, I realized that I can only cry for so long. No amount of tears can bring back the past. More importantly, I came to realize that the best solution is Special Autonomy. The Special Autonomy is the solution that is endorsed by the world community. This is the solution that is the most practical, good for Jakarta, good for the Papuans" (quoted in the Federal News Service 2010). Further, Messet entreated activists outside of West Papua "not to make tensions worse because when things get worse in West Papua, you stay here in your comfort and we suffer" (Federal News Service 2010). This plea does need to be considered by advocates for West Papua, with its suggestion that standing up for human rights will only serve to entrench abuses against West Papuans by Indonesian colonizers. It reinforces, however, the claims of many other West Papuans and observers that a climate of human rights violations and impunity is ubiquitous in West Papua[3]—surely not the message Joku and Messet were hoping to convey.

In 2011 Messet e-mailed me the following: "I hope that one day all the dream[s] may come true but I am very skeptical about it. . . . An Independent State in the near future is only an impossible dream" (2011). Messet believes in the value inherent in the dream of independence but has given up on the likelihood of achieving it. His ideas about what will meet Papuans' needs have been influenced by Indonesian cultural and political hegemonic discourses, evidenced by his justification on the Indonesian government's behalf of Special Autonomy's shortcomings: "We are given millions of pounds to establish [Special Autonomy], to make that. But we are lazy. We are [too] lazy to do that" (Federal News Service 2010). Here, Messet's words reflect the effects of what Ngũgĩ has called the "culture bomb," the "biggest weapon wielded and actually daily unleashed by imperialism against . . . collective defiance. . . . The effect of the culture bomb is to annihilate a people's belief in their names, in their languages, in their environment, in their heritage of struggle, in their unity, in their capacities and ultimately in themselves" (1981, 3). In describing West Papuans as lazy, it is possible Messet is suffering from what African American sociologist W. E. B. Du Bois termed "double consciousness," the act of judging one's own people as if through the eyes of their colonizer (1903, 8). Had Memmi had the opportunity, he might have responded to Messet by asking, "Can one accuse an entire people of laziness? . . . One can wonder if their output is mediocre, whether malnutrition, low wages, a closed future, a ridiculous conception of a role in society, does not make the colonized uninterested in his work. . . . The independence of the accusation from any sociological or historical conditions makes it suspect" (1965, 81).

The views put forward by Joku and Messet endorsing Special Autonomy rather than total decolonization via independence are those of a minority of West Papuan leaders. This is evidenced by the ever-increasing size and frequency of protests for a referendum taking place across West Papua and supported by a broad representation of West Papuan leaders working in unison within the ULMWP. In Eagleton's words, "Hope is . . . a species of permanent revolutions, whose enemy is as much political complacency as metaphysical despair" (2015, 69). The apparent political complacency displayed by Joku and Messet indicates that they had been affected by Indonesia's "culture bomb" to the extent that they had lost hope in the vision of *merdeka*. Overwhelmingly, though, the majority of West Papuans I have consulted over the course of my research in West Papua and in the diaspora do not believe that *merdeka* is possible without independence. And while Joku and Messet may have given up on independence, many West Papuan leaders declare an unwavering belief that West Papua will become independent. The perspective of West Papuan–Papua New Guinean activist David Tekwie, a leader of UPNG's West Papua Student Association in 2008, sums up the view of many West Papuan leaders when he states: "What we want is . . . to help ourselves first . . . whether it's going to be autonomy first, or independence first. . . . I want independence and I'll do anything it takes (Interview, 2009).

It is difficult to tease out the various dimensions of *merdeka* because its many facets are mutually dependent. Even the most basic elements of decolonization are nearly always mentioned in conversations about *merdeka* in tandem with the need for political independence. Some critics deem West Papuans' insistence on their right to self-determination as "folly" and "unrealistic" (see McGibbon 2006, x). It is not entirely clear why they single out the desire for the realization of this particular right (self-determination) for condemnation but not others (for example, West Papuans' desire for freedom from physical violence), but it is likely a combination of hoping to appease Indonesia and a postmodern sense of unease regarding the idea of nationalism. The problem with such reasoning, as political scientist Sankaran Krishna argues, is that "if identities such as the nation or ethnicity, or notions such as 'traditional homelands' of native peoples, can be shown to be historical and social constructions or fictions, governments and elites can use such ideas to deny their responsibility for past crimes or to oppose current claims for reparation or redress" (quoted in Byrd 2011, xxxiv). Golden writes that the pursuit of *merdeka,* like cargo cults, leads to "dangerous scenarios, because it inspires both unrealistic expectations and the willingness to sacrifice everything to achieve them" (2000, 30). In his report *Pitfalls of Papua,* McGibbon argues, as noted, that "efforts by the West Papua constituency [in Australia] to contest Indonesian sovereignty, including calls for a [United Nations] review of Papua's political status, or the introduction of foreign forces to enforce a peace deal are folly. They lack realism and make the situation worse" (2006, x). Worse for whom, one might ask? There is significant consensus among West Papuans that international support for *merdeka* via an act of self-determination (often visualized in the form of a referendum) is potentially life-saving for West Papuans as a people. *Merdeka* will finally enable, in the words of the West Papua National Committee's (KNPB) spokesperson, Victor Yeimo, "self-determination without colonization by Indonesia. . . . There is no peace or justice under Indonesian control; independence is the best solution to achieve peace and justice in West Papua" (Interview, 2010).

Perhaps where Golden's and McGibbon's comments of this nature have been useful in some regard to Papuans, however, is by putting a greater onus on Papuans to present coherent, unified, and forward-thinking strategies for achieving independence. The formation in 2015 of the ULMWP has been a signal accomplishment to this end. Such accomplishments will go some way toward allaying regional fears concerning the "Balkanization" of Indonesia, or a future failed state of West Papua. The survey of West Papuan thinking on the issue of independence in this chapter has demonstrated some of the links between international theorization of decolonization and West Papuan understandings of *merdeka* and the ways in which such understandings constitute a common West Papuan leadership vision for the future. For West Papuans, *merdeka* is total decolonization, indivisibly physical and spiritual—and decolonization in the West Papuan context includes the right to exercise self-determination with the option of an independent state. The opportunity to choose an independent state is a necessary step toward the actualization of *merdeka,* even though *merdeka* comprises more than political independence alone.

Regardless of whether sovereign state status is recognized by the international community in West Papua, Papuans still face a maze of decolonization challenges in working toward the other dimensions of *merdeka* discussed in this chapter. These may include intertribal and ethnic tensions, corruption, elite exploitation, endemic violence against women, global capitalist neoimperialism, development decisions, resource management, and tensions between diaspora and in-country leaders. However, in the event of attaining independence, these would be West Papuan problems (many inherited from more than a century of colonialism [Trask 1993, 133]), and it would be the responsibility of the West Papuan polity to decide how to address them in line with common West Papuan understandings of *merdeka* (O. Ap, interview, 2008) and international human rights mechanisms. In terms of uniting West Papuans in a common vision, the dream of *merdeka* serves a similar purpose to the OPM, which some say stands for *om, paik, mak* (sun, moon, stars; Sharp 1994, 97). "As long as those three objects, the sun, the moon and the stars, are still shining, our fight for liberation will always be there," promises Papuan independence activist Henk Rumbewas (quoted in Webster 2001–2002, 523). The sun, moon, and stars—particularly the Morning Star—are the symbols of West Papuans' radical hope, and "hope is the crack in the present through which a future can be glimpsed" (Eagleton 2015, 44).

2

DREAMS

What Does the Future Hold?

> One of the strategies which indigenous peoples have employed effectively to bind people together politically is a strategy which asks that people imagine a future, that they rise above present day situations which are generally depressing, dream a new dream and set a new vision. The confidence of knowing that we have survived and can only go forward provides some impetus to the process of envisioning.
>
> —*Linda Tuhiwai Smith,* Decolonizing Methodologies

It was the year 2000, and a young West Papuan girl, perhaps four or five years old, held her father's hand as they stood in a large crowd. Her father, an indigenous Papuan, was a journalist with an Indonesian government news agency, and he had taken his daughter to town for the day. People were milling excitedly in the streets of Jayapura, waving Morning Star flags, the cherished nationalist symbol of the Free West Papua Movement. This was the era known as the Papuan Spring, when the Indonesian government had decreed the Morning Star flag could be flown, and talk of *merdeka* filled the air. The little girl, however, was worried. She tugged on her father's hand, nervously asking him, *"Bapak, kalau kita merdeka, Mama nanti ke mana?"* (Dad, if we become independent, where will Mama be then?). Her mother, a resident in West Papua, was from Makassar, and the girl wondered whether a nonindigenous Papuan like her mother was included in the crowd's vision for an independent West Papua. But her father answered reassuringly, "Mama will still be here. Mama is part of us."

This vignette, recounted to me in 2009 by the late Clemens Runawery, a West Papuan refugee in Papua New Guinea (PNG), illustrates the questions on the minds of West Papuan citizens and leaders as they imagine what an independent West Papua might be like. To preface the importance of such political imaginings, which extend to constitutional matters and cultural policy, this chapter starts by assessing what indigenous West Papuans believe will happen to them if the current political situation remains; that is, the conditions of genocide to which they are already subject will soon render them a culturally and land-bereft minority in Indonesia—a people no more. West Papuans widely broadcast that they are subjects of Indonesian genocide in their campaign for independence, perhaps because they take a view similar to Amilcar Cabral that "it is impossible to struggle effectively for the independence of a people... unless we really know our reality and unless we really start from that reality to wage the struggle" (1979, 44). They aim to inform others of just how grim they believe the reality to be and how important it is to take urgent action.

Although different political ideas for governing West Papua after independence have been debated, one outstanding point on which the majority of West Papuans I have interviewed agree is that West Papua will, one day, become independent. The "when" and "how" of independence varies in these visions but the "why" does not—many West Papuans believe that God is on their side, that they are morally justified in their struggle, and that their position of righteousness will eventuate in political independence. The origins of this "discourse of righteousness," which infused nearly all of my interviews with West Papuans, are examined in detail.

This chapter also looks at the extent to which West Papuans believe themselves prepared for independence. Critical considerations, including appropriate leadership and ideas about migration and citizenship eligibility in an independent West Papua (including the future status of "mixed-race" and immigrant Papuans such as the young girl's mother mentioned above) are touched upon. Finally, West Papuans' political models for postindependence are canvassed, with a view toward gauging the level of consensus on the appropriateness of particular options.

Genocide

A commonly and staunchly held belief among West Papuans is that they, as a people, are victim to a "slow-motion," but systematic, genocide (Elmslie and Webb-Gannon 2013). That is, in the words of West Papua–based student activist Victor Yeimo: "In West Papua we don't have to think [an] emergency is like a bomb, like war... systematically, we have... an emergency. People from outside, they come and they have [jobs on] every side, and we are dying. Genocide is still happening in West Papua. And we are saying that it is an emergency for us!...You cannot see it physically in West Papua, but systematically, every day, people still die" (Interview, 2010).

Genocide, as defined by Article II of the United Nations Convention on the Prevention and Punishment of the Crime of Genocide (United Nations General Assembly 1948), includes "any of the following acts committed with intent to destroy, in whole or in part, a national, ethnical, racial or religious group, as such:

1. Killing members of the group;
2. Causing serious bodily or mental harm to members of the group;
3. Deliberately inflicting on the group conditions of life calculated to bring about its physical destruction in whole or in part;
4. Imposing measures intended to prevent births within the group;
5. Forcibly transferring children of the group to another group."

West Papuans recognize genocidal patterns in their treatment by Indonesian political and military institutions. Many believe that Indonesia is inflicting upon them conditions of life calculated to bring about the destruction of the West Papuan people (see 3 above). Leading West Papuan activist Markus Haluk argues:

> There are many ways and forms of abuse and elimination of Papuans, first by stigmatizing and linking cases with separatism, then direct killings, the equivalent of slaughtering...animals. Colonial subjugation takes many forms, through family planning (why not in Java?), assimilation, forced marriages, transmigration, and exclusion of Papuans from jobs—[even] public service positions are dominated by the military. There are also massacres....Special Autonomy is another form of subjugation through money—local officials are allocated so much money they have lost their integrity and dignity [through] excessive drinking [and by]...spreading HIV/AIDS.[1] Forced decentralization [*pemekaran*] is another form of killing by dominating all the positions in the bureaucracy [and] denying Papuans important positions of decision-making. (Interview, 2008)

West Papuan women's rights advocate Frederika Korain articulates the concerns of many West Papuans when she discusses the rapid decline in West Papuan birth rates compared to the climbing birth rates of Indonesian migrants in Papua and with those in neighboring PNG. She cites a 1961 census taken in (what are now) PNG and West Papua and compares the birth rate statistics then to the results of the census from each territory since 2000. Korain says that "if we discuss... genocide, [impeded population growth] is part of the picture" (Interview, 2008). She claims that part of the problem is that the Indonesian government in West Papua provides for the growing population of urban migrants with infrastructure, resources, and necessary facilities but neglects its duty of care to West Papuans, particularly those far from urban centers.

West Papuan decolonization leaders carry on their activities while knowing they might be killed for their leadership (see 1 above). The murder of independence advocate Theys Eluay in 2001 by Indonesian Special Forces is frequently cited by Papuan leaders as evidence that they could meet a similar end. According to Markus Haluk, "My feeling is the Indonesian government deliberately plans to eliminate our people. If Papuans are killed, they are happy. Those who commit the crimes are not punished; instead, they are promoted. Take, for example, the case of Theys Eluay: those who... killed him were released" (Interview, 2008). Similarly, Zachi Sawor asserted, "Theys Eluay, you know, they killed him.... So you have to be careful because Indonesia is very bad, try[ing] to wipe out our people" (Interview, 2008).

Serious bodily and mental harm is another category of genocide (see 2 above) that applies in the West Papuan context. Amatus Douw, a West Papuan refugee and student in Melbourne who is also president of the International Youth Coalition for the Liberation of West Papua, recounts how West Papuan people "disappear every day, and killings [are] going on every day, but we have no guns to fight with [Indonesia]. And now they send... TNI [Indonesian military] soldiers there just to control our minimum space" (A. Douw, A. Galilee, and P. Florentinus, interview, 2009). The degree to which the military controls West Papuans' "minimum space" through torture and intimidation was evidenced in two YouTube clips posted by the Asian Human Rights Commission in October 2010 (one of which was subsequently removed from YouTube due to its graphic nature). These depict West Papuan men being tortured for information about hidden weapons. A burning stick is applied to one man's genitals, another man is suffocated with a plastic bag, guns and knives are held to the faces of two men, and other Papuans are kicked in the head by Indonesian troops (Asian Human Rights Commission 2010b; on torture in West Papua, see Hernawan 2018).

Certainly, leading academics, as well as the late US Congress delegate representing American Samoa, Eni Faleomavaega, take West Papuan claims of genocide seriously. In 2009 scholars of West Papua Jim Elmslie (2009), Stuart Upton (2009), and Richard Chauvel (2009) debated in the online magazine *Inside Indonesia* whether West Papuans' demographic status as a minority in their own land constitutes genocide. Elmslie, in arguing that West Papuan concerns about genocide have merit, writes: "Up to six large passenger ships now arrive each week in Jayapura, the province's capital city, to deliver thousands more migrants. Demographic swamping does not constitute genocide, but it does lay the foundations for it" (2009, n.p.). Upton, in a contrasting piece to Elmslie's using the same statistics, argues that the huge in-migration occurring does not point to genocide because the indigenous population's numbers are merely relatively diminishing (in other words, the migrant population is increasing), not diminishing in total (2009, n.p.).

Be this as it may, genocidal intent on behalf of the Indonesian government via its transmigration policy in Papua, as well as its practices of cultural devastation, cannot be ruled out. Chauvel, in a response to Elmslie and Upton, writes that even though the pattern of in-migration within eastern Indonesia represents less of a migration flow to Papua than to other eastern Indonesian provinces, Papuans view in-migration as genocidal in West Papua because they understand it to "be a consequence of the territory's incorporation into Indonesia: a very different situation from East Kalimantan or other high immigration provinces" (2009, n.p.).

In 2004 a group of scholars at Yale Law School reported that "the available evidence [provides] a strong indication that the Indonesian government has committed genocide against the West Papuans" (Brundige et al. 2004, 1). John Wing and Peter King (2005) of the West Papua Project at the University of Sydney addressed the issue in a report titled *Genocide in West Papua? The Role of the Indonesian State Apparatus and a Current Needs Assessment of the Papuan People* and concluded that a genocide "may be underway" in West Papua. In 2008, international relations scholar King wrote: "Indonesian policy in Papua seems to qualify for an inquiry under the [Genocide] Convention on points (a) to (d) [listed above] at least" (2008, 2). Genocide analyst Kjell Anderson describes the conflict in West Papua as a "cold genocide" (as opposed to "hot genocides" such as the Holocaust, which occurred over a relatively short period of time) that has been taking place over generations and is "rooted in the victims' supposed inferiority" (2015, 9). Adding to the list of scholars giving credence to Papuan genocide concerns, Eben Kirksey writes that in December 1961, "The Indonesian military invaded [West Papua] and began what was arguably genocide according to international law. During the coming decades of Indonesian occupation, thousands of indigenous Papuans were killed in bombing raids, displaced by military operations, subjected to arbitrary detention, executed, or 'disappeared.' Forced sterilization campaigns and neglect of basic public health programs resulted in slower, perhaps more insidious, declines in Papuan populations" (2012, xi). In a September 2010 US congressional hearing on human rights abuses in West Papua convened by Congressman Faleomavaega, Faleomavaega introduced the hearing by appealing to Indonesia to answer accusations about "the potential of the terrible act that may be called genocide" in West Papua (Federal News Service 2010). And in earlier work on which I collaborated with Jim Elmslie, we found that "actions carried out by the military and police are the result of explicit government policies aimed at countering West Papuan 'separatism.' The goal is to 'destroy' that part of the West Papuan 'group' who are pro-independence: a very substantial part of the West Papuan population" (Elmslie and Webb-Gannon 2013, 144). Papuan leaders with whom I have spoken are very much united in their belief that the survival of their peoples, lands, and cultures is under serious threat. In light of such concerns, "it is axiomatic that the West Papuans will continue their struggle for independence.... From [Papuans'] point of view they have no choice" (Elmslie 2002, 8). Fear of genocide is a catalyst for the active and increasing resistance against Indonesian authority (Elmslie, Webb-Gannon, and King 2010). To the minds of many, independence is the only possible future they can contemplate. The alternative is their own demise, the ultimate outcome, West Papuans believe, of the genocidal processes they have described.

Discourse of Righteousness

> As the sun goes down and pass[es] the horizon and the land fall[s] into darkness[,] [d]o not be troubled and have worries; we know that this is just a state for [the] time being. Tomorrow the Morningstar will rise to a new dawn. Just have faith in God, righteousness and justice and love for Papua; we will not be abandoned, because we are all children of God.
>
> —*Joseph Prai*

"Do you believe West Papua will attain independence?" I asked Rex Rumakiek, secretary of the United Liberation Movement for West Papua (ULMWP), in Sydney. "Yes, I believe in it. Otherwise I wouldn't be working for it," he replied (Interview, 2010). Whenever I posed this question to West Papuans, the answer—in West Papua, in Vanuatu, in Sweden, in the United Kingdom, in the Netherlands, and in PNG—was affirmative, almost without exception. Rather than determining how realistic this level of certitude might be, the point of this chapter is to demonstrate the degree to which—and why—West Papuan leaders are unified in their pursuit of independence as a means of decolonization and in their visions for their future. This is an important part of the book's mounting argument that the independence movement is growing in cohesion and, as a result, is gaining increasing international support.

When I asked West Papuans why, against incredible odds, they have continued to fight for what has long appeared to be the highly unlikely goal of independence, the answer was unanimous—independence is a West Papuan entitlement; a God-given right and a human right. Within this discourse of righteousness, it appears self-evident to West Papuans that, in God's time, they will receive the political independence that is rightfully theirs. West

Papuans' belief in a good God who will deliver them in their time of trial echoes a similar hope that may have sustained the Native American Crow as their buffalo were being destroyed and their traditional ways of life eradicated. According to Jonathan Lear, Crow leader Plenty Coups may have been thinking during that experience, "Ah-badt-dadt-deah [the Crow god]—is good. [Crow] commitment to the genuine transcendence of God is manifest in commitment to the goodness of the world transcending our necessarily limited attempt to understand it. [Crow] commitment to God's transcendence and goodness is manifested in my commitment to the idea that something good will emerge" (2008, 94).

A customary leader in Merauke, West Papua, told me in 2008, "God always arranges [for Papuans] . . . [which is why] Papuan people have spirit. . . . God will save us" (Interviewee C, 2008). Similarly, two elderly Organisasi Papua Merdeka (OPM) soldiers in Port Moresby, PNG, told me that they continue to struggle for independence because their hope is in God. According to Robin Osborne, the "TPN's [OPM's armed wing] ideology was essentially Christian . . . [with] much talk about God being on the side of Papuan nationalism" (1985, 52). Papuans "have the hope, the faith that someday it will arrive. Faith that what they are struggling for is right, and because it is right, God is on their side" states a West Papuan source cited by Danilyn Rutherford (2006, 120). Followers of Koreri also draw "their strength from the secrets of Manseren Nanggi, Almighty God, through the agency of Sampari-Kumeseri, the Morning Star," according to Noni Sharp (1994, 62–63).

I encountered an example of this discourse of righteousness during an interview with a West Papuan refugee and former OPM soldier turned church minister in Port Moresby in 2009. He told me: "God is our creator and he knows; he listens to our cries. He is the one who worked through Moses and Aaron and is the one who worked through the Gentile King Cyrus. For me, my faith has not wavered, because my faith has already spoken to me last year in Vanimo" (Interviewee A, 2009). The minister explained that one morning in Vanimo, PNG, he arose at 5:00 a.m. to pray. There, God communicated with him, saying, "I am the one, the creator of heaven and Earth. I can honestly tell you that West Papua will become independent. . . . At that time you will be unified" (Interviewee A, 2009). It was significant, according to my interlocuter, that some West Papuans who had been to Israel had had similar prophecies about West Papuan independence verified by Jewish spiritual leaders. He, like many other West Papuans, believed that the similarities between the West Papuan political situation and those of the Jewish peoples who yearned for Zion are promising for West Papua.[2]

A website focusing on the activism of the late Theys Eluay provides further comment on the Judeo-Christian element of the West Papuan struggle: "There always was the understanding among Papuans [including Eluay] that the Papuan struggle was to be peaceful. It was in fact a religious struggle, comparable to that of the Israelites who were led by Moses out of the bondage of Egypt" (*Wapedia* 2010). During an interview for the *Far Eastern Economic Review* (2000), Eluay relayed the instructions West Papuan leaders had given independence demonstrators during recent protests in Jayapura, Fak Fak, and other towns. "Take to the streets at 3 a.m.," demonstrators had been told, "and circle each town seven times." The *Review* states, "The action harks back to Biblical days, when the Israelites laid siege to Jericho" (2000). "'Indonesia is our Jericho,'" Eluay had told the interviewer (*Far Eastern Economic Review* 2000). Zionist affinities also motivated a delegation of thirty-four West Papuans to visit Israel in 2007. The delegations' members, having come across the Bible verse Zechariah 6:17—"And the distant ones will come and build the Temple of God"—decided that their self-designated status as figural Israelites obligated them to travel to Israel to donate gold from West Papua for the rebuilding of the temple on Jerusalem's Temple Mount (HaLevi 2007).

West Papuan Zionist sympathies are also evident in the ubiquitous display in West Papua of the Jewish Star of David next to the prohibited Morning Star flag symbol featured on stickers on guitars, on wall calendars, and in *nokin* (woven bags) embroidery (see figure 3). The apparent similarities between the West Papuan and Jewish historical plights, including genocide of the Jews in World War II and Papuans' perception of their own genocide and the extant political/religious tensions with surrounding Muslim populations, provide a felt affinity among Papuans for Israel's political situation. Jewish symbols therefore act as powerful, unifying symbols of hope for Papuans too. Belief in the same God as that of the Israelites has led to a popular interpretation of another Christian Old Testament verse cherished by West Papuans in the diaspora, a verse that was, in fact, the topic of the sermon at a West Papuan church service I was invited to attend in Port Moresby in 2009. The verse, Jeremiah 29:11 (New International Version), states: "'For I know the plans I have for you,' declares the Lord, 'plans to prosper you and not to harm you, plans to give you hope and a future.'" That hope and future is foreshadowed for West Papuans by the Jewish people's inhabiting of their own (highly contested) "Promised Land." The establishment of a Jewish state has contributed to West Papuan certainty that they will attain their own *merdeka*, an independent West Papua, in the future.

Interestingly, Palestinian decolonization politics are also watched closely by West Papuans, in hopeful anticipation that Jakarta might take note of these. West Papuan refugee in Melbourne Jacob Rumbiak told me that he has tried to "give this argument about Special Autonomy [to Jakarta]: This is like the Palestinian system. If Jakarta wants this huge permanent great autonomy like Hillary Clinton mentioned in June [2009] to the Indonesian government for Papua, that means our position, standard great autonomy, must be

FIGURE 3. A wall hanging in Sentani, West Papua. Photograph by Camellia Webb-Gannon.

like the Palestinian [one]. We must have [a] prime minister, ministers, and twenty-five members under our Special Autonomy [that] must not work with . . . Jakarta" (Interview, 2009).

Perhaps, as a result of West Papuan empathy for both sides of that protracted Middle East conflict, constitutional arrangements for the compassionate acceptance of "both" Papuan populations (indigenous and nonindigenous) might be made in an independent West Papua.

The discourse of righteousness that emphasizes a God-given right to independence in West Papua is closely related to Papuans' firm belief that their right to self-determination will ultimately be realized because it is also a human right. John Tekwie, in explaining why he is certain that West Papua's independence is impending, told me simply: "Well, first of all, [with] West Papua, the case is a human rights issue. . . . It's nothing more than that. It's a human rights issue" (Interview, 2009), implying that the ease of moral diagnosis guarantees a just outcome. Similarly, the late Seth Rumkorem remarked to me in 2008 that he had no doubt that West Papuans "will show to the world we are a people, and we are a race. We know—as human beings—we know our rights. As people, we know our right to self-determination. No one will take it from us" (Interview, 2008).

The following story, told to me by Freddy Waromi, the leader of a group of TPN/OPM refugees that has resided in Port Moresby since 1981, demonstrates West Papuans' pride and belief in the righteousness of their struggle. Since 1997 the group of 158 people have been moved five times to different locations in the city and have recently been involved in a legal battle with the PNG government over their treatment and lack of security. Waromi and the group believe these forced relocations, which cause continual distress to group members, are "because of political reasons, and because of security reasons, and because of our involvement in the [West Papuan] struggle"

(F. Waromi, interview, 2009). The enforced instability stems primarily, in Waromi's view, from the refusal of the refugees to apologize to the government over the following incident.

In September 2006, the then governor of Papua Province (in West Papua), Bas Suebu, was invited by the PNG government to celebrate PNG's independence day in Port Moresby. According to the refugees, an unauthorized visit was made to their camp at Eight Mile by a PNG-government-chaperoned Governor Suebu. The purpose of the visit, from Waromi's point of view, was to add names to a repatriation list of West Papuans that PNG and Indonesia hoped to convince to return to West Papua and accept Special Autonomy. However, in Waromi's words:

> We [were] fighting for years in the jungle, not for greater autonomy... [but] for full independence. So, we don't want to go back to West Papua before West Papua gets its own independence. (Interview 2009)

He continued:

> When [the] governor's delegation... visited us, we chased them out. We damaged two of their vehicles, and we busted some of the members that they brought with them into Eight Mile block.... So, because we chased them out and damaged their car, two days later police... issued us a letter warning us to immediately apologize to both the Papua New Guinean and Indonesian governments. But we refused to apologize because we didn't invite them, and they didn't notify us about their intention to visit, and [the PNG government must] always [keep] in mind that we, as members of [the West Papuan] National Liberation Army, we are always the enemy [of Indonesia] because we are still fighting for independence. They should [keep that] in mind... but they failed. (Interview, 2009)

The refugees were made essentially homeless for their refusal to apologize, yet they were so sure of the fundamental morality of their cause that they would not relent.

Other than belief in the God-sanctioned righteousness of their struggle and in the ultimate triumph of human rights, West Papuans provide several other reasons for sustaining the goal of independence. Jacob Prai cites the "many groups still fighting against the same government, [the] same enemy" as proof that independence will come. "There are the Acehnese, there is... Poso, [and] there are the Moluccans.... The Indonesian government, since they got independence... they just depend on the Western proxy. They have no capacity to deal with their own nation. You see, there are many,

many factors that I can [use to] convince you [that in the] West Papuan struggle, independence we will get, sooner or later" (Interview, 2008).

His words are reminiscent of Cabral's (1979) declaration in relation to African decolonization that "no crime, no power, no manoeuvre or demagogy of the criminal... colonialist aggressors can halt the march of history, the irreversible march of our African people... towards the independence, peace and genuine progress to which they have a right" (297): in other words, according to this way of thinking, wrong cannot ultimately trump right. Perhaps Prai's confidence derives from the advantage identified by Césaire that West Papuans believe they hold over Indonesia: "They know that their temporary 'masters' are lying [about the legitimacy of their sovereignty in West Papua]. [And] therefore that their masters are weak" (1972, 32).

Other Papuan leaders state that faith in the younger generations, in the increasing quality of the education that many of these up-and-coming leaders are acquiring (A. Ajamiseba, interview, 2009; J. Tekwie, interview, 2009), and in the strength of the West Papuan spirit keep them hopeful. As an example of the latter, the reverend Benny Giay described to me a "kind of a 'we' feeling, a kind of an awareness that we are one, [by] which... I mean... one population, church, [and] militia that makes, somehow, this awareness... that we should be united, we should be one... that keeps [us going] somehow" (Interview, 2008). This sense of unity in belief and belief in unity is apparent in other indigenous sovereignty struggles. For example, Ray Halbritter, founder of a successful gaming enterprise and Harvard Law School graduate of the Oneida (US) Indian Nation, argues that "the essence of my people is belief itself. It's the ability to hold on to that belief. It's the fire of our people. It goes back to a spiritual aspect, and our belief that the Creator made us and put us here, and it is his will that we live" (quoted in Alfred 2005, 213).

From the preceding examples, it is evident that within the West Papuan discourse of righteousness, eventual independence is considered an inevitable achievement.[3] In the words of West Papua analyst Peter Savage, independence, from a West Papuan perspective, "no longer remains a question of 'win or lose' but rather a question of 'how and how long'" (1978, 994). This triumphalist discourse is more than optimism: it is a combination of radical hope (see Lear 2008) and faith. Literary theorist Terry Eagleton writes that optimism is facile and futile, while hope and faith are based in principle and in a belief in a power greater than chance. In the view of Taiaiake Alfred, such belief is critical for warriors of indigenous culture (2005, 85). It "provides emotional stability in the face of constant conflict and danger" (85). Plenty Coups, for example, chief of the Mountain Crow tribe (US) from 1876 to 1932 (see chapter 1), whose biography Jonathan Lear traced in his 2008 book *Radical Hope*, did not give up hope for the cultural rebirth of his people despite the cultural devastation they faced. A possible reason for this, according to Eagleton, is that Plenty Coups was "a baptised Christian, one who regarded his commitment to God as sustaining his trust in a future that outstripped his own efforts to grasp it" (2015, 114).

Many philosophies and movements have been sustained by a belief in the ultimate triumph of good over evil; right over wrong. Marxism professes faith that capitalism is not sustainable because the proletariat will not countenance exploitation forever. Cabral noted that the decolonization movement of Guinea-Bissau and the Cape Verde Islands was "strengthened by the certainty that we [were] right" (1979, 44). For Spartacus, Terry Eagleton commented, "The slaves' struggle [was] not simply to improve their condition, but a principled rebellion in the name of freedom; so that even if they [were] all slaughtered, their insurrection will not have been in vain. On the contrary, it will have manifested their unconditional commitment to emancipation" (2015, 130).

While hope desires, faith anticipates. West Papuans hope for *merdeka*, and they have faith that they will attain it. In general, Eagleton observes, "the more rational one's grounds for faith, the more one may hope, since the more probable it is that one's faith will be vindicated" (2015, 42). It is evident that many West Papuans have a Christian-based faith in the ultimate triumph of their struggle, but their hope is also anchored in the rational basis for their faith—that is, the precedent of East Timorese independence from Indonesia, against all expectations, in 2002 (see the conclusion). The West Papuan discourse of righteousness is a "steadfast conviction" that God and the international community will not abandon West Papua, and in Eagleton's words, "To trust that one will not be abandoned is the foundation of hope" (2015, 41).

What Comes after Independence?

So far, I have established that a discursive certainty about the inevitability of independence circulates among many West Papuans, as does a conviction that the alternative to independence is genocide. But to what extent have West Papuan leaders planned for West Papua's future if independence is indeed attained? This has been a concern of at least a few West Papuan intellectuals, as well as outside observers of the struggle. How can independence do more than fulfill a human and, in West Papuans' eyes, God-given right? How can it enable more than the mere survival of a people? Upon what foundations will a decolonized West Papua be built? And where would independence leave West Papua's relationship with Indonesia?

During the period of African decolonization, Senegal's first president, Leopold Senghor, pronounced: "It is not the colonial past that characterizes us as Africans. We share it with all the other peoples of Asia and America. It belongs to the past—at any rate, it will belong to the past tomorrow. It lies behind us now that our task is to build our future" (quoted in Kohn and McBride 2011, 19). As they continue laying down their own decolonization path, West Papuans are also deciding what, beyond common suffering at the hands of their colonizer, unites them as a body politic. One important unifier is the concept of *merdeka,* the vision for the future held by many West Papuans (see chapter 1). Another is the strong West Papuan identification as Melanesian (see chapter 3), which serves as a basis of regional unity and pride in much the same way that Césaire's and Senghor's "development of the concept of negritude" (Kohn and McBride 2011, 20) has done for black Africans at home and their descendants in diaspora since the 1930s (see Webb-Gannon, Webb, and Solis 2018). Under Indonesian occupation, Benny Wenda contends, West Papuans find it difficult to celebrate what binds them together—their Melanesian customs and identity; Indonesia accepts such cultural expression only to the extent that it provides entertainment for tourists and objectifies Papuans (Interview, 2018). This "limits us in expanding our wings... but when West Papua becomes independent, we can share our [Melanesian] values and vision together more strongly," Wenda reasons (Interview, 2018). Both of these unifiers—the vision of *merdeka* and Melanesian identity—depend on indigenous imaginings and thus allow West Papuans to avoid, to some extent, Indian author Rabindranath Tagore's warnings of the dangers inherent in founding a state on foreign models of nationalism (Kohn and McBride 2011, 19).

Some observers anticipate that the proximity of West Papua to Indonesia, like East Timor, precludes its economic independence even if West Papua does obtain political independence. But to many West Papuan leaders, independence does not mean cutting off all ties with Indonesia. After all, Indonesia's wealth is also West Papua's: "Indonesia owes us a lot," Rex Rumakiek contends (Interview, 2018). Fanon wrote of the commonly held perception in the so-called Third World that colonial powers achieved their wealth on their own merits and of the feeling among newly postcolonial nations that they must prove they are similarly capable (1963, 54). But "posing the problem of development of underdeveloped countries in this way seems... to be neither right nor reasonable" (Fanon 1963, 52), he surmises. In line with Fanon's thinking on this matter, it seems West Papuan leaders do not feel the need to prove themselves "absolutely" independent given the decades of exploitation to which they have been subject. A relationship of interdependence with Indonesia, leaders have commented to me, will be carefully established, considering the needs of the Indonesian population living in West Papua and the specific trade and business interests of West Papuans (R. Rumakiek, interview, 2018; B. Wenda, interview, 2018).

Other West Papuan leaders, including the late Catholic priest and academic Neles Tebay, have voiced concerns that insufficient thought has gone into constructing a political foundation for an independent West Papua: "I ask [Papuans calling for independence]: 'So suppose if you are my leader, do you have any vision for an independent West Papuan state?' And they have no idea. No idea. So…I have come to realize we have [fewer] leaders who really have a vision. So, fighting, fighting, but fighting for what? No idea. For separation from Indonesia, that's all. And then what? And then what kind of society do you want to set up here?" (Interview, 2008).

To assuage the concerns of intellectuals such as Tebay, many West Papuan political leaders have been involved in debating significant issues likely to face a West Papuan state, including ensuring competent leadership, dealing with migration and settlers in the nation, and weighing up the merits of various governance structures for an independent West Papua.

LEADERSHIP

Political leadership in the West Papuan decolonization movement is presently highly contested and characterized by considerable factionalism (see chapter 4). John Tekwie contends: "The problem with the West Papua struggle is not an issue of understanding and knowing where we want to go, everybody knows [that] already.…The issue of West Papua is an issue of leadership.…You can quote me on this. West Papua will only get independence—and they will get it…[when we] answer this problem; the question of leadership" (Interview, 2009).

Less controversial than the topic of leadership now is the topic of leadership after independence: leaders of most current factions largely agree that they do not presume they will automatically assume leadership positions in an independent West Papua (A. Ajamiseba, interview, 2009). Suriel Mofu, a West Papuan academic who was living in Oxford when I interviewed him in 2008, believes that those who lead West Papua in the future will be those who prioritize both peace and justice. He anticipates that the present internal politicking will abate once leaders experience the freedom to meet and to discuss differences through democratic processes (Interview, 2008). According to Rex Rumakiek, the ULMWP reminds people "that we are not there [in an independent state] yet so don't try and do something to create problems that might defer independence even further: why don't you wait until we achieve independence, then we can sort out our differences.…We are aware that we are so many tribes that these things can happen, and we will not allow the differences to divide our nation" (Interview, 2018).

For leaders such as Rumakiek who have dedicated most of their lives to the struggle, the postindependence period may present an opportunity to make up for some of that time, rather than continuing in a national leadership position. "I have been away from my own tribe for a long time so I have to repay the damage; I have to do something for my own tribe as well," Rumakiek reasons (Interview, 2018).

Customary leadership is considered an important part of West Papua's cultural heritage and future, and leaders as geographically distant from each other as the late Erna Mahuze from the Majelis Rakyat Papua (MRP;

Papuan Legislative Council) in Jayapura and the late political activist Zachi Sawor in the Netherlands have stated that leadership representation from the Dewan Adat Papua (DAP; Papuan Customary Council) will be important in an independent West Papua (E. Mahuze, interview, 2008; Z. Sawor, interview, 2008). Female leadership in an independent West Papua is also considered critical among female and male independence campaigners—the MRP currently features a one-third compulsory female leadership policy (F. Korain, interview, 2008; E. Mahuze, interview, 2008), but the ULMWP, according to its chair, Benny Wenda, is committed to equal representation of women and men at the leadership level (Interview, 2018). West Papuan activist Leonie Tanghama (based in the Netherlands) previously held a place on the Executive Committee of the ULMWP, and Paula Makabory (based in Australia) currently sits on the committee. Rex Rumakiek anticipates the establishment of "a special ministry [for] women" in an independent West Papua and an acknowledgment in the constitution that women have "suffered double and triple. They have [had] to [see] their children be killed. They give birth to children not to be killed but they are always killed, and their husbands are killed, and their family members are killed. They have suffered a lot" (Interview, 2018).

The West Papua National Authority (WPNA—the self-proclaimed West Papuan provisional government that holds considerable influence on the ground in West Papua) has promulgated the idea that in order for the government to remain in touch with the needs of "the people," the future leadership of West Papua should come from those within rather than from those who have spent considerable time in the diaspora (J. Rumbiak, interview, 2009; H. Wainggai, interview, 2009). However, not all leaders in the diaspora or from factions other than the WPNA necessarily agree with this; the most well-known West Papuan independence leaders on the global stage at present live in the diaspora. There is a strong sense, however, among young and old Papuans at home and abroad, that the current generation of youth and student leaders in Papua is powerful, highly educated, technologically savvy, well versed in theories of global political economy, and able to mobilize the West Papuan masses. Faith that this generation will produce solid future leaders for an independent West Papua prevails (R. Runawery, interview, 2009; H. Wainggai, interview, 2009; V. Yeimo, interview, 2010).

But the question remains for West Papuans of how "leaders evolve from being critics of colonial regimes and instigating revolutionary political change to being able to establish a stable, political alternative" (Kohn and McBride 2011, 5). Can and should the current leaders of West Papua's independence factions take on leadership positions in an independent West Papuan government, or is an entirely new set of leaders required to lead a new country forward? Benny Wenda acknowledges that while "we carry the legacy or spirit of our elders . . . the world is changing. There might be a new generation taking the leadership.... When the time comes, it is up to the people" (Interview, 2018).

MIGRATION POPULATION ISSUES

West Papuans have identified catastrophic effects on their cultural identity from in-migration from other parts of Indonesia, and they frequently lament their minority status in their own land (E. Mahuze, interview, 2008; F. Yaboisembut, interview, 2008). Neles Tebay worried out loud to me: "In all major Papuan towns, two-thirds of the population [is] non-Papuan. And [all] development activities [are] concentrated in towns. So... we ask, who enjoys, who benefits from development if not Papuans?... The consequences are very big" (Interview, 2008).

Very soon, Tebay anticipates, the mayors of the cities will be non-Papuan because in a democratic society everyone gets to vote, and the majority migrant population will vote for non-Papuans. He thus reasons that democracy, if West Papua remains within Indonesia, will ultimately work against West Papuans. To counter this threat, Benny Giay speaks of the need to limit migration: "I mean we have maybe four or three boats from Jakarta.... I talked about [this] with Father Neles [Tebay]. 'Father, this is [a] sign of [the] times. Maybe God is telling us something about this for us to react, we have to respond.... I mean, this is a real threat.'... [We] said alright, we have to think about a movement to stop this.... We have to limit... the population" (Interview, 2008). Similarly, Neles Tebay, whether by way of prediction or prescription, told me that when "West Papua gets independence... the consequence of this is... there will be no [im]migration" (Interview, 2008). To suggestions that restricting migration from Indonesia to this extent might be considered racist, West Papuan responses tend toward the position that if that were the case, their racism is defensive rather than aggressive. Memmi has described this sort of racialist response on the part of the colonized as "neither biological nor metaphysical, but social and historical" (1965, 121; see also Trask 1993, 55, on this point).

Very few West Papuan leaders appear to have plans that would change the postindependence status of Indonesians who have already made West Papua their home, provided that members of the latter group decide to become West Papuan citizens (A. Ajamiseba, interview, 2009; R. Rumakiek, interview, 2018; B. Wenda, interview, 2018). The predominant sentiment among West Papua's current independence leadership regarding the plight and rights of nonindigenous West Papuans and so-called mixed-race West Papuans in an independent West Papua is captured by the late West Papuan activist Clemens Runawery: "My personal view is... I don't want to see the transmigrants stay on in West Papua.[4] But, from a humanitarian point of view... some of them have been there for quite a long while, not at their fault. So we need to be... compassionate about that; we need to see some ways that we can also accommodate them. Those are the negotiating issues—so there [is] room" (Interview, 2009).[5]

Citizenship for West Papuans and nonindigenous Papuans in an independent West Papua is outlined in a proposed West Papuan constitution known as the *Basic Guidelines of the Federalist States of West Papua*. Included in section 32, under the heading "Citizens," are the following propositions: "(1) Those who may become Citizens are The Papuan and Melanesia[n] Ethnic by origin and other Ethnics....; (2) The State of West Papua acknowledges and respects double [dual] citizenship as far as [citizens conform] to societal order in The State of West Papua" (West Papua National Leadership 2010, 33). Notes provided to this constitution by West Papuan philosopher Don Flassy mention Benny Giay's book, *Menuju Papua baru* (Toward a New Papua). This book urges Papuans in the process of building a future for West Papua to "strengthen a culture of forgiveness" toward nonindigenous Papuans while simultaneously reversing the "Indonesianizing" of the "Nation of Papua...both in attitude and behaviour" and advancing the "Papuanizing [of]...the Nation of Papua" (West Papua National Leadership 2010, xvii). While the *Basic Guidelines* document is not necessarily the constitution that West Papuans will use after independence, it demonstrates an acceptance among certain leaders of the reality of a multicultural West Papua, the management of which will need to be sensitively handled.

GOVERNANCE

Taiaiake Alfred asks, with regard to indigenous American peoples, "How can we regenerate ourselves culturally and achieve freedom and political independence when the legacies of disconnection, dependency, and dispossession have such a strong hold on us?" (2005, 20). The same question faces West Papuans as they attempt to build the apparatus of an independent West Papuan state while still in the grips of colonialism—a state that, even postindependence, will still feel the impact of decades of colonialism. Even if a new state is established, governance systems will need to be put in place that encourage decolonization of the mind (see Ngũgĩ 1981; Tuhiwai Smith 1999, 23). While independence might mean that "colonialism in its formal sense [has] been dismantled...many of the problems of [the new state are likely to be] products of the old colonial state" (Césaire 1972, 27). Césaire warns of the dangers inherent in postcolonial states where the primary difference between the new and the colonial state "is the presence of black faces" in positions of power (1972, 27). What might a "truly" postcolonial West Papuan state look like?" ask many leaders. It is not possible to go back to the conditions of precolonial Papua. Neither will it be possible for West Papua to completely ignore models, or aspects of models, presented by current examples of other nation-states if it hopes to be a participating member of the global system of nation-states. For an independent West Papua, Papuans will need to develop a model, therefore, that balances governance solutions deriving from the present "colonized time [drawing on contemporary nation-state models], and the time before that, pre-colonized time [when the many nations residing in the territory that is now West Papua did not require the governance of a state]" (Tuhiwai Smith 1999, 24).

Various governance structures building on contemporary democratic philosophy and West Papuan customary systems have been proposed over the course of the struggle, some of which retain currency to this day. At the left-leaning end of the spectrum is advocacy for a social democratic structure of governance in West Papua, sometimes expressed as the more radical goal of "Melanesian socialism," an idea originating at the beginning of the struggle in the late 1960s and early 1970s. The philosophy was espoused by the first prime minister of Vanuatu, Father Walter Lini. He linked Melanesian socialism with the Melanesian way, emphasizing a "sustained awareness for the need for a communal discipline" and common roots and traditions among Melanesians, including the custom of giving, receiving, and sharing according to need (Linnekin 1990, 167). Lini was influenced by Julius Nyerere's ideas of African socialism in Tanzania (Rich 2006, 121). New Caledonia's resistance movement (FLNKS; Kanak Socialist National Liberation Front) also links the pursuit of sovereignty with a socialist philosophy (Waddell 2008).

Peter Savage wrote in 1978 of the "rise [in the late 1960s] of the younger, more left-wing, and more strategically adventurous [West Papuan leaders such as] Jacob Prai . . . and the development of a more obviously anti-capitalist, anti-imperialist rhetoric which [was] being supported by combat action" (1978, 991). West Papua scholar Beverly Blaskett has also commented on Prai's socialist politics, writing that in 1977, "Jacob Prai issued a press release which claimed that a new slogan had been adopted by his group: 'Without Socialism There Can Be No Independence'" (1993, 323). She notes that a West Melanesian Socialist Party was formed in the late 1970s that supported Jacob Prai's jungle government (1993, 323). When I visited Prai in exile in Malmö, Sweden, in 2008, he had maintained his socialist-styled resistance even there—he and his son Joseph had established a European OPM headquarters in Malmö that existed on the strength of political support from the socialist Swedish Social Democratic Youth League, a branch of the Swedish Social Democratic Party.

Jacob and Joseph told me they were guided by the OPM constitution, which claims: "The ideology of the OPM is one that promotes an equalitarian [*sic*] society with an equitable division of political, economic and social power, with respect for the rights and dignity of all citizens. This may be described as MELANESIAN SOCIALISM" (OPM Department for External Affairs, n.d.). Similarly, Seth Rumkorem, who had joined Prai's guerrilla forces in 1970 to offer professional army training, talked to me in 2008 about his welfare state governance vision, which is based, he asserted, on the land reform policies of Ho Chi Minh:

> A West Papuan state [will be] a legal, democratic state [with] respect for human rights. There are three bases already in . . . our constitution . . . [and our] OPM . . . program. It is already laid down, what we'll do in the future. First of all, one of the most important programs . . . [is] the . . . Program for People's Development—I [will] give you an example: most of the revolutions, they get to reach welfare state through land reform. From Latin America to [the] Pacific Islands, just land reform is [the] means to reach [a] welfare state. . . . Only Ho Chi Minh . . . failed not. Nine years of fighting, and they didn't lack . . . food. . . . Vietnam is [the] number one rice producer country. And [in] West Papua: land, [there is] plenty. . . . We have fish in our rich land. We have trees, jungle, [and] forest. We have oil [and] gas. (Interview, 2008)

According to Otto Ondawame, before joining the TPN/OPM Seth Rumkorem was a member of the XVII (Irian Jaya Province) Communist Party during his time in the military training school in Bandung (Ondawame 2010, 48). Beverly Blaskett notes that Jacob Prai referred to Rumkorem, in various letters, as a "Communist" (1993, 323).

The socialist-inspired philosophy lives on in the West Papuan struggle for independence on the ground in the form of stringent anticolonial and anticapitalist critiques from the younger generation of leaders today. In Port Vila, Vanuatu, in 2008, at the West Papua Coalition for Liberation's leadership summit, several of the student delegates from West Papua vociferously opposed suggestions of accommodating Special Autonomy or any other "stepping-stone"-type plan that entailed working gradually toward the realization of human rights in West Papua. This they saw as tantamount to allowing the ongoing economic exploitation of West Papua not only by Indonesia but also by the United States and other foreign powers. Many of the younger, left-leaning leaders view global neocolonialist structures of oppression, including economic exploitation, as just as harmful to West Papua as Indonesian occupation. It remains unclear what influence this "socialist"-styled critique might have in an independent West Papua, however, as radical critique tends to be discouraged by some of the more "centrist" second-generation leaders. One executive and politically seasoned member of the independence movement later mentioned to me that he wished the student movements would "tone down" their expressions of opposition to neocolonial exploitation in West Papua and abandon their more radical ideologies, as these detracted global attention from the struggle against the main enemy—Indonesian colonialism. This, coming from an original member of the OPM, could be considered an example of the phenomenon of "middling out," which has occurred in other liberation movements such as the "Provisional Irish Republican Army (IRA), Palestine Liberation Organization (PLO), or African National Congress (ANC)...in the 1970s and 1980s...[each of these movements] supported radical socialist, Marxist, or anti-Western ideas but have since moved firmly into the political mainstream as their leadership has aged" (Schulze 2003, 247). Apart from attempting to negotiate post–Cold War politics (Schulze's explanation), the advocacy of a less radical political stance by older Papuan leaders could also stem from efforts to appeal to an uncertain "market for transnational support...in competition with a host of other worthy movements, and in the face of limited attention and resources" (Bob 2005).

The idea of social equity as a principle of governance is often linked by independence leaders to visions of a future independent "federal republic of tribes." Benny Wenda speculates that prior to colonial occupation the governance system he imagines probably existed in West Papua was that of loose tribal federations and that this system should be resurrected (Interview, 2008). The rationale behind such an idea is that a state governance system that does not respect the regional and customary diversity represented by West Papuan tribes will not make for effective unity. Indeed, Otto Ondawame noted, "It is often argued that a federal system is more likely than a unitary state to guarantee justice to all groups of peoples, large and small" (2010, 248). Drawing on the Acehnese independence leader Hasan di Tiro's appraisal of federalism, Ondawame commented: "Federalism is an implementation of democracy: it aims to harmonise diverse cultures, traditions, ways of life, economic concerns, races and religions in a framework which serves their common interests" (2010, 248). Suriel Mofu, too, advocates a governance system that honors, unites, and respects the "250 tribes and leaders" of West Papua so that what happened in Indonesia, where "one tribe leads many," will not be replicated in West Papua (Interview, 2008). Viktor Kaisiepo described this idea as "confederation":

> Independent West Papua should be designed in a political process or political structure that is called confederation. Confederation...simply [takes into account] the internal differences in West Papua. Like in Papua New Guinea [where there are] 775 tribes...[and]...250 something in West Papua—by definition, that is already conflict!...If you want to meet the new-world criteria of nation-state, what is required to compose a nation-state?...If you want my opinion, confederacy is the best solution for West Papua. Let the highland community decide on the highlands, how it [will] flourish. But when we talk West Papua, let them delegate, mandate some of their representatives

> up to an upper house [that] will discuss West Papua, but not the highlands because that's the prerogative and the right of the cultural groups in the highlands to make their own decisions, similarly to the lowlands and the islands. And then see how we can mesh these, too, with the modern and the traditional life. That's my idea.... That's what I dream of, of a free West Papua, that it's going to be organized that way, with respect for the community, and that's the starting point. (Interview, 2008)

At the bare minimum, Kaisiepo recommended that some sort of tribal governance structure be appended to whatever becomes the dominant system of government in a free West Papua, similar to the Great Council of Chiefs that existed in Fiji until 2012 or the Vanuatu Malvatu Mauri (National Council of Chiefs; interview, 2008).

Like Kaisiepo, West Papuan theorist Sem Karoba proposes that a "tribal democracy" (an idea he credits to Nelson Mandela) might be the most appropriate way to govern West Papua. Karoba is concerned that the killing and exploitation that have been committed under Indonesia's reign will continue in an independent West Papua unless Papuans are careful to avoid having a foreign governance system imposed upon them (2009). "All systems of government in this earth are imperfect and some principles only appropriate for certain groups," Karoba writes (1999, n.p.). He predicts that a Western-style liberal democracy will perpetuate exploitation in West Papua. A tribal democracy, on the other hand, will facilitate equal representation for each West Papuan tribe at the national level, recognize and work with West Papuan constituents as both tribal people in a modern world and modern people in a tribal world, and govern according to a more holistic, less anthropocentric view of the world than might a nontribal democracy (Karoba 2009).

Such a tribal democracy, federation, or confederation might be configured loosely along the lines of the current DAP structure, which, according to its chairperson Forkorus Yaboisembut, was

> established [in 2002 of] individual tribal councils and expand[ed]... to link with others to establish a common social culture. During the Dutch Administration there were seven cultural regions. The region starting from the Mamberamo [River] to the border with PNG [is] called Mamta. [There] is one cultural group called Tabi, and I am the chairman. The [other] regions, Biak, Serui, [and] Nabire/Waropen [form] another cultural group called Saireri. Then Sorong... is another group. The Fak Fak, Kaimana, Bintuni group is region four, called Bomberai. The Asmat, Merauke... region, five, [is] called Animha. Region six comprises Wamena... [and] is called Lapago. Then region seven,

> the Paniai region, [is] called Mepago. The Papua Tribal Council represents all those seven cultural groups. [These groups are connected through] shared cultural values and issues such as the same faith, historically... and the same suffering [and] oppression. (Interview, 2008)[6]

Other federation-inspired ideas extend to the suggestion that West Papua eventually join together with the neighboring Melanesian countries to form a Melanesian federation. "My father was a big fighter for the [idea of a] Melanesian federation. He was looking for a co-operation between the Melanesian countries—that was his dream, his idea. When I was young, [my father] created the airlines... called MAS—Melanesian Air Service" to service and represent the federation should it become a reality, reminisced Viktor Kaisiepo (Interview, 2008).

Andy Ajamiseba, the late Vanuatu-based member of the ULMWP, argued for the currency of the idea, professing to strongly

> believe that... Melanesia will eventually become a federation... a sort of union, with an executive of para-legislatures.... A federated state of Melanesia [with] a state parliament [and]... a federal parliament which is very good because then we will become a bloc, an economic bloc, a political bloc, much stronger because then a country like Vanuatu could become our capital of the federation or something. In a smaller country, we could supply our [own] oil, or maybe we could build a refinery here, and supply the whole Pacific.... A federation of Melanesia, you're talking about ten million people. (Interview, 2009)

The idea of a Melanesian federation is a fitting example of Tuhiwai Smith's postcolonial governance recommendation that any new governance model incorporate elements from "the time before, colonized time, and the time before that, pre-colonized time" (1999, 24). Federation has its origins in colonial thinking and in postcolonial regional sentiment while it simultaneously honors indigenous West Papuan federalist preferences (Waters 2010). In the 1950s, the former governor-general of Australia, Justice John Kerr, was a vocal advocate of a Melanesian federation that, had it come to fruition, would have seen a united PNG, West Papua, and Solomon Islands. Due to shifting regional politics, his idea was ultimately abandoned by Australia, but the concept captured the imagination of many West Papuans at that time who had envisaged becoming part of a united New Guinea state (independence leader Nicolaas Jouwe, for example, was an avid supporter). Rex Rumakiek recalls, "We never dreamed that there would be two separate countries. We always dreamed that Australia and the Dutch were actually working on a scheme that the whole island would be independent, and there [would not] be any boundaries" (Interview, 2010). He remembers, with irony, a school soccer match in the pre-PNG-independence era in which a team from the PNG side and a West Papuan team competed against each other. The West Papuan team had uniforms, but the PNG team wore *lap laps* (wraparound skirts). Because of this the West Papuans felt sorry for the (soon-to-be) Papua New Guineans. Rumakiek says, "We felt that... it would be our duty that as soon as we got our independence, *we* [would] help *them* to get their independence, not the other way around!" (Interview, 2010)—the idea of independence linked in his imagination at the time to a rejection of traditional attire.

Many of the older generation of West Papuan leaders and some within the middle and younger generations who resent the artificial border and the colonial imposition that it signifies still harbor hope for a unified New Guinea State. More leaders, however, are skeptical about the viability of such a future, believing that the disparate colonial histories of the two sides of the island have rendered the nationalist visions of each too different (A. Ajamiseba, interview, 2009; S. Rumkorem, interview, 2008). There are also conflicted feelings among West Papuans about PNG's role in their struggle. On the one hand, many West Papuans are grateful for the civil society solidarity of Papua New Guineans, but on the other, they are also deeply disappointed by the PNG government's lack of support. As Freddy Waromi observes: "In culture, you can call everyone [a] friend, but in politics, you can [be an] enemy to your brother or your sister. It is [a] fact that we are [the] Melanesian brother of Papua New Guinea, but because of political reasons, because of the bilateral relationship [with] Indonesia, Papua New Guinea denies us" (Interview, 2009).

Many West Papuans believe that PNG had "their freedom handed over by Australia... as a gift, so... they [Papua New Guineans] don't feel the pain like we are feeling" (O. Ap, interview, 2008) and that PNG takes its independence for granted. Therefore, Papua New Guineans are sometimes seen as merely "lip-service brothers" (O. Ap, interview, 2008) or "puppets of Indonesia" (Jacob Prai, interview, 2008) who offer little genuine support to West Papuans.[7] PNG's official reticence to deny Indonesian sovereignty in West Papua is perhaps understandable from a realpolitik point of view, given the threat that the Indonesian military poses to PNG, with whom Indonesia shares a border. The PNG Defence Force, for example, numbers approximately 2000 personnel (*Post Courier* 2017), compared to Indonesia's approximately 436,000 (Global Firepower 2018). Overall, the most common West Papuan view now is that a unified government, however idyllic in theory, would not work in practice.

Currently, there are five West Papuan constitutions in circulation (O. Mote, pers. comm., 2018), all of which will be consulted, leaders say, when the official constitution is drafted (if and when West Papua becomes independent). For the ULMWP, however, the OPM constitution developed in 1971 (the "original constitution," according to Benny Wenda) will provide the foundation for the new constitution, although elements of the other constitutions will be taken into consideration during the ongoing effort to bring the OPM constitution up to date (B. Wenda, interview, 2018).

Ultimately, West Papuans whom I have interviewed anticipate that their future government will comprise some form of representative democracy that values the will of the people—a "luxury" they have never experienced under Indonesian democracy. If there is one thing West Papuans do have in abundance, it is experience in how not to structure their democracy. UK-based West Papuan activist Richard Samuelson once asked a British MP why, since Indonesia is a democracy, West Papuans are not allowed to form Papuan political parties. The MP, not sympathetic to West Papua's plight, responded that Indonesia is "a different type of democracy." This "different" type of democracy, West Papuans agree, is not the type they envisage for their own state (R. Samuelson, interview, 2008; B. Wenda, interview, 2008). "The time has long passed when we will adopt somebody else's political model for our struggle, including our path towards nationhood," Hawaiian decolonization scholar Haunani Kay Trask wrote in 1993 (1993, 269); West Papuan leaders appear to think similarly. There is an apparent consensus among West Papuan leaders that a British-style Westminster system would be unlikely to work for West Papua. As Viktor Kaisiepo argued: "If we... adapt a system, a foreign system and... adjust [it] to us, then we will get lost like PNG. Then we will get lost like Vanuatu because we are making the music from the party tunes from overseas. It's not the flute, the bamboo flute, the *kundu* [drum], from our own community" (Interview, 2008).

Whatever political form a West Papuan state may assume in the event of independence, whether it be a federation of tribes or a unitary republic, and whatever competing forms of governance might be advanced, West Papuans still believe that their independent state will assume the generic function of a state, which is "to bring together or articulate into a complexly structured instance, a range of political discourses and social practices which are concerned at different sites with the transmission and transformation of power" (Hall 1985, 93). What they are acutely concerned with is that their hoped-for state is structured to be culturally responsive to the needs of a diverse population.

Many West Papuans believe that the alternative to independence is genocide—that Indonesia is currently engaging in genocidal measures against the Papuan population—and that if the current political status quo is not urgently replaced with an opportunity for self-determination, the survival of West Papuans is uncertain. This position is only growing in strength among the younger generations and is a point of bonding between multiple generations of West Papuan independence leaders. Further, there is a strong consensus among many West Papuans that independence will be achieved. It is perceived to be a predestined, God-given, West Papuan entitlement and a human right.

However, the staunch unity that exists around West Papuans' fierce insistence that their future consists of either independence or obliteration, but that God will ensure it is the former, becomes somewhat less obvious in discussions about what West Papua might look like postindependence. Some Papuan intellectual leaders are worried that political leaders have failed to give enough thought to what lies ahead in terms of governing an independent state. The West Papuan human rights advocate John Rumbiak expressed such fears during his active campaigning days. He was concerned that West Papuans might be overcome with euphoria upon attaining independence. This, he argued in an interview with West Papua observer Jim Elmslie in 2005, "is not 100 per cent wrong, that's fine, but rationalising it... is extremely important." He was equally concerned about the potential desire for revenge: "It is the psychology of people who are oppressed. It happened to the South Africans, it happened to everyone else who was once colonised. Once you understand that, what you have got to do is to develop processes by workshops and education to release the people from this psychological scar and to be rational so that they don't [seek] revenge" (quoted in Elmslie, unpublished data). This fear is constructive to air because it may prompt West Papuan leaders to continue to produce viable ideas for living peaceably together and with Indonesian settlers. While leadership is currently hotly contested in the extant proindependence movement, most leaders do agree that the current leadership will not necessarily be the leadership of the future. The latter will be determined democratically when the future becomes clearer. Migration-related issues—both managing ongoing migration and working out the status of established migrants—will perhaps be the Achilles' heel of an independent West Papuan government. In a democracy, there will need to be some provision for political representation from nonindigenous Papuans. Dealing with land ownership issues, retraining TPN/OPM forces into a national military or reintegrating them into society, and reintegrating disparate diaspora populations will also comprise major hurdles, as they did in independent East Timor (Scheiner 2006).

West Papuans agree that they want a democratic government, although the type of democratic system is up for debate. The establishment of, and membership within, a greater Melanesian political union (one more comprehensive than the current Melanesian Spearhead Group) has also been proposed. Ultimately, though, there is a strong leaning toward some sort of "federation of tribes" governance structure, which, it is hoped, could accommodate the great diversity of West Papuans within a harmonious, unified body politic. Analyst of East Timor politics Charles Scheiner has commented:

"Nearly every new nation in history, including many which are affluent and long-standing today, took a decade or more to establish peace, national unity, stable constitutional government and rule of law. Nation-building requires patience, time and trial-and-error" (2006, 6). This will certainly be true for an independent West Papua. But above all, the foregoing analysis has shown that the West Papuan independence leadership does agree, to borrow words from Cabral, on the importance of "unity and struggle. Unity . . . to struggle against the colonialists and struggle . . . to achieve our unity . . . to construct our land as it should be" (1979, 33).

3

CONSTELLATIONS

Cultural Performance as Resistance at Home and Abroad

> We use [culture] as a tool.... [Culture is a] messenger, you know...something everyone can see.
>
> —*West Papuan university student, 2009*

During my work with West Papuans over the past thirteen years, I have heard many at home and in diaspora express the sentiment that it is just as important to be "culturally" West Papuan as it is to be "politically" so (N. Jouwe, interview, 2008; S. Karubaba, interview, 2009; F. Makanuey, interview, 2009). In exploring such claims, I have come to understand that at times an emphasis on the identity politics associated with being West Papuan (for example, being black with curly hair [*hitam keriting*], indigenous [*orang asli*], and Melanesian), rather than on overt political demands for nation-statehood, is strategic. Culture binds people outside of the factions and generational conflict that nation-state politics creates (see chapter 4). Culture has a corporeal quality—it can be performed, worn, sung, tasted, spoken, and seen. To many West Papuans, the cultural expression of West Papuanness ensures the survival of West Papuan politics and people (F. Makanuey, interview, 2009; J. Tekwie, interview, 2009). It "opens up mental space for political analysis to slip in," according to Trask (1993, 275). West Papuans recognize the same principle that Cabral put forward in 1979 in relation to the Guinea-Bissauan and Cape Verdean decolonization struggles: such struggles are "based on culture, because culture is the fruit of history and it is a strength" (58).

Some scholars have argued that the development of West Papuan nationalism (a pan–West Papuan political culture) is primarily a reaction to Indonesia's violent occupation of the territory (see Ballard 2006, 11; Chauvel 2004, 6; Webster 2001–2002, 513). Historian David Webster writes that West Papuan nationalism "could have been mobilized in the interest of union with Indonesia, in particular [because of] the common language,[1] raising the question of why emergent nationalism was eventually realized on the lines of West Papuan rather than Indonesian identity. Without the separation from Indonesia, it seems unlikely that Papuan nationalism would have emerged, at least not in the same form. Both 'pro-Dutch' and 'pro-Indonesian' streams existed within Papuan elites" (2001–2002, 513). Webster assumes "Indonesia" holds the primary national identity within which "West Papua" could have been incorporated—without establishing what it is that gives "Indonesia" a more legitimate and fundamental identity, or makes it more worthy of a state for its nation(s), than West Papua. Similarly, Chauvel argues: "That Papuans should have developed a pan-Papuan identity separate from an Indonesian one was not a forgone conclusion, for ever since the Pacific War Papuans have been confronted by a number of alternate visions of their future" (2005, 83). He describes the Indonesian nationalist Soegoro's postwar vision for West Papua as part of an independent Indonesia and Dutch educator in West Papua Van Eechoud's vision of a Melanesian future for West Papua (2005, 83). But where in these theories of the development of West Papuan nationalism does Papuan creativity, cultural expression, and political agency fit? West Papuans have been as actively involved as any outsider in deciding what it is, under conditions of modernity, to "be West Papuan."

West Papuans' post–World War II Melanesian identity is at least as much a consequence of precolonial Melanesian Asian antagonisms and their shared histories and cultures with other Melanesian peoples with whom they share a region as it is a result of Dutch identity construction or a reaction to conflict with Indonesia. Migration to New Guinea, from Africa, via Asia, commenced at least forty thousand years ago (Moore 2003, 21). Over one thousand different languages, and many more dialects, are spoken in New Guinea and fall into two main groups—Austronesian languages, brought by settlers around four thousand years ago, possibly originating in Taiwan and traveling south via Southeast Asia, and Papuan, a much older group of languages spoken by most New Guineans today (Moore 2003, 35–36).

Clive Moore submits that the Malay world through which the Melanesian Papuan and Austronesian populations traveled to get to New Guinea and the Melanesian world in which New Guinea is anchored "blend together over several hundred kilometers of ocean and islands" (2003, 57). By the eighth century, this meant that certain Papuans and Malukans at the periphery of both worlds were able to form lucrative *sosolot* (trade) enclaves and intermarry, creating privileged communities that would come to enjoy economic advantage over both European and other local traders in the region (Goodman 1998, 1).

But in New Guinea, these *sosolots* only benefited a Papuan elite. The elite New Guineans participating in the *sosolot* exchange received highly valued *kain timur* (woven cloth) in exchange for procuring slaves and other items, as well as "brass wire, swords, steel chopping-knives and axes, porcelain cups and bowls, basins, rugs, glass beads, armlets, tobacco, [and] rice" (Moore 2003, 70). The numerous Papuans who became "objects" of exchange (slaves) were not so fortunate, often being sent far from home. For example, Chinese records from the eighth century note that the Sumatran king of Shrivijaya gifted the emperor of China "two dwarfs, a number of parrots, and some 'Seng-k'i girls'" (the term "Seng-k'i" is thought to refer to Papuans; Souter 1963, 17). And from the fourteenth century, New Guinea was plundered for its "exotic produce," including "slaves, cockatoos, lorikeets and crowned pigeons, bird-of-paradise plumes and other bird pelts and plumes, beche-de-mer, pearls, turtle-shells, and ambergris," to supply Asian trade networks (Moore 2003, 63). The plundering of slaves from New Guinea was "substantial" (Moore 2003, 68), taking "advantage of the regions' ethnic and linguistic groups" that prevented organized resistance (67): "Each year for several centuries hundreds of New Guinean slaves—children and adults—were transported east into the Malay Archipelago, usually never to return" (68).

The roots of Melanesian Asian antagonism date back to the formation of this largely exploitative trade network in which the sultans of the Malukan states of Tidore and Ternate extracted slaves, exotic goods, and tribute from New Guineans. From at least the fifteenth century, those sultanates claimed to exercise over certain areas of west New Guinea (Moore 2003, 62) what was known in European international law of the time as suzerainty. Suzerainty entails the control by one polity of another's foreign relations but not of their internal governance. New Guineans had little to gain and rather much to lose in their suzerain relationship with Tidore. The rule of the sultan of Tidore in Papua, according to eyewitness and Dutch government accounts at the time, was characterized by campaigns of terror and depredation. "The sultan wielded…his rule over the region [through] the appointment of headmen, the collection of the tribute, and, should this not be produced, the sending of a fleet of armed war canoes, the so called hongi" (Huizinga 1998, 386). While "theoretically the mission of the hongi expedition was to collect tribute and enforce order[,] in reality, they turned out to be raids, bring[ing] death, slavery and devastation in their wake" (Huizinga 1998, 415). "The very sight of them caused the local inhabitants to panic and flee inland. Those who did not manage to escape in time were robbed of all their possessions, murdered, or carried off as slaves" (Drooglever 2009, 6). According to historian Pieter Drooglever, "governance [of Papua by the sultan of Tidore] in the true sense of the word did not actually materialize" (2009, 6). He expressed his authority and leveraged his influence solely through the periodic deployment of the *hongi* (Drooglever 2009, 6). Thus, we can see that conflict between the Melanesian populations of New Guinea and the Asian populations with whom they were in contact became apparent centuries before Dutch and then Indonesian colonizers attempted to shape West Papuan identity.

Far from being passive subjects of a national identity formation, West Papuans have also drawn on a long autochthonous cultural history to shape the Melanesian trajectory of their national identity. Moore maintains that fundamental differences have long existed between Oceanic/Pacific cultures and Asian and European ones: Pacific concepts of time are cyclical, not linear (2003, 8); spirit worlds link the present, past, and future (8); and social relationships and behaviors are governed according to wider cosmological beliefs (9). Melanesian society is founded on networks of relationships based around land, exchange and trade, language, and parentage/ancestry (Moore 2003, 11). "Such was the strength of the core culture of New Guinea and Island Melanesia," Moore writes, "that later Austronesian migrants only managed to have a peripheral affect [*sic*]" (2003, 33): "New Guinea clearly hosted an affluent human society many thousands of years before the same could be said of Southeast Asia. Sahul's [the Pleistocene-era continent comprising New Guinea, Australia, and Tasmania] people practiced large-scale hunting and gathering, tree-cropping and tree-cultivation. They were sailors capable of moving long distances. They perfected fire-stick farming and developed complex agricultural practices, including drainage and irrigation" (Moore 2003, 33). And when Sahul separated into the landmasses that would become New Guinea, the Australian mainland, and Tasmania, Papuan cultures became increasing distinctive: "Papuans formed into clan cultures. [They] cultivated taro and root crops adapted to their islands [as opposed to their Malay neighbors who were grain growers], and are famed for evolving persuasive individual leaders that scholars have called 'Big Men'" (Matsuda 2012, 13).

Because of this history, and because of the ongoing politics of difference emerging from the Indonesian-Papuan conflict that poses an essentialism between "Asian" and "Melanesian" identities rather than the heterogeneous assemblage forms these often take, many West Papuans view themselves as more like other Melanesian peoples than Indonesians, whom they view as Asian. As Otto Ondawame explains: "I don't feel Indonesian. I'm uncomfortable staying in Indonesia, or Asia, or Malaysia, or Singapore, or whatever. I feel comfortable when I stay in Melanesia, like Vanuatu or Solomon Islands. I feel like it's my home. I feel that we share [the] same culture [and] traditional way of life" (Interview, 2009). This identity, both a construct and a lived reality, persists despite Melanesian countries' disparate colonial histories. While, as anthropologist Chris Ballard writes, at least some of "the seeds of [a political pan-]Papuan identity [were] born of suffering" (2006, 11), West Papuan national identity is now a complex phenomenon with transnational articulations. Globalization has increased the interaction between the West Papuan diaspora and the homeland, and as a result, West Papuan cultural nationalism has begun to flourish even outside of Melanesia.

In this chapter I develop the argument that West Papuan nationalism is more than a reactive phenomenon that, had the Indonesian regime not been violent, may never have arisen or otherwise taken on a more "Asian" than "Melanesian" character. That Dutch preparation and Indonesian violent opposition were in fact the circumstances under which contemporary West Papuan cultural nationalism did take root does not preclude the strong possibility that, in an era of "Third World" nationalisms and decolonization, black power politics, and globalization, West Papua may have developed a national identity separate to Indonesia's, with Melanesian linkages, regardless. This is important because their cultural distinctiveness, or at least their cultural "Melanesianness," is one of the attributes that West Papuans contend defines them as a people, a unit separate to "Indonesia" and worthy of self-determination. First, I canvas the ways in which, "in the context of Indonesia, [West Papuan] cultural performance as a representation of nationhood is conceived as an activity of resistance" (Glazebrook 2004, 1). I look at Indonesia's belief that West Papuan culture threatens its own nationalism and examine whether Indonesian criminalization of West Papuan symbols, institutions, and cultural practices could be considered cultural genocide. Second, I look closely at what the West Papuans whom I have interviewed identify as the crucial and unifying aspects of their pan–West Papuan culture, at the central importance West Papuans place on their culture for their survival, and the ways in which West Papuans position culture as a resistance strategy. I contend that even though West Papuan cultural nationalism did not emerge solely as a reaction to Indonesian hegemony, it has subsequently been situated by West Papuans as a powerful form of resistance to the same. Finally, I draw on examples from West Papuan diaspora communities in Australia, Vanuatu, Sweden, the UK, the Netherlands, and PNG to demonstrate the articulated nature of some of the disparate yet connected West Papuan diaspora nationalisms. In doing so, I am conscious of cultural theorist Stuart Hall's problematization of identity, a phenomenon "not as transparent or unproblematic as we think. Perhaps instead of thinking of identity as an already accomplished fact, which the new cultural practices then represent, we should think, instead, of identity as a 'production,' which is never complete, always in process, and always constituted within, not outside, representation" (1993, 222).

On many occasions West Papuans' cultural identity is mobilized as a "decolonization production," one that is vibrant and flexible in an attempt to ensure the continuing existence of the West Papuan peoples and the unification of the many diaspora and in-country Papuan populations and their customs. West Papuan cultural nationalism not only constantly sharpens the blade of resistance to Indonesian occupation (Glazebrook 2004, n.p.) but continuously marks West Papuans as a distinctive ethnonationalist group in pursuit of a state for their robust nation.

Cultural Genocide and Survival

The primary aim of colonialism, according to scholars Ngũgĩ wa Thiong'o (1981, 16) and Nicholas Thomas (1994, 2), is to gain control of another population's wealth. The most straightforward way of achieving this, Ngũgĩ argues, is through "dominating the mental universe of the colonised. . . . Economic and political control can never be complete or effective without mental control. To control a people's culture is to control their tools of self-definition in relationship to others" (1981, 16). As in the North American context described by Taiaiake Alfred, it might be said that cultural desecration in West Papua "has placed [West Papuans'] continuing existence as peoples, or as nations and distinct cultures, in imminent danger of extinction" (2005, 30; see also see Barber and Moiwend 2011, 45–49). Raphael Lemkin, the Polish law professor who coined the term "genocide" in 1944 after narrowly escaping the Nazi occupation of Poland, also lobbied to have "cultural genocide" enshrined in the Genocide Convention. Lemkin defined cultural genocide as

> a coordinated plan of different actions aiming at the destruction of essential foundations of the life of national groups, with the aim of annihilating the groups themselves. The objectives of such a plan would be disintegration of the political and social institutions, of culture, language, national feelings, religion, and the economic existence of national groups, and the destruction of the personal security, liberty, health, dignity, and even the lives of the individuals belonging to such groups. Genocide is directed against the national group as an entity, and the actions involved are directed against individuals, not in their individual capacity, but as members of the national group. (Quoted in Nersessian 2005)

While the convention ultimately only recognized biological genocide, the 2007 United Nations Declaration on the Rights of Indigenous Peoples (UNDRIP), to which, ironically, Indonesia is a signatory, prohibits cultural genocide (although the declaration is not legally binding). What Lemkin describes as cultural genocide, Ngũgĩ has called the "cultural bomb" (1981, 3)—that is, an attempt "to annihilate a people's belief in their names, in their languages, in their environment, in their heritage of struggle, in their unity, in their capacities and ultimately in themselves" (3). Although West Papuans are resisting it, their cultures, and therefore their existence as a people, are currently threatened by the cultural bomb dropped on them by the Indonesian occupation.

In 1984 West Papuan musician and curator/anthropologist Arnold Ap was assassinated by the Indonesian military as a result of his culture-affirming work collecting songs and dances from around West Papua. His son, Oridek Ap, living in The Hague in the Netherlands, spoke to me about the legacy of his father's work, which, Oridek contends, lives on despite Indonesian attempts to suppress the power embodied in West Papuan song and dance:

> [Arnold Ap] was a musician, he was an anthropologist, his work was to unite our people with our culture, so it was something that I got to learn when I started to make music, and I started to understand why he made the choice [to put the well-being of his nation before his personal safety] and how important the choice was, because it was the right choice. . . . It was good for my people; he gave them hope by singing the old songs, by telling the old stories, by dancing our dances. It was a simple thing, but it was the soul of my people. It was almost gone, but he managed, together with his friends from Mambesak [Ap's performance group], to keep it alive, and they managed to promote it through the people, so I was proud and I accepted his choice finally. . . . We still have our elders in Papua, and let's hope that they tell the old stories and they still sing their old songs because that's our hope; when people are singing their old songs—that's our hope. But when they are singing the new songs, composed by, you know, Indonesians or other people, the old songs will disappear. And as soon as the songs, the old songs disappear, our people also disappear. (Interview, 2008)

Arnold Ap practiced resistance through his museum work, and Mambesak embodied resistance in its performances through the use of local metaphor, regional languages (as opposed to Bahasa Indonesia), and costume (or lack of it—the members of Mambesak once danced unclothed to protest a state campaign to ban *koteka,* the traditional Papuan highlands penis gourd; Glazebrook 2004, 9). Each of these actions served to mark out a non-Indonesian, West Papuan identity and in so doing served three purposes: they demonstrated opposition to the homogenizing strategies of Indonesian rule, they worked to preserve endangered West Papuan cultural practices, and they celebrated West Papuan cultural distinctiveness.

In addition to West Papuan songs and dances, indigenous Papuan languages have been the victim of various Indonesian interventions. The targeting of indigenous languages is particularly strategic. Ngũgĩ identifies language as "the collective memory bank of a people's experience in history.

Culture is the most indistinguishable from the language that makes possible its genesis, growth, banking, articulation and indeed its transmission from one generation to the next" (1981, 15). If language, "key to worldview and the embodiment of Indigenous cultures," is lost, so, too, is the culture that depended upon and supported it (Waziyatawin and Yellow Bird 2005, 5). When in elementary school, Neles Tebay recalls not being allowed "to speak in local language.... If we students were found speaking in our native language, then we got a penalty.... So, by those kinds of things, they were saying that our local, native language is bad" (Interview, 2008). Viktor Kaisiepo spoke mournfully to me of the loss of local West Papuan languages through Indonesianization: "The Indonesian education system says that as soon as you go to school, primary school, you have to speak Indonesian. By the end, you end up at university at the age of twenty-something and you don't speak your mother tongue anymore, so what's the use of education? Educate to gain knowledge, not to lose knowledge!... It is creating distance between the cultural patterns" (Interview, 2008).

The dominant religion in West Papua is Christianity, and this has also been targeted through Indonesian campaigns singling out church leaders for attack. For example, Reverend Socrates Sofyan Yoman, chair of the Papuan Baptist Synod, is listed in Kopassus (Indonesian Special Forces) secret documents leaked in November 2010 as the number one state "enemy" in West Papua (Nairn 2010). In response to the news of his status in these files, Reverend Yoman responded that "he has received anonymous death threats 'all the time, everywhere,' but that as a church leader he must endure it" (Nairn 2010).

Various of my West Papuan interlocuters commented on the culturally myopic nature of their early education, which focused on Indonesian history, for example, but discounted Melanesian history and Melanesian ways of knowing. Admittedly, this experience is not restricted to Papua but is part of the Indonesian national curriculum that for years ignored local histories and cultural identity politics. Refugee and West Papuan activist Herman Wainggai believes that through schooling, "starting from primary school to high school and then university, Indonesia tries to... change Papuan young generations' brains... [to] brainwash them with their curricula, to change our identity as Melanesians" (Interview, 2009). Benny Wenda recalls the moment he realized that West Papua (then known by the Indonesian name, Irian Jaya) was part of the island of New Guinea, a greater landmass that did not in its entirety belong to Indonesia, and that it occurred to him that this fact had been purposely hidden from school students. "As soon as I grew up and I went to high school, then I understood [that we were not isolated as we had been led to believe]; I saw the map. On the map [was] just one line, [and I thought] okay, I know there must be another side" (Interview, 2008). Wenda claims that in school he was taught only of the limits of Indonesian (including West Papuan) territory—"Sabang to Merauke"—but he became curious about the "straight line" that he had seen on the map: "Then one time, I went with a few friends to the headmaster's [office], and I saw the globe. [I noticed that] the island is connected down there!... Then I put my finger and turned it around while they were speaking and, in my mind, [I thought] 'there's a connection.' Then they said 'Papua New Guinea.' And that's one word we cannot say—'Papua'—at the time. Papua, this [word is] taboo. [And I realized] Papua New Guinea is Papua; okay that is the connection!" (Interview, 2008).

More than endangered songs, dances and languages, and selective education, Neles Tebay believes that Indonesian-sponsored transmigration and encouraged in-migration from other Indonesian islands pose the biggest threat of cultural genocide to West Papuans. He says of the great influx of migrants who now outnumber indigenous West Papuans in Papua:

> When they are many in terms of number, then their culture will be dominant whether you like it or not.... Papuans are having [a] crisis of cultural identity. And I think this is the very big problem we are facing now.... Papuans want to express themselves as Papuan, but their way of expressing themselves is different from the *pendatang* [migrants]... from Malays. So when... the migrants are big in terms of number... they will judge everything from their cultural norms.... I think that's why many people are getting drunk.... When they get drunk, then they can express themselves. [But] without having drunk, it's like they cannot... express themselves; what they think, what they feel.... The presence of others also challenges our worldview. I'm not talking culturally in terms of music or songs but how we perceive the world, how we interpret events and things happening around us. All these things are challenged, really challenged by the different culture, Malay culture. (Interview, 2008)

That Indonesia would go to such efforts to stifle the dissemination of West Papuan songs and dances, ban the use of indigenous languages, target West Papuan religious leaders, censor elementary school curricula, and promote mass migration to West Papua points toward the threat it considers West Papuan cultural nationalism to pose to its perceived sovereignty and territorial integrity. Although their cultures are eroded by these processes, West Papuans are working hard to hold on to them. At the same time, in recognition of the political power that their threatened cultures hold, activists in West Papua and in diaspora are repositioning and politicizing culture as a tool of resistance. Culture is both the thing fought for and fought with. Nancy Jouwe, daughter of the late West Papuan veteran freedom fighter Nicolaas

Jouwe, living in Utrecht, the Netherlands, describes how cultural identity develops into a strategy of survival: "The thing about culture is, in the best sense, it's very much, to its fullest, expressing who you are. And if you constantly have the feeling that who you are is not being seen . . . or is threatened, in the Papuan Indonesian context, then culture really becomes an important strategy, [an] identity marker, but also a strategy to keep your voice alive" (Interview, 2008). Similarly, West Papuan refugee Opina Sapioper, in The Hague, explained to me: "We are real active with our culture because we want to keep it as long as we are outside our own country, but [the Dutch government] also knows the background of why we continue doing our culture. The main thing is [that] we just want independence, but we can't just go out [and] shout outside on the street that we want independence. . . . So we're doing it under the [cover of], as we call it, culture" (Interview, 2008).

So far, this chapter has shown that "imperialist domination has the vital need to practise cultural oppression" and that therefore "national liberation is necessarily an act of culture" (Cabral 1979, 143). The remainder explores how West Papuans continue, in the tradition of Arnold Ap, to use their cultures to build unity within and between West Papuan communities at home and abroad in order to oppose Indonesian hegemony and ensure the survival of their people and nation.

West Papuan Cultural Identity

Cultural identity can be understood in two primary ways, according to Stuart Hall. The first involves an essentialist interpretation of culture whereby a given group promotes the innateness of its identity, often employing a form of strategic essentialism to withstand oppression (Spivak 2012) or a staunch cultural nationalism, hypersensitive to any hint of the colonizer's cultural hegemony (Trask 1993, 53). This might include a narrative of a shared history or ancestry that binds the group together in a perceived oneness, as did, for example, the experience of blackness that "was at the centre of the vision of the poets of 'Negritude'" (Hall 1993, 223). In the West Papuan context, a shared Melanesian history and culture is often promoted by West Papuans as the essential West Papuan unifier (see Stephanie Lawson [2013] on the power that the idea of "being Melanesian" holds in Melanesian politics throughout the region, despite the many potential pitfalls of appealing to ethnicity as the foundation of a national cultural identity). The second interpretation of cultural identity, Hall writes, "recognizes that, as well as the many points of similarity, there are also critical points of deep and significant difference which constitute 'what we really are'; or rather—since history has intervened—'what we have become'" (1993, 225). This second perspective recognizes that we are always still becoming who we are—it is oriented toward the future as much as it is to the past (Hall 1993, 225).

In what follows I explore what it means to West Papuans to be Melanesian in terms of cultural identity and political strategy and how this is played out in the two senses identified above. In what ways do West Papuans identify as pan-Melanesian in order to connect with a cultural-political power bloc that operates separately to Indonesia, I ask, and in what ways do they distinguish themselves as distinctively West Papuan Melanesian (rather than Papua New Guinean Melanesian, for example)? How does "being Melanesian" "offer a way of imposing an imaginary [yet vitally important] coherence on the experience of dispersal and fragmentation" (Hall 1993, 224) under Indonesian occupation in West Papua? I also examine the differing ways in which West Papuan cultural identity is expressed between diaspora groups as each operates under diverse cultural conditions to create and recreate sustainable (while ever-changing) West Papuan identities that articulate with "in-country" identities yet expand the possibilities of what it means to "be West Papuan." In this analysis, the continuities and ruptures between what West Papuans value of their past and the critical elements of present-day West Papuan cultures under conditions of dispersal will become apparent. During interviews with West Papuans from different generations, factions, and diaspora populations, I encountered a near-ubiquitous identification with Melanesian culture and with what my West Papuan interlocuters described as Melanesian values. It is their Melanesian identity that many West Papuans believe differentiates them culturally, spiritually, and politically from Indonesians. West Papuan Melanesian identity extends to Christian beliefs, attitudes toward land and resources, ideas about community and communal living, political sensibilities, a felt "roots" connection with the Melanesian region, and a sense of "togetherness" achieved through performance.

Christianity, the common religion of Melanesia, was first brought to Dorei Bay in West Papua by German Protestant missionaries in 1855 who were joined by members of the Dutch Protestant Mission Union in 1862. Catholic missionaries came to West Papua in 1888 (Moore 2003, 123–124). Up until 1960, "before the occupation," writes Otto Ondawame, "93 per cent of the population of West Papua were Christians" (2010, 41). Indigenous West Papuans are still predominantly Christian (although there is a growing indigenous Muslim population), while Indonesians in West Papua are primarily Muslim (Ondawame 2010, 156). As such, Christianity forms an important shared cultural identifier among Melanesians (Douglas 2002; Farhadian and Babuljak 2007, ix, 173). Reverend Benny Giay explains: "We have this Bible which I see is a global thing. We make use of this to communicate. Whether we like it or not, Christianity is a bridge to the world community.... We are part of a bigger tribe" (Interview, 2008). At the same time however, Giay is interested in how West Papuans can "indigenize" Christianity. He is committed to "understanding how my people adopted Christianity... [and in developing] a new understanding, a new theology, a West Papuan theology" (quoted in Farhadian and Babuljak 2007, 28) that is not simply a religious colonial transplant. This is one way in which West Papuans' identification as Melanesian, through the region's predominant religion, takes on a distinctly West Papuan character. Here, European or Melanesian "religion is not a fixed set of elements but a dynamic web of shared meanings [that can be] used in different ways in different contexts" to link distinctly West Papuan theologies with the Christianities of Melanesia (Magowan 2007, 462; see also Neilson 2000, 263). Through an identification with a West Papuan indigenous Christian theology, for example, West Papuans can experience being part of a global and Melanesian Christian transnation and a West Papuan Christian nation at the same time. Christianity in this sense has been described by the West Papuan Koreri follower Markus Kaisiepo as "a mask" that is recognizable to everyone. "The contents behind the mask," however, "belong to us," according to Kaisiepo (quoted in Sharp 1994, 84).

Ways of valuing land, water, and other resources, even across the large expanse of sea that connects Melanesian islands, also locate West Papuans within broader Melanesian cosmologies. Ron Crocombe argues that in Oceania, the "smaller original ethnic communities have become less significant, and more geographically spread owing to extensive mobility. The nation-state as an ethnic identity (or, in the case of multi-racial states, the indigenous people of the state) has become very significant, and [regionalist] ethnic identity above that level is of increasing importance" (1993, 195).

When I was in Port Vila, Vanuatu, in 2009, I interviewed Chief Selwyn Garu, secretary of the Malvatu Mauri (Vanuatu National Council of Chiefs), about why the Vanuatu chiefs and people support a decolonized West Papua. He told me that

> the chiefs support Melanesian traditional values, and we look across the nations at West Papua and Kanaky [New Caledonia]; these are Melanesian nations, and the values that they share are similar. So that's where we, the Vanuatu chiefs... identify with them, because they share the same respect for life, for land.... Melanesia is not a concept; it's a reality... because of the values that [Melanesians] share.... One of the values that they share across Melanesia is the word "respect," and the value and respect of the land, respect for the sea, respect for the relationships that people have.... These are things that kind of tie people together, and I think one of the things that makes Melanesia what it is is this respect that can be accorded to everything, as though everything is alive. (S. Garu, interview, 2009)

The cherishing of community was also identified to me by some West Papuans as a distinctively Melanesian value. Oridek Ap described a traditional West Papuan "acceptance that you don't need many things—that's the Melanesian thought, because we are social you know, and we share" (Interview, 2008). And John Tekwie of PNG justifies caring for West Papuan relatives on the other side of the colonially imposed border thus: When "one of our brothers is suffering, us Melanesians, we, in terms of caring and thinking of our other relatives, go beyond third and fourth and fifth generations; they are still our relatives" (Interview, 2009).

Geopolitically, as well, West Papuans identify strongly as Melanesian. This is for strategic reasons and because of felt cultural affinities. Jacob Rumbiak recalls how the now deceased West Papuan independence and cultural leader Thomas Wainggai, in the late 1980s, started to "call the territory of West Papua, West Melanesia. That was strategic...we used it to influence Papua New Guinea, Solomons, Fiji, and Vanuatu that they must back up their own family" (Interview, 2009). Herman Wainggai adds that there was another strategic dimension to this nomenclature—he says that Indonesians "sometimes use [the name] Papuan [as if] we are dirty...so that's why [some] people use the [word] Melanesian...rather than Papuan, or Irian" (Interview, 2009).

A sense of Melanesian "roots" connecting them to the region has been described to me by several West Papuans. Of West Papuan descent but born in the Netherlands, Nancy Jouwe remembers the sensation of visiting her "home" in West Papua for the first time: "I'm not the sort of person who was heavily looking for their roots, I wasn't, but [I had] a sense of coming home....I had this physical sensation of roots coming from my feet and [I could] sort of...feel the earth.... You become one with the earth" (Interview, 2008). Viktor Kaisiepo similarly told me that although he became a Dutch citizen, "I am not a Dutch person by birth, by design, by genes, by DNA. I can be a Dutch person...with a passport from the Dutch and protection from the Dutch, but I cannot act like the Dutch.... I can to a certain extent try, but there will be things in my system that will connect me to my roots, which are Melanesian" (Interview, 2008).

Neles Tebay, from the Mee people in the highlands of West Papua, has had a similar "roots" experience connecting him to his kinship group, his nation, and his region, describing how "the more I keep my distance, or the more I am away from my home village, I come to realize that I belong to the tribe of Mee. But the more I am away from this island, then I come to realize that I am Papuan, I am Melanesian" (Interview, 2008).

The centrality of music and dance to group identity culturally connects West Papua to Melanesia too. Across Melanesia, anthropologist Deborah Van Heekeren contends, songs "bring people together in more than a social way. They promote the modes of being that are most highly valued" (2011, 55). And anthropologist Bruce Knauft concurs; in Melanesia, he explains, the performing body celebrates "social and cultural vitality." The singing voice is "an index of relationships between the internal self and the social collective" (1999, 84). In West Papua, also, David Tekwie, a young man of West Papuan and PNG heritage, explains that identity is expressed through "our culture's song and dance" (Interview, 2009). That the work of Arnold Ap is still revered among Papuans today is evidence of this.

Social groups involving young West Papuans living in Port Moresby, including the performance group Tabam Ramu, center around performances of singing and dancing. These performances are seen as a celebration of West Papuan culture and an expression of a unified identity that transcends factions, as well as a means of attracting Papua New Guineans' attention to Papuan politics (S. Karubaba, interview, 2009). As youth leader and West Papuan refugee Sonny Karubaba explains:

> If [a West Papuan faction] is [trying] to do a promotion or [raise] awareness for West Papua, the other group won't show up. But you know, if we use culture to do our promotion, everybody comes because they say, that's my culture. So the strategy that we started off when I was back at university is we get the kids, the young people . . . and tell them hey, let's practice some West Papuan culture. . . . We have regular training practices . . . and then the parents who were interested . . . bring their kids to practice the culture as well. . . . In the process the parents come . . . together to unite, and they say, "Oh, this is very good" . . . [because] previously they [did not talk much] because of their differences. But through the culture they were able to talk to each other. . . . They appreciate West Papuan dance, and everybody feels proud if the West Papuan traditional dance is performed in the school or anywhere. They really appreciate it, you know, despite the fact that we also perform dances where it covers all of the West Papuans and not only one particular area. (Interview, 2009)

Expressive culture and performativity are central to Melanesian life. As Karubaba described, West Papuans, as Melanesians, make use of their traditional and contemporary cultural performances to unite conflicting West Papuan groups and to demonstrate to other Melanesians their cultural similarities and differences. Ray Halbritter of the Oneida Indian Nation (US) relates a similar experience of the uniting power of cultural tradition among his people: "Our people are so not used to success . . . that they don't have a concept of how to work together. . . . That's where tradition comes in for me. The whole essence of our traditional teachings in the Great Law is one thing: unity. We are to be unified and forgive one another and work with one another" (quoted in Alfred 2005, 218). The extent to which an anticolonial movement depends upon cultural performance to bring an oppressed nation together prompted Fanon to declare: "The conscious, organized struggle undertaken by a colonized people in order to restore national sovereignty constitutes the greatest cultural manifestation that exists" (1963, 178).

Performing West Papuanness in the Diaspora

The second half of this chapter addresses the cultural politics of being West Papuan in the diaspora. A history of conflict between diaspora and internal activists exists in the West Papuan decolonization movement, as it has in many decolonization movements around the world, for reasons outlined clearly by Cabral:

> At the start of the struggle there were some who preened themselves because they were inside the land. They thought that those outside were afraid and did not do much, as they were outside. Anyone who in a struggle like ours hangs on to this idea or other complexes of vanity and fear, because he is inside or is outside, has not understood our struggle. But anyone who has never left the bush and has withstood seven years of struggle but has failed to understand the significance for the struggle inside the land of the work of those who are working outside the land, has not understood anything either. And someone who is outside, seated in an office or somewhere, and has failed to understand the value of those who are inside the land and who are opening fire, or preparing the political ground and suchlike, and the value of the latter, has also not understood anything. (1979, 65)

The discord between West Papua's activists "inside" and "outside" traces to the period shortly after West Papua was handed over to Indonesian administration in 1962, when Nicolaas Jouwe and other first-generation West Papuan decolonization activists decided their efforts would best be spent engaging in diplomacy in the Netherlands. This decision raised the ire of their compatriots who thought the battle ought to be waged inside West Papua. What has proved a unifying force between West Papuans at home and in diaspora over many decades has been the articulation of West Papuan national-cultural diaspora identities with homeland, West Papuan Melanesian identities. The result, observable in the following survey of West Papuan diaspora nationalisms, is a loosely unified international West Papuan cultural identity that exhibits a distinctive local character in each host country. It is within this expansive identity that West Papuans at home and abroad are able to let go of "insider/outsider" distinctions and work complementarily, in different parts of the world, toward a common goal. The role of diaspora West Papuan identity is important in progressing the struggle overall because, immersed in host country cultures, diaspora groups are able to translate and adapt West Papuan political identity into cultural performances and expressions that encourage solidarity from host country populations. (Exceptions might include diaspora communities that sense hostility toward their plight on the part of the host government, as in the case of Freddy Waromi's community in Port Moresby, PNG [see chapter 2] and become inward focused as a result.) The following examples demonstrate how West Papuan diasporic communities establish their presence in host countries and become "West Papuan abroad." Such West Papuans in dispersal maintain and develop new forms of West Papuan Melanesian cultural nationalism in their now internationally networked struggle for cultural and political survival.

AUSTRALIA

What follows is an extraordinary story of survival marked by culturally influenced expressions of spiritual faith. On January 17, 2006, forty-three West Papuans arrived in an outrigger canoe at Weipa, Queensland, after four days at sea. Each, fleeing persecution in his or her homeland, had headed to Australia in pursuit of asylum with the "shared intention of going outside to campaign for West Papua's independence" (Nichols, n.d., 9). They chose Australia as their country of asylum because of its historical geographic Melanesian links as well as the international attention they would receive (A. Douw, A. Galilee, and P. Florentinus, interview, 2009). The journey was simultaneously a bid for help, a political statement, and an expression of cultural identity. The vehicle for the trip, and hence for their political message, was of critical cultural importance. While still in West Papua and preparing for the voyage, the leader of the forty-three, Herman Wainggai, "commissioned [a] boat to be made [an outrigger canoe]. It was to be wooden, suitable for ocean sailing, as my ancestors had made for hundreds of years" (quoted in Nichols, n.d., 7). The group's crossing, expected to take sixteen hours, took nearly six times that due to the failure of one of the outboard motors, wild storms and flooding of the boat, and navigational error. They took little food with them, and the captain fell ill.

During this time the passengers' Christian faith was sorely tested, but this faith, they believed, is what saw them through the journey. Some of the Papuans in the boat saw lights coming from the depth of the ocean, which they interpreted as the destructive spirits of the ocean conspiring against them (Nichols, n.d., 22). Others experienced visions of Jesus wrapping his arms around them. Such visions are a common West Papuan element of faith. "For Christians from their homeland," writes Alan Nichols, the author of a book about the saga, "visions like this were not unusual" (n.d., 20). The group prayed and sang songs together and followed the dolphins and birds, which guided them, along with a compass, to land (A. Douw, A. Galilee, and P. Florentinus, interview, 2009). Their canoe carried a Morning Star flag and a large sign reading: "Save West Papua people soul from genocide, intimidation and terrorist, from military government of Indonesia. Also we West Papuan need freedom, peace, love and justice in our homeland [*sic*]." By making a spectacle of their highly risky asylum journey by using traditional Melanesian transportation, flying a banner, and revealing how they relied on religious visions and communication with animals to survive the journey, "the forty-three" were able to "market their rebellion" to an unusually responsive Australian media and public (Bob 2005).

Since arriving, the forty-three have formed a community with other West Papuans living in Australia and with the Australian public to actively share their political message through cultural means. For example, the International Youth Coalition for the Liberation of West Papua, established by members of the forty-three and headed by Amatus Douw but supported by Australians too, uses "cultural fundraising nights" to raise money to bring more Papuans out of West Papua (A. Douw, A. Galilee, and P. Florentinus, interview, 2009). The cultural politics of the West Papuan struggle so touched Australian filmmaker Charlie Hill-Smith that he featured several of the forty-three in his film about West Papua, *Strange Birds of Paradise*. Hill-Smith says of his film's subject (which incorporates West Papuan music), "Art is a weapon and culture is life, as long as [West Papuans] can sing they will prevail" (ABC Radio National 2010). Politics has been deeply embedded in culture and culture in politics in the Australian West Papuan diaspora's expression of national identity, and the coming of the forty-three with their creative display of culture and politics reinvigorated the Australian solidarity movement for West Papua.

UNITED KINGDOM

The cultural importance of political and religious expression to the establishment of a West Papuan identity abroad can be seen in the ways in which West Papuan refugee Benny Wenda and his family have worked to forge relationships with their local community in Oxford, UK. Benny escaped from prison in West Papua, where he was detained for allegedly inciting an attack on a Jayapura police station. He was granted political asylum in 2002 in the UK. I met with Benny and his family for the first time at Benny's house in Oxford in 2008. Shortly after settling in Oxford, Benny and his wife, Maria, joined a church in the area. As they became acquainted with the community, they introduced indigenous West Papuan (Lani) cultural arts, particularly music, to the congregation and communicated the tragedy of their personal and national struggles. As a result of the members' relationship with the Wendas and in solidarity with Papuans, the church decided it would call itself a "Papuan Church" and determined to become bicultural. To this end, the Wendas' church in Oxford established connections with the Protestant Church in West Papua (the Gereja Kristen Indonesia [GKI]).

Subsequently, a young couple belonging to the Wendas' church arranged to have the West Papuan Morning Star flag flown during their wedding and asked Benny to speak at their reception. They also distributed Morning Star flag stickers to each of the several hundred guests present to attach to their clothing (B. Wenda, interview, 2008). Standing Rock Sioux (US) theologian and activist Vine Deloria Jr. has questioned whether indigenous religious "ceremonies are restricted to particular places" and limited by geography, becoming "useless in a foreign land" (2003, 69). It would appear that in the Wendas' circumstances, however, religious ceremonies have been a political conduit across geographic boundaries, inviting solidarity rather than creating cultural silos.

Since 2008, when the Wendas related this story to me, they have gone on to build a flourishing West Papua campaign (the Free West Papua Campaign), with headquarters in Oxford and offices throughout the world. The success of the campaign appears, based on personal observation over more than a decade, to have been accomplished similarly to the way in which the Wendas built up local community solidarity in Oxford. Dressed in a traditional highlands headdress and often with a ukulele in hand, ready to sing about West Papua, Benny discusses politics with world leaders and the media while offering up his culture as a gesture of common humanity.

"In a world shaped by diaspora, migration, hybridity, and movement," writes Chickasaw (US) scholar Jodi Byrd, "the very idea of indigeneity can be [seen as] dangerous and xenophobic when combined with nationalism or anticolonial struggle" (2011, xxxiii). Indonesia has certainly interpreted Benny Wenda's winning combination of anticolonial politics and indigenous cultural expression as dangerous. In 2011 Indonesia successfully requested an Interpol red notice for Wenda's arrest, limiting his ability to travel internationally to speak about West Papua. Fortunately, Fair Trials International was able to convince the Commission for the Control of Interpol's Files that Indonesia was "abusing the red notice system for political purposes," and Interpol subsequently dropped the notice (Tinsley 2012, n.p.). The support elicited for West Papua when the Wendas took the initiative to introduce their culture and politics to their Oxford community is an example of how community rituals and cultural politics can combine to create a diaspora culture that links home and host cultures. It was also a demonstration to the Wenda family and other West Papuans that the national and cultural identity they share with receptive foreigners is one that can be simultaneously celebrated in public and intimate ways around the world.

VANUATU

One of West Papua's most treasured cultural icons, the reggae/rock band the Black Brothers, has played a significant cultural role in representing the West Papuan diaspora in Vanuatu and garnering support for West Papua's independence struggle. David Bridie, an Australian musician and producer who works alongside many Melanesian musicians, comments, "From Suva to Noumea to Vila and Port Moresby, [the Black Brothers] were arguably the most important band in this region" (Eliezer 2005). From their name to their Afro hairstyles and reggae influence, the Black Brothers were an important symbol in Melanesia of the black civil rights movement that emerged in the United States in the 1960s and connected with black consciousness movements globally around that time.

The band's manager, the late Andy Ajamiseba, had lived periodically in Port Vila, Vanuatu, since 1984 when the band was invited to Vanuatu to set up a support base for West Papuan independence (Dummett 2003). In his later years (until his death in 2020), he managed the West Papua People's Representative Office in Port Vila and was a member of the United Liberation Movement for West Papua (ULMWP). However, in 1988 the band members and their families were temporarily deported from Vanuatu as a result of political conflict between Vanuatu's political leaders (Paterson and Early 2006). West Papuan Organisasi Papua Merdeka (OPM) member Rex Rumakiek, who was stationed in Vanuatu at the time with his work on the Pacific antinuclear movement, interpreted the political conflict in Vanuatu as influenced by tensions between the Anglophone and the Francophone Ni-Vanuatu populations. He recalls rumors circulating among Francophone communities that the Black Brothers, using the immense popularity of their music on every island in Vanuatu, had assisted the Anglophone Vanua'aku Party with winning three national elections. Hence, after taking government office in 1991 for the first time since Vanuatu's independence, Francophones, under then prime minister Maxime Carlot Korman, were keen to remove the Black Brothers from the Vanuatu political scene (R. Rumakiek, interview, 2010). In an unexpected twist, Rumakiek (who had positive political relationships with both Anglophone and Francophone parties) describes how he used the Black Brothers' popularity in Vanuatu, as well as the Vanuatu people's support for West Papua as a fellow Melanesian nation, to bring about greater unity within Ni-Vanuatu politics while simultaneously promoting West Papuan decolonization:

> I knew that I had no problem with the Francophone [people in Vanuatu] because while I was with the Vanua'aku [Anglophone] Party, I always had secret meetings with the Francophone people. They always advised me, "We all support you, no problem, but these bloody Anglophone people want to dominate us, so we don't like it. But we all support your struggle, [although] we don't like this tension." I remember when [the Black Brothers] played the first time.... I wore two hats, [one for] the antinuclear movement and the [other for the] OPM and walked all over from island to

> island.... So when I came to finish one of the trips at a nearby island, Malakula, Tautu village (Tautu village is the place where the Vanua'aku Party was born), I used it as the last point for my [antinuclear work] tour, showed my slides, and then... the chiefs came and formed a council meeting that night, a chiefs' council meeting, and they decided to give me a chief's title. So the next day, I killed a pig, and they gave me a title.... I was not prepared for it, and I did not know what to say. I just pulled [the words] out of my hat, just like that—I said, "Since all of you are fond of the Black Brothers, they are in Holland, but I will try to bring them back here. And when they come here, I promise you, the first place they will [play] is here." It spread like fire [throughout] the whole island from end to end—"The Black Brothers are coming!"—even though it was not really finalized yet! (Interview, 2010)

According to Rumakiek, the national government was swayed by the excitement of the Malakula people and, fortunately for Rumakiek's reputation, allowed the Black Brothers to return. Rumakiek continues:

> When [the Black Brothers] arrived, they did actually... play first in Malakula—it was beautiful! And in fact, that was a political statement as well because [the Anglophone] people are very strong in north Malakula.... For two weeks [beforehand], they worked to build... the fence around the place where [the Black Brothers would] play.... People from everywhere came and built the stage.... [When] the Black Brothers finally arrived,... some [people had] already come days ahead, sleeping about, waiting, from everywhere; it was so crowded. And then the conflict started. The Francophone people wanted to come in, but the Anglophones [who outnumbered Francophones] wouldn't let them. But... [because] I was now a chief [in Malakula] myself, I had to be part of the decision-making body.... So we sat in the meeting and they discussed whether the Francophone [people] could come in or not. The majority didn't want them to come in because the [Francophones had not traditionally supported] independence [for Vanuatu]. (Interview, 2010)

But when they asked Rumakiek for his opinion, he told them:

> Well, my position is that the OPM needs everybody—needs Francophones, needs Anglophones—and everybody's support [keeps] us strong. I think if that means that you deny them, then you deny support for West Papua as well because this band is

> West Papuan. They come because of the struggle; that's why [these people] are here. So my position is—I think they should come in. (Interview, 2010)

According to Rumakiek, there were already truckloads of Francophone people waiting outside the gates to enter the concert arena, so the organizers opened the gates and

> they all marched in [and] embraced everybody inside! So it was politics outside, but actually [they were all the] same families anyway, so they were all embracing each other, happy.... Everybody spoke about the West Papuan struggle and supported [it]. It was because of the West Papuan struggle that we were all there. (Interview, 2010)

And so it was that the West Papuan struggle for independence and Vanuatu's love of the Black Brothers' West Papuan music helped to unite opposing political sides in Vanuatu, the country that has turned out to be West Papua's longest-term nation-state advocate for independence. The Black Brothers' popularity and significance lives on in Vanuatu; as recently as 2005, the Black Brothers headlined Vanuatu's annual music festival, Fest Napuan. Their legacy also continues. Fest Napuan (2010) featured the West Papuan band Tabura (based in Melbourne, Australia), which, as their write-up on the festival's website claims, "invigorate[s] music of Papuan legend, song-man and musicologist Arnold Ap, and [the] famous Black Brothers, to underline [their] deep commitment... [to the] West Papuan legacy and raise awareness of the struggle facing the indigenous people in their country." This story provides a fascinating example of how, in the words of diaspora scholar Michel Laguerre, "a local political problem created in the homeland [is] thus shifted from homeland politics to hostland politics and... [is] reinscribed inside the transnational field of diasporic politics. This is an instance where the local becomes globalized and the global becomes central in the production of a local solution" (2006, 15).

NETHERLANDS

A West Papuan Melanesian identity is often taken on even by West Papuans born in the diaspora. For example, West Papuan indigenous and women's rights activist Nancy Jouwe, born and raised in the Netherlands, describes her own sense of West Papuan identity thus:

> I was born and I grew up here, so in a sense I don't know any better, but... I talked about this with a couple of black friends of mine. Just recently we were reminiscing, and I was saying, "I

> remember going to Papua New Guinea, [and] I remember having the sensation of 'Wow, the majority is black and it's their country,' and it's a very powerful sensation!" So you know [you are] a cultural minority [in the Netherlands] in a couple of ways, and you start to live by it; you have survival strategies that you develop because you live here and because you have to. But that it can be different is an important experience to have, and I think [that's] why many second-generation Papuans also go to Papua to see and hear a sense of home, a sense of identity, a sense of a place that's theirs, that's ours. (Interview, 2008)

In this sense, West Papuan identity is as much "chosen" as it is "born into." Connections to their parents' and grandparents' homeland are forged by diaspora-born West Papuans through trips to West Papua, through socializing within diaspora communities, and through celebrating West Papuan and other Melanesian traditions in the host country. West Papuan identity in the Netherlands anchors black Melanesians to a history and home outside of the predominantly white European Netherlands.

Jouwe identifies three aspects of West Papuan identity in the Netherlands that color the Dutch West Papuans' sense of Papuan national-cultural identity: gender, generation, and Melanesianness. It turns out that each affects the others. Jouwe is concerned about what she describes as the "third-rate citizen" status of Papuan women in West Papua, explaining that it is the "women who are raped by the military . . . [and then] ousted by their community because they are sort of damaged goods." It is women, too, who suffer from "internalized racism," Jouwe observes, when Papuan men fetishize Asian women and choose them over Papuan women for marriage partners (as men are then exempt from dowry obligations; interview, 2008). To remedy what she describes as "the invisibility of Papuan women" in the Netherlands, Jouwe has been involved in organizing a March 8 (International Women's Day) celebration of West Papuan heroines together with first-, second-, and third-generation Papuan and Malukan women. According to Jouwe, "We [celebrated] . . . Papuan heroines from the past, one of them being Dorcas Tokoro Hanasbey . . . one of the first female politicians in Papuan history. . . . [The March 8 celebration was] about honoring those women and giving them the floor, celebrating them" (Interview, 2008). Occasions such as these are important for building political confidence in often marginalized diaspora women.

Generation as well as gender has an impact on Dutch West Papuans' cultural identity. For example, there is a group of male, second-generation West Papuans in the Netherlands that Jouwe calls "the lost generation." These men "never got over [being refugee children] and have a real hard time connecting to life and making the best of it. So that's, you know, also a sad thing to see" (N. Jouwe, interview, 2008). On the other hand, the second generation of West Papuan women in the Netherlands, according to Jouwe, "are really strong women, and a lot of them did studies and have good jobs . . . so it's also good to see that within one generation [the women have] really progressed. As opposed, a lot of the time, to the men. When you look at the nineties, the strong, second-generation people were the women; they were actually doing the politics" (Interview, 2008).

The third major influence on West Papuan identity in the Netherlands is the emergent trend of celebrating "Melanesianness," evident in the desire of the Malukan community to form a common identity with the West Papuans. Jouwe recalls:

> My father has always stressed that point that we are Melanesian, not Asian. So . . . that sense of a Melanesian identity comes quite naturally. . . . I see it as a political identity, I guess. But there's definitely that whole ethnic, cultural sense of being one, being part of a same group. And the interesting thing is that third-generation Malukans are totally embracing that whole Melanesian thing. . . . We, as Papuans, look at that also a little bit like "hmm, interesting." (Interview, 2008)

She elaborates on the latter part of her comment:

> You can debate about if [Malukans] are actually Melanesian or not—they're sort of on the borderline. For them it's a political link, a political strategic identity, whereas for the Papuans it's also very much a natural identity. When we come together we have . . . a vibe . . . together as Melanesians. It's funny. It does bring up some discussion among Papuans because, for instance, there's always been a very interesting connection between the Malukans here and the Papuans, a common enemy [Indonesia] if you will. [But] a lot of Malukans, for the longest time, have been living in Papua as teachers and clergy for church, [and] there was . . . this sense of them looking down on Papuans, and Papuans know that very well. . . . So this whole notion of us being the cool ones now as Melanesians is quite interesting! (Interview, 2008)

"Between the 1890s and World War Two, Dutch New Guinea was administered through the Malukan Residency," notes Clive Moore (2003, 182). The Dutch "greatly appreciated" the "highly efficient manner" of the Moluccans who administered Papua for them and gave them positions as government assistants, police officers, medical officers, and teachers (Drooglever 2009, 65). Ironically, although the Moluccan administrators were also ethnically and geographically Melanesian, "their contempt for the Papuans was set in stone," according to Pieter Drooglever (2009, 65). However, as Nancy Jouwe's analysis above has demonstrated, "Melanesianness" as a political identity, and thus solidarity with West Papuans, is now being used as a political strategy by Moluccans, too—particularly by the Moluccan movement seeking independence from Indonesia, the Republik Maluku Selatan, which is also active in the Netherlands. The Papuan second generation and Malukan third generation have now collaborated to organize two Melanesian culture days in the Netherlands, which, according to Jouwe, are extremely popular. Pacific peoples from many different countries now residing in Europe, including Kanaks, Tongans, and Solomon Islanders, attend the Melanesian culture days.

This brief example of West Papuan cultural and identity politics in the Netherlands shows the complexity of establishing a sense of belonging in a host country while maintaining or reestablishing connections to the homeland, particularly for non-first-generation diaspora members. Gender, generation, and the politics of belonging (to West Papua, Melanesia, and the Pacific, more broadly) shape individual diaspora members' experiences and political collaborations differently. Yet West Papuans in the Netherlands have worked hard over a number of generations to commemorate West Papuan heroes and keep the struggle alive, inspiring younger generations to celebrate the cultures that connect them to West Papua and to other members of the Pacific residing in the Netherlands and that simultaneously distinguish them from Europeans.

PAPUA NEW GUINEA

West Papuan diaspora cultural politics are highly sensitive in PNG, the country that shares West Papua's Melanesian people and Indonesian border. Nevertheless, a great portion of PNG's civil society and a number of prominent PNG leaders vocally support West Papuan decolonization, including the former governor of Sandaun Province John Tekwie, who, in addition to his political advocacy, adopted a West Papuan refugee, Michael Horota Tekwie. Tragically, in 2008 Michael, at just twenty-four years old, collapsed in his room while studying and died (*National PNG* 2008). According to his siblings and others who had studied alongside Michael at the University of Papua New Guinea (UPNG), he had been very charismatic, a natural leader, and president of the university's West Papua Student Association and vice president of the university's Student Representative Council. In life, Michael had championed West Papuan rights and celebrated West Papuan cultural traditions. His funeral was conducted in a similar fashion—with a spectacular West Papuan political and cultural celebration—which had significant political ramifications for the PNG government. The story of the cultural and political impact of the funeral, which involved the participation of the West Papuan diaspora and Papua New Guinean supporters of West Papuan freedom, was recounted to me by two people close to Michael: his brother by adoption, David Tekwie, and his friend, fellow West Papuan refugee Sonny Karubaba. Tekwie recalls:

> During [Michael's] time [as West Papua Student Association president, he] laid a foundation [and] raised the flag one more time on campus so people realized that West Papua's [flag is] flying again.... His personality attracted a lot of people, and we had a very big following on campus.... And when he passed away, we had like the biggest festival ever, [a] funeral on campus, [on] the home square. Thousands of people attended. And the Indonesian government was a little bit afraid of that so they called the [then] prime minister, Sir Michael Somare, and... they asked him if he could stop the funeral. So what Sir Michael Somare did was he told them, "For goodness' sake, it's a funeral. Not even I as the head of state can stop a funeral. They are not doing a protest; they are just having a funeral." But we seized... the moment, and we made a very big noise. We came in colors, our traditional colors. And although it was a very sad moment, it was an opportunity for a lot of people to actually see who he was.... A lot of people on campus, administration, academic staff—they kind of respected and admired him, his leadership, so everybody attended, and we had a very big crowd on the day. That kind of made the Indonesian embassy scared. (Interview, 2009)

Karubaba adds:

> We made it more political. We had our flag on top of [the coffin], everybody dressed up in traditional dress, we were singing West Papuan political songs, [and] we were carrying the [West Papuan] flag and [the] PNG flag as well. [We sang our West Papuan] national anthem and a couple of other songs that we sing, all political stuff... and people were walking on the streets in the campus. (Interview, 2009)

This remarkable story demonstrates how in some instances, the power of diaspora cultural politics can transcend the power of state politics. Even the PNG head of government did not feel comfortable curtailing West Papuan political-cultural expression at Michael Horota Tekwie's funeral, despite requests from the Indonesian government to do so. A young West Papuan refugee, well integrated into his host country and new family yet committed to his homeland politics, through his untimely death brought together his diaspora community, his university community, and his fellow Melanesian

(Papua New Guinean) supporters in the celebration of his life that was his funeral. The political significance of this event is evidenced by the response of the Indonesian embassy in PNG and in the fact that, according to community organizer Frank Makanuey, "The university had not allowed any funerals to be held in that area [of campus], whether it was the vice chancellor or some academic who has taught at the university for a while. But they did it for this West Papuan kid from the refugee camps in Kiunga" (Interview, 2009).

SWEDEN

I interviewed Joseph Prai, Swedish citizen and highly accomplished son of one of the founders of the OPM, Jacob Prai, in Malmö, Sweden, in 2008. Joseph was born in the jungles of PNG along the West Papuan border in Sekotiau in 1971. He is the only one of his brothers to have been born outside of Sweden, and he believes that his Melanesian birth has instilled in him a consuming desire to work for the freedom of West Papua. Instead of merely seeking to accommodate West Papuan/Melanesian cultural traditions within his Swedish lifestyle, Joseph is also concerned with how to apply European political strategies to the West Papuan independence struggle. Thus, his West Papuan and Swedish identities are highly integrated in purposeful, strategic ways. He describes his West Papuan, Melanesian identity as

> a fixed point in my life. I don't think I [would] achieve anything in this country if I didn't have that in me. So because of that... I have to win everything here [so I can] some[how] get back to this Melanesian soul of mine, to find my roots. I don't know how, but I will go back someday, and what I have learned outside here I will take back one day, hopefully, and build a nation. And the political structure, how it is built up here, I will take the best from here [and] take it back and just take away the barricades. For instance, I am [currently] studying telecommunications. I want to build my country in communications—I know everything now. So when I [go] back, I know we are a very rich country with natural resources. We have money; the only thing we need is know-how. Now I know who to contract.... This is still in my soul, always telling me, "You have to go back—even if Sweden is your new country, your soul belongs to that country." (Interview, 2008)

Joseph's West Papuan national and cultural identity is very much influenced by his father's biography. He believes he has a responsibility to the struggle "because I am my father's son [and] because my father was the symbol for freedom.... Even if I have my own agenda, my dreams, I have to put them aside because this is bigger than me" (Interview, 2008). Joseph is very proud of his West Papuan heritage and of the cultural symbols of the West

Papuan political struggle. For example, when I met Joseph with his father in Malmö, he excitedly unfurled for me the original Morning Star flag that was raised during the 1971 OPM proclamation of independence in Markus Victoria, PNG. Nevertheless, in his position as OPM European spokesperson (to which he was appointed by his father's international OPM office established in Malmö in 1992), Joseph is committed to bringing to his West Papuan identity, and to the struggle, a thorough understanding of Swedish, European, and international politics, as well as his training in civil engineering and communication technology, his close relationship with the Swedish Social Democratic Youth Party, and his knowledge of multiple languages. "We have to [understand] that time changes, and politics change, too, with time," Joseph asserts. "That's why I'm sitting on [the] city council today. I have learned how things work here, and I try to see [from a] global perspective [what] I can do for Papua" (Interview, 2008).

Discussion

The idea of "roots" (or of a tangible or performed connectedness to a West Papuan history and nation) that runs through many of these stories is key to understanding the complex and at times seemingly contradictory nature of West Papuans' collective national/cultural identity, particularly in the diaspora. Roots to some West Papuans signify a primordial connection to a past and an identity so profoundly other to that of Indonesians that the former may as well belong to an alternate moral order—one in which they are a chosen people destined, by dint of their prolonged, innocent suffering under Indonesian rule, to realize what they perceive to be their divinely ordained right to self-determination (see chapter 2). Roots to others (including many of the younger generations and those living in diaspora settings) are phenomenological, felt during experiences of solidarity with other West Papuan, Melanesian, and/or black peoples from other parts of the world or during visits to the "homeland." Roots signify connection, a belonging to a people, a place, and a story that acts as an anchor in a sea of colonial and host country indifference or hostility to West Papuan difference. And West Papuan roots are also asserted metaphorically by West Papuans who employ essentialism as a strategy, who recognize that claims of irreconcilable differences in origin stories between West Papuan and Indonesian bodies politic can further the West Papuan national agenda of decolonization.

It is critical to point out that although these positions may appear at first to be incommutable with one another, many West Papuans hold more than one of these perspectives at any given time. These concepts emerge from a common West Papuan history of hurt, pride, and hope—what West Papuans call their *memoria passionis*. Hurt based on decades of oppression. Pride in Papuans' creative, powerful cultures. Hope that there is some merit to the idea of the incontrovertibility of human dignity and rights, including the right to self-determination. Or that if powerful nations view such rights as mere constructs, they nevertheless will honor their tacit commitment, by virtue of United Nations membership, to ending formal colonialism anyway. Hope that other black and indigenous peoples who have achieved a workable form of sovereignty in their own contexts will provide a solidarity sufficiently formidable to shift West Papua's nonsovereign status. The shared idea of common roots among Papuans comes out of their history, their *memoria passionis,* whether experienced directly by Papuans living in country or as a result of intergenerational trauma experienced by second- and third-generation Papuans in diaspora.

Each of these concepts of roots, of cultural identity, is also oriented toward a shared goal—that of decolonization. What varies is the environment surrounding different root networks as the networks support new branches of the independence movement to reach out toward the nourishing light of decolonization. In other words, what leads various members of the West Papuan body politic to express their political identity in any of the specific ways outlined above depends very much upon context and audience and how West Papuans consider these best handled to optimize political gain. Nancy Jouwe, for example, an accomplished scholar of identity politics and black histories, can talk about the physical sensation of roots growing out of her feet to ground her when reminiscing nostalgically about her first visit to West Papua while at the same time recognizing at an academic level that roots are a cultural construct, a metaphor employed at strategic moments by West Papuans to signify their closeness to West Papuan land and Indonesians' foreignness to the same. To Nancy, roots—and identity—are at once phenomenological, strategically asserted, and metaphorical.

To erudite and cosmopolitan Viktor Kaisiepo, who believed that in an era of globalization West Papua must be outward looking and recognize its interdependence with Indonesia, the concreteness of his perceived Melanesian roots still held a firm grip. As nonessentialist as his political outlook may have been when it came to models of national identity, "by DNA," in his "genes," Kaiseipo described himself as Melanesian (not Dutch, even though he was a Dutch citizen).

To Joseph Prai, roots are spiritual. His soul, he believes, is rooted in West Papua. For Prai this means that his life in Sweden is at all times oriented toward seeking freedom for West Papua. But while Prai's ethnopolitical identity, his roots, are a "fixed point" in his life, bound up in a territorially grounded spirituality, they provide a pivot point that allows him to be flexible in responding to the fickleness of international politics concerning West Papua. Roots, to Prai, are simultaneously foundational and dynamic, allowing him to excel as a fundamentally indigenous West Papuan change agent in a continuously transforming world.

As I have shown, performed West Papuan national identity is amorphous in politically significant ways. Early on, it adopted an ethnonationalist liberal democratic focus intended to appeal to the post–World War II powers brokering worldwide decolonization. As time stretched on and appeals to the dominant European model of nationalism, with its focus on the self-determination of the ethnos, appeared to fall on deaf ears, alliances were built with indigenous peoples elsewhere, including West Papua's Pacific neighbors. This has led to rather more counterimperial expressions of identity that celebrate indigenous ideas about sovereignty and lean on pan-Oceanic cultural tropes. One such important trope is that of *wansolwara* (Melanesian pidgin for "one ocean," signifying one people), an idea that builds on Epeli Hau'ofa's theorization of the Pacific "sea of islands," in which Hau'ofa argues that the ocean is what connects rather than divides the Pacific community (2008). Identifying with indigenous and Pacific decolonization movements does not, for the most part, demonstrate that West Papuans believe all models of sovereignty are equal, however, or that an alternative form of sovereignty to independent nation-statehood would be acceptable to them. Rather, it indicates a shift in strategic thinking, an openness to the idea that there might be more effective ways of achieving independent nation-statehood than appealing endlessly and only to the United Nations, for example. West Papuan political identity is not an "either/or" phenomenon—one grounded either in a fixed view of history and ethnic belonging or in an understanding of identity as purely mercurial, contextual, and opportunistic. It is both of these things at once: in short, it is an identity of suitable complexity for a colonized people trying to work out how best to survive and thrive in a postcolonial world.

Some scholars have questioned why post–World War II West Papuan national identity took on a Melanesian character rather than an Indonesian one, positing that this development was by no means a certainty. Probably, they assert, this was a result of Dutch intervention and the viciousness with which Indonesians have maintained their rule in the colony. Of course, these explanations have merit. The Dutch did indeed encourage West Papuan nationalism to take an "anti-Indonesian" direction. And, governing by military, Indonesians have made few friends in West Papua. This chapter has attempted to demonstrate, however, that West Papuans' agency and creativity have possibly had as significant an influence on the development of a Pacific-oriented West Papuan national identity as the other pieces of the puzzle—Dutch intervention and Indonesian brutality. The forms that West Papuan nationalism has taken over the past five decades have roots that precede Dutch colonialism and are more embracing of a celebratory "Melanesianism" than an identity born primarily out of opposition to Indonesian colonialism might suggest. The "Melanesian" characteristics of West Papuan cultures are not inconsistent with the cultural similarities that West Papuans traditionally shared in the precolonial era, and still share, with other Melanesian cultures. Adversity often expedites and solidifies identity-forging processes and articulation (Ballard 2006; compare, for example, the strength of West Papuan identity compared to the much less forceful pan–Papua New Guinean identity across the border). However, that West Papuan identity took on particularly strident Melanesian characteristics cannot be reduced to the actions of Dutch and Indonesian colonizers. This point is significant for the West Papuan argument that they are "a people," separate from "the Indonesian people," still awaiting the fulfillment of their right to self-determination.

This chapter has also demonstrated the various ways in which West Papuan cultural nationalism, leveraged as a form of resistance to Indonesia and practiced in order to survive, searches the primordial past for inspiration even as it is continuously constructed (see Hall 1993, 223–225). In the face of cultural genocide, looking backward and forward is critical, West Papuans believe, to the survival of their people. For many West Papuans, it is their perceived "Melanesian roots" that bind them and connect them psychologically and emotionally to their homeland as they simultaneously adapt their cultures to fit changing political circumstances within host countries. Otto Ondawame believed that those in the diaspora and those struggling inside West Papua must work together to achieve decolonization—both groups have important roles to play. He explained: "People inside . . . know the political situation inside, but . . . they don't know about the diplomatic [situation], what language they have to use, or about international political relationships . . . so one must complete the other. . . . Other liberation movements indicate clearly that both must play an important role. In East Timor the guerrillas continued to fight, fight, fight . . . but if people outside did not speak out strongly, it could not have gone anywhere" (Interview, 2009).

Under present circumstances, West Papuans are gravely concerned that many of their unique cultures are unlikely, in the long term, to survive in any meaningful way. The extent of in-migration from Indonesia to West Papua spells the rapid proportional decline of the indigenous West Papuan population compared to the settler population. In this context the specter of the fate of Australian Aboriginal and Native American cultures looms large. The indigenous peoples of each of these settler colonies have become a small minority of the overall populations and are severely marginalized, even as their cultures are appropriated and commercialized by the occupiers of their lands. Even if Indonesian democracy was, at this late stage, to change tack to the extent that it legitimately embraced and encouraged West Papuan expression of their own cultures, my research suggests that this would be too little, too late: West Papuans' desire for independence would continue to lead to efforts to perform their cultures in ways that "emphasize the differences between West Papuans and other Indonesians" (Blaskett 1993, 333). In any case, the prospect of Indonesian democracy changing sufficiently radically for West Papuan cultures to flourish freely is more hypothetical than likely given the extent to which pan–West Papuan culture is viewed by Indonesia, quite rightly, as deeply tinged with anti-Indonesian nationalism. An unfortunate paradox, then, remains: West Papuan political identity and cultural expression are, for the time being, strengthened in some ways by Indonesian oppression. However, if the West Papuan nationalism that drives the struggle for decolonization does not result in an independent nation-state, this same Indonesian oppression will likely be the ultimate undoing of much of West Papua's cultural diversity.

The cultural expression of nationalism is one of the strongest points of similarity between West Papuan populations living throughout the world. West Papuans have faith that their cultures (and people) will not have to succumb to the devastation of cultural and biological genocide because, they believe, independence is inevitable (see chapter 2). While from an outside observer's perspective it is difficult to agree that independence is inevitable (although this book demonstrates that it is certainly not impossible), the upsurge in recent years of West Papuan cultural-political activism indicates that the decolonization movement is gaining steady momentum. To maintain this momentum, West Papuans are working to develop dynamic, forward-looking political cultures at home and in diaspora. At the same time, to ensure unity, as one young West Papuan woman living in Port Moresby explained to me, West Papuan political leaders continue to appeal "to our roots. It's the culture that will keep us together" (Interviewee B, 2009).

4

WRESTLING IN THE DARK

Three Generations of Factions

> Decolonization is a long, generational process.
>
> — *Haunani Kay Trask,* From a Native Daughter

The importance of generations has frequently been overlooked in explanations of political conflict in West Papua, an oversight given West Papuans' own emphasis on the ways in which generational belonging has shaped the direction of their decolonization movement. West Papua's culture of resistance, with its attendant ways of managing internecine conflict and strategizing for independence, is a creation of the generational genealogy of West Papuan resisters whose own ideas have been molded by their historical milieu.

To Haunani Kay Trask's observation that "Marxists see class, not culture; white feminists see women, not people and liberals see only individuals . . . none of these groups understand Native nations" (1993, 273), might be added, in the context of West Papua's conflict, that "the postcolonial world sees only Melanesian disfunction," viewing *wantokism* as nepotism and "Big Man" politics as egotism, and so on.[1] Examining factionalism within the decolonization movement, as I do here, in terms of an unfolding genealogy of political generational perspectives, rather than as a polyphany of primordial contestations, is therefore a decolonial methodology.

What follows is a brief history of factionalism in West Papuan decolonization politics, drawing on the perspectives of three generations of leaders broadly defined. It shows how unfolding generations of West Papuan activists have learned to work with or temporarily mask over factionalism for the benefit of the decolonization movement. In various strategic instances, due to the articulated and polycentric (Kirksey 2011, 281) nature of West Papua's decolonization struggle, factional divides in the movement have led to critical progress and a rapid expansion of the battlefield, signalling positive change for West Papuans.

The origin of disunity in West Papua's decolonization movement is frequently traced to the 1976 Organisasi Papua Merdeka (OPM) feud in the West Papuan jungles of Keerom (Blaskett 1993; Elmslie 2002; Ondawame 2010; Osborne 1985). There, Jacob Prai, a founder and political leader of the OPM's National Liberation Army of West Papua (TPN), and the TPN military strategist Seth Rumkorem, had a falling out so monumental that the OPM split into two major factions. For the five years prior to their misunderstanding, Prai, a former law student with family roots in the Keerom region, managed a TPN command with the Biak-born Rumkorem, a defector from the Indonesian army, at the TPN headquarters known as Markas Victoria. Prai provided political education for recruits, teaching the significance "of unity, where different tribes learnt the importance of fighting the Indonesians rather than each other" (Rumakiek and Elmslie 2017). Rumkorem offered standardized military training, which "lifted morale and confidence at Markas Victoria, as well as in the other field commands" (Rumakiek and Elmslie 2017).

The high point of the men's collaboration consisted in their declaration via short-wave radio of West Papuan independence, a bold act that accompanied their troops' attack on a nearby military post in 1971. On behalf of the West Papuan nation, the two men proclaimed: "Today, July 1st, 1971, the land and people of West Papua have been declared free and independent.... Let it be known to the world, that the sincere wish of the Papuan people to be free and independent in their own country is hereby fulfilled" (Osborne 1985, 56). While the declaration received little acknowledgment outside West Papua, it nevertheless functioned as an important unifier and confidence-booster for West Papuans throughout the territory, renewing their desire for struggle (Ondawame 2010, 76). Following the declaration, Prai and Rumkorem were elected to senior positions in the newly formed Revolutionary Provisional Government of West Papua. According to OPM spokesperson Otto Ondawame, who worked closely with Prai after the leadership split, the establishment of the new government was a national success. An effective leadership was created to oversee new policies, programs, and committees, and political and military structures were strategically improved. The OPM was carried forward by this momentum until March 23, 1976, when Prai and Rumkorem parted ways.

Diverse accounts of the Prai-Rumkorem rupture emphasize different contributing factors: strategic differences, tribal clashes, a battle of egos, and ideological disagreement. It is likely that each of these factors played a role in the split. Rex Rumakiek, who worked for Prai and Rumkorem at the time of the conflict, attributes the tensions between the two to an intelligence leak. Rumakiek, then based in Port Moresby, Papua New Guinea (PNG), sent a man claiming to be a representative of the Nigerian government, one of the few West Papua–friendly governments at that time, to visit Prai at Markas Victoria. The man in question claimed he was reporting to African supporters on the efficacy of the OPM-TPN. When Rumkorem found out about the visit, he was incensed that Prai had provided the visitor (who, it was later revealed, according to Ondawame, was not Nigerian but a Central Intelligence Agency [CIA] agent) with TPN intelligence and had Prai arrested by a section of their own armed forces (Ondawame 2010, 80). This account would suggest that the split was triggered by strategic differences between the men (that is, in beliefs about who should and should not be made privy to the more intimate details of OPM-TPN operations).

The late West Papuan activist Wim Zonggenau attributed the dispute to region-of-origin tension: "People do not forget that Prai comes from Keroom [*sic*] region. If Rumkorem treated his people badly, Prai as a local leader has to stand up and defend them" (quoted in Ondawame 2010, 80). Scholars Beverly Blaskett (1993, 221) and Robin Osborne agree with Zonggenau, with Osborne pointing out that the troops who remained with Rumkorem after the split were mostly from Biak (1985, 65). Others attributed the dispute to personal issues and a clash of egos (see Elmslie 2002, 29): Prai could never forget that Rumkorem had once served in the Indonesian military (Osborne 1985, 53) and accused him of being authoritarian and "pro-Indonesian" (Ondawame 2010, 80); Rumkorem resented Prai taking a Biak woman as a second wife (Ondawame 2010, 80). Both men were from elite families, but Prai was a scholar and considered Rumkorem, with his military ways, to be somewhat brutish and belligerent (Ondawame 2010, 80), while Rumkorem thought of Prai, with his lack of military training, as weak and ineffectual (Rumakiek and Elmslie 2017).

Ideology may have also played a role. Rumkorem had been a "strong supporter of the Indonesian Communist Party in the 1950s and 1960s" (Ondawame 2010, 79) and believed that the TPN would be well served soliciting weapons from the Eastern Bloc—a suggestion Prai vehemently opposed (Osborne 1985, 55). The two men and their respective followers set up different camps, each camp regarding the other as "the enemy under the same mosquito net" (Osborne 1985, 65) and each holding the same two goals: to overthrow the Indonesian occupation and to destroy the other camp. It was not until 1984, when both men were living as asylum seekers in different European countries, that the "resistance began to develop a unified command" once more (Osborne 1985, 65).

Such is the story of the factionalism in the resistance movement that has been its most maligned characteristic ever since. Problematically, the literature about West Papua focuses on stories like the Prai-Rumkorem dispute that emphasize dissension among West Papua's leadership, exacerbating the tendency among observers of the region to pathologize Melanesian political culture as parochial, unstable, and hopelessly fragmented (see, for example, Doumenge 2002 and Reilly 2000). West Papuans, including Simon Sapioper (Interview, 2008), Joseph Prai (Interview, 2008), Clemens Runawery (Interview, 2009), and Sonny Karubaba (Interview, 2009), have stated their concern to me about outsiders' perceptions of the struggle as incompetent and divided. Jacob Rumbiak told me that Michael Somare once informed him: "We want to support you, but you people are split; you fight each other" (Interview, 2009).

This chapter offers an alternative perspective—that West Papuan politics revolve around, and are capable of achieving, periodic strategic consensus. This perspective has come into sharper focus under the guidance of the current West Papuan leadership. Working toward consensus through debate and disagreement as West Papuans do is democratic; it is also a key characteristic of Melanesian political "style," which reflects Melanesia's traditionally acephalous social structures (May 2004). When consensus is necessary, it is to be arrived at without concession to hereditary or imposed authority.

In a 2018 conference presentation in Adelaide, Australia, West Papuan activist Ronny Kareni (2018) explained that different groups within the resistance movement are free to pursue different decolonization ideas and strategies, confident that when it matters, everyone will work together to use what they have learned along their diverse paths in support of their common goal. Kareni's view of consensus, of unity of purpose, is similar to that espoused by Amilcar Cabral: "The basic principle of unity lies in the difference between the items" (Cabral 1979, 29). He elaborates: "Each one can preserve his personality, his ideas, his religion, his personal problems, even a little of his style of play, but they must all obey one thing: they must act together to score goals against any opponent with whom they are playing. . . . They have to form a unity. If they do not do this, there is no football team, there is nothing" (Cabral 1979, 29). To achieve this unity, Cabral contends, "It is necessary to struggle" (1979, 33). Ray Halbritter of the Oneida Indian Nation in the United States takes a similar perspective when reflecting on tensions in indigenous North American politics: "I believe it's possible to get to a place of consensus. It doesn't mean everyone agrees, but it means that they're at least willing to go along enough to not object" (quoted in Alfred 2005, 215).

In many ways it is remarkable that it took eleven years from the OPM's inception in 1965 for factionalism to become pronounced, given the tensions outlined above that many resistance fighters besides Prai and Rumkorem encountered as well. Various of these tensions not only endure today but have been exacerbated by Indonesia's exploitation of leadership fissures. For example, the practice of *pemekaran,* or the rapid creation of new administrative and budgetary units by the Indonesian government in West Papua, is viewed by many West Papuans as an Indonesian "divide and rule" tactic in which a small minority of West Papuans are given limited control over continuously divided regions (B. Wenda, interview, 2008). But what Indonesia stirs up is not necessarily "traditional opposition" between West Papuans: "It is the opposition between the colonized excluded from the benefits of colonialism and their counterparts who manage to turn the colonial system to their advantage," as Fanon discovered in Algeria in the 1960s (1963, 67). Colonialists leverage the antagonism they create to splinter nationalist parties, mobilizing "the population in the mountains and the interior against the urban population [and] set[ting] the back country against the coast [to] revive tribal identities" (Fanon 1963, 67; on this phenomenon, see also Cabral 1979, 40, and Ngũgĩ 1981, 1).

But what is critical to emphasize is that such tensions, whether endemic or colonially manipulated, have never overwhelmed the movement. Indeed, as Ondawame points out, "The split created some productive competition between the two main factions, which encouraged West Papuans to participate in the struggle, expanding the areas of struggle and creating new approaches" (2010, 81). The split was an equalizer of sorts, taking the fight out of the hands of its elite leadership and delivering its control to localized commands throughout West Papua. Fanon described this phenomenon as typical of decolonization struggles in their foundational years: "During this period, spontaneity rules. Initiative rests with local areas.... The action of each and every-one substantiates the nation and undertakes to ensure its triumph locally" (1963, 83). As in decolonizing Africa of the 1980s, observed by Ngũgĩ wa Thiong'o, the resistance tradition gradually became one of the "working people (the peasantry and the proletariat) aided by patriotic students, intellectuals (academic and non-academic), soldiers and other progressive elements of the petty middle class" (1981, 2).

As the struggle has progressed, what has become ever more apparent to the generations of resisters following Prai and Rumkorem is the value, in terms of garnering international support, of the show of unity despite internal factional differences. Over the decades, disagreements have thus begun to coalesce more around intergenerational choices of strategy, while differences such as place of origin, for example, have taken on less significance. The first generation did not—could not—envision the seeming interminability of the struggle, nor was it aware in the first few years how necessary to the success of its goal it would be to enlist the support of the majority of the world. Its members had no idea, in the beginning, that their disagreements would be viewed by outsiders as symptomatic of a stereotypical Melanesian political incompetence.

As subsequent generations have become involved in the struggle, they are aware, in ways that the first generation of resisters was not, that they are dealing with complex global politics and a context in which formal decolonization has been withheld indefinitely. These generations have the benefit of being able to look back on failures and forward to potential solutions. While many of the first generation of resisters are still involved in the struggle, and some even work alongside later generations, their politics were shaped early on by a set of historical events and global political circumstances that the latter have not experienced. Thus, decolonization politics within the West Papuan movement have become longitudinal, focused on building bridges across rifts between generations with different strategic insights.

Generational Politics

Leaning on the ideas of generational scholars Mannheim (1927), Strauss and Howe (1991), Pilcher (1994), Dunham (1998), and Rintala (1963), I apply the concept of political rather than biological generations to an analysis of West Papua's leadership. Political generations are delineated by a subjectively experienced rather than a numerically measured period of time (Pilcher 1994, 478) and are in a constant state of flow: multiple political generations are participating in politics at any given time. Nevertheless, biological age does hold some significance for political generation affiliation. Generational scholar Marvin Rintala argues: "Late adolescence and early adulthood are the formative years during which a distinctive world-view emerges, which remains essentially unchanged through old age. The crucial years are regarded as approximately seventeen to twenty-five" (1963, 513). It is during this time period, generally speaking, that a new social generation develops its generational consciousness and distinguishes itself from the previous generation.

In West Papua, where in the face of cultural genocide there is so much at stake in the bequeathing of cultural practices to new generations, the development of new generational consciousness is especially fraught. Because the political "coming of age" theories I refer to are European and American derived, I apply them cautiously to the Melanesian context. They do seem particularly fitting, however, to the case study of West Papua's decolonization struggle, given that the struggle commenced under Dutch colonization and continues to be carried out via appeals to European and international political institutions. West Papua's cosmopolitan politicians have come of age under conditions of globalization that make sense in the terms of such theories. Mannheim's observation that "the continuous emergence of new human beings (generations) certainly results in the loss of accumulated cultural possessions" but also "facilitates re-evaluation of our inventory and teaches us both to forget that which is no longer useful and to covet that which has yet to be won" (1927, 294) accurately describes the processes taking place within West Papuan intergenerational politics.

Intergenerational conflict occurs as new political generations come of age with a different appreciation of what is required for decolonization at that particular point in time. Rather than being detrimental to a decolonization movement, however, intergenerational conflict can drive it, writes Memmi: "The conflict of generations can and must be resolved by social conflict; conversely, it is thus a factor in the movement and progress. The young generations find their solution to their problems in collective movements. By choosing a movement, they accelerate it" (1965, 97–98).

WEST PAPUAN GENERATIONS

West Papuans frequently speak, in general terms, of the "older" and the "younger" generation(s) when explaining major shifts in the movement's momentum. For example, after Jacob Prai and Seth Rumkorem's OPM leadership split in the 1970s, OPM member Jacob Rumbiak, their junior, recalls thinking, "We must set up [an] understanding in [the] new generation, especially [of] how we [will] educate them [in] nationalist thinking" (Interview, 2009). Otto Ondawame, a contemporary of Rumbiak, thought of generations in terms of the degree of openness to Indonesian culture among different West Papuan age groups. "[The] young generation of people feel more Asian," he reflected, "but [the] old generation, my generation, we don't feel it" (O. Ondawame, interview, 2009). Similarly, Jacob Prai's son, Joseph, younger than both Rumbiak and Ondawame, fears that young West Papuan generations have become Indonesianized, culturally bereft, and depoliticized (Interview, 2008). By contrast, activist Victor Yeimo, a member of the "young" generation referred to by Rumbiak, Ondawame, and Prai, asserts, "In reality, we know that the elders have failed" (Interview, 2010). He goes on to explain that the failure is not the elders' fault but rather is a result of "Indonesian repression [and] intimidation" (Interview, 2010). It is important, in his view and in that of activists of his generation, that "elders and youngsters . . . work together for independence," each generation needing the insights of the other to defeat Indonesia (Interview, 2010).

Based on my research with West Papuan decolonization activists involved in the struggle from the 1960s to the present, including interviews with factional leaders and with their international allies, I have discerned three broad generations of leaders in the movement. Each generation is distinguishable according to the strategies and ideologies it has applied to the struggle, from guerrilla warfare to identity politics networking (see figure 4). Liem Soei Liong from Tapol, a human rights advocacy organization that focuses its attention on Indonesia, argues there may be reason to speak of four generations in order to include the activists prior to Rumkorem and Prai: the political elite, prepared by the Dutch for leadership of an independent West Papua, who went into overseas exile with the Dutch after the failure of the Act of Free Choice (for example, Nicolaas Jouwe and Marcus Kaisiepo; interview, 2008). Because these leaders supported the OPM in various ways while in exile, however, I consider them to be members of the first of the three identifiable generations in this book's schema. Historian John Saltford plots West Papuan political generations in terms of the presence of internal movement unity and external solidarity. Early on (in the 1960s and 1970s), he argues, West Papua was plagued with the problem that many independence movements face—a struggle for a united front: attempts at unity "didn't always work, and people would kind of speak out of turn.... There were quite a few rivalries" (Interview, 2008). The decade of the 1980s, Saltford continues, was characterized by trying to heal the rifts of the 1970s. The following generation then realized that possibly more important than focusing on achieving consistent internal unity was "press[ing] the right buttons with the global community," focusing on "peace, human rights and environmental issues" (and to this list I would add contemporary identity politics) as they concern West Papuans (Interview, 2008). A movement with such concerns, this generation reasoned, would likely gain more sympathy from the international community than would "a traditional liberation movement—especially if that liberation movement is unlikely to actually achieve on military terms what it wants" (J. Saltford, interview, 2008).

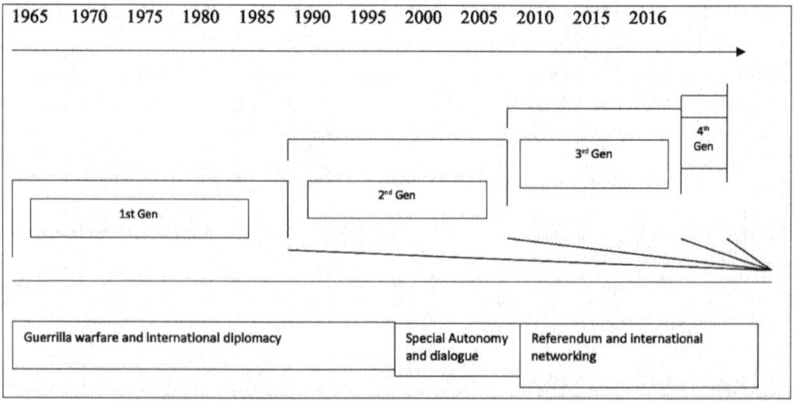

FIGURE 4. Time line of generations and faction affiliations.

Benny Wenda, a leader representing the "younger" political generation, elaborates on the shift identified by Saltford: The "vision, the goal [of each generation] is the same, but my generation is very different because [of] globalization and technology" (Interview, 2008). He believes that communication, as a result of Internet access and the proliferation of social media, is more fluid than it ever has been. West Papuans can seek out information about world politics from the relative safety of their own mobile phones and, similarly, can disseminate information about their own situation using Facebook, Twitter, and YouTube. As a result, Wenda believes, his generation is the most politically savvy to date (Interview, 2008). Richard Samuelson, a UK-based West Papua activist and close supporter of Wenda, provides more context:

> The first generation's only way was to fight in the jungle.... But they also had a very high expectation of western democracies. They all thought that the British, the Americans, the Australians, if they knew, then they would come and help. They didn't know the truth about British and... Australian and... American foreign policies and the support for Indonesia.... And, of course, now, [Wenda's] generation, they know the truth.... [They are] fired up because... from a young age, they've known everything. They can also read... much more about what's going on in the outside world. (Interview, 2008)

Samuelson's point supports the insights of Saltford and Wenda: the latest generation of West Papuan leaders has access to more and better digital resources than their predecessors and therefore can more strategically orient their struggle to match the immediate priorities of international governments and civil society. Samuelson's, Wenda's, Saltford's, and Yeimo's perspectives on the strength and spirit carried by younger generations counter the more pessimistic views concerning those generations expressed by Rumbiak, Ondawame, and Prai. It is understandable that as Indonesian migration to West Papua increases and more Papuans are forced to leave their ancestral homelands as a result of Indonesian military operations, the earliest generations of the effort are concerned that the urgency of resistance and the importance of cultural heritage will not assume political priority for the newer generations. The accounts above, and the lives of many other "younger"-generation West Papuan activists that I have observed during my thirteen years of research with the movement, however, reveal otherwise. The younger resisters driving the struggle now, in partnership with various of their older compatriots, appear to be the most powerful and effective yet.

My schema of three generations of West Papuan leaders follows Rintala's advice that "politically, one must not give a generation more than, at most, 15 years" (1963, 517). Each of the seventy-five leaders I interviewed during my research for this book was born in a specific fifteen-year period between 1933 and 1986. According to this schema based on birth years, a fourth generation now exists. However, I have seen no evidence yet that a new set of leaders has emerged from this generation or that it promotes substantively different strategic preferences from those of the third generation. Perhaps this is a result of the unprecedented degree of unity within the movement, fostered in part by a particular convergence of historical and technological circumstances that have presented West Papuans with opportunities to reflect on the importance of demonstrative unity and to connect with global contemporary indigenous, black power, and decolonial movements (see Webb-Gannon, Webb, and Solis 2018).

The First Generation of the struggle comprises leaders born between 1933 and 1948; the Second Generation, between 1950 and 1965; and the Third Generation, between 1971 and 1986. Each of these generations has been influenced during its formative political years by a different set of events of marked significance that has shaped its initial, and in some cases ongoing, perspectives on how the struggle should be carried out. (On the importance of such events to the development of a generation's political consciousness, see Rintala 1963, 513.)

The leaders who composed the First Generation were all at least seventeen years of age (which is when, according to Rintala, political consciousness begins to develop) on the significant date of December 1, 1961, during which the first New Guinea Council formally adopted West Papua's national symbols. These leaders started out full of hope—their Dutch colonizers were preparing them to lead an independent West Papua. After Indonesia invaded West Papua, they maintained hope that the United Nations (UN) would bring justice to their nation-in-waiting. Following the bitter blow that the outcome of the 1969 Act of Free Choice represented to these leaders, many stopped looking outside of West Papua for help, mobilizing to form the OPM instead, with limited weaponry but expansive networks and knowledge of their own land.

Members of the Second Generation were coming of generational age around either the time of the 1971 OPM declaration of independence in Markus Victoria, the subsequent split of the OPM in 1976, or the Jayapura Uprising of 1984, in which a failed flag raising in Jayapura resulted in such extreme reprisals that up to twelve thousand refugees fled from West Papua to PNG. This generation bore witness to internal unity followed by rupture and exodus. Aware of its own vulnerabilities, it sought out compromise with the more powerful Indonesia in the form of Special Autonomy and, when that failed, dialogue.

Many of the Third Generation remember clearly the 1998 Biak Massacre, when the Indonesian military shot into a crowd of nearly two hundred people participating in a several-day-long flag-raising event in Biak, and all experienced the exultation of the Papuan Spring of 2000, a period during which, following East Timor's referendum on independence, they expected their own to be realized. This generation has seen that Indonesia was able to be persuaded on the issue of a referendum in East Timor and now demands the same for West Papua. Members have also been able to connect, through social media and the hosting of events, with activists outside of West Papua to bring attention to the mass human rights violations that occurred during their formative years. One such event was the 2013 collaboration between Australian-based academics and indigenous Biak activists in the form of a "citizens' tribunal" at the University of Sydney, staged to bring global attention to the ignored Biak Massacre (Biak Massacre Tribunal 2013).

While each generation cannot help but be affected by the events and political milieux informing the political orientations of subsequent generations, what is apparent from my research is the tendency of West Papuan leaders to form factions with other members of their same generation (albeit with some generational slippage). These factions have a propensity to favor, over time, the political outlooks and decolonization strategies pursued at the time their members were coming of political age. Of course, within each generation frictions and different factions exist. "Every generation speaks out with more than one voice... there is polyphony within each generation as well," Rintala contends. This horizontal friction internally divides generations into what Mannheim calls "generation units"—groups within generations that are oriented toward each other in conflict. Mannheim explains: "Youth experiencing the same concrete problems may be said to be part of the same actual generation; while those groups within the same actual generation which work up material of their common experiences in different and specific ways, constitute separate generation units" (1927, 304).

Generational units occur more frequently among the First and Second Generations than the Third. What is remarkable about the Third Generation is the ways in which it has been able to minimize internal conflict and work productively alongside members of contentious generation units in the First and Second Generations. To understand the evolution of this phenomenon, I turn now to a closer consideration of the factionalism that has characterized West Papuan politics since the struggle's inception.

Factionalism

The formation of factions in politics is a common phenomenon, with negative and positive effects, and can have many causes. Early scholars of factionalism Bernard Siegel and Alan Beals describe factionalism as "essentially a phenomenon of socio-cultural change. Hence its origins could presumably be attributed to external pressures of various kinds which either create conflict or lead to the re-channeling of conflict along the lines of pervasive factionalism" (1960, 300). In West Papua, factionalism results, in part, from the Indonesian government's repression of regionally based political parties (on this issue in other regions of the world, see Bujra 1973, 145, and Schwartz 1969, 1099). Because formal political parties are banned, West Papuan aspirations for independence are channeled through the formation of unofficial (in Indonesia's eyes) political action groups that I categorize here as "factions."

The decolonization movement factions to which I refer are qualitatively different from the type examined by scholars of West Papua Jaap Timmer (2005) and Richard Chauvel (2004), who focus on factionalism within the territory's local administration units, an effect of *pemekaran* that has created a local circulation of elites oriented less toward the task of governing than with maintaining power. It is important to recognize that "factions are 'amorphous,' elusive, and 'refractory to the usual analytic methods'" (Schwartz 1969, 1088) and include a range of possible groupings, including generation units and intergenerational collaborations. Even as I write, West Papuan factions are changing. Instead of claiming a definitive knowledge of West Papuan factions, therefore, I hope to illuminate some of the ways in which factionalism and unity interplay in West Papua's dynamic decolonization politics, representing, so to speak, two sides of the same strategic coin.

Factionalism can induce setbacks in the momentum of political movements and has done so, at different times, in the West Papuan decolonization struggle. Over the years, factions have formed and fractured in response to interpersonal conflict, different levels of leader charisma, rivalry around power accumulation, personal vendettas, and distrust that other leaders are being bribed by Indonesia or are "Indonesian puppets." But factionalism is not always destructive. Bujra writes that factional conflicts are "essentially a preview to new kinds of cooperative activities and new social alignments" (1973, 141). Schwartz concurs. Factionalism may, he argues, have

> a creative influence in that it can provide an important avenue for leaders to emerge...an opportunity for more opinions and sentiments to be openly expressed... [and] more flexibility in the search for solutions to the new problems. (1969, 1066)

Further, Schwartz continues:

> In the absence of durable national political parties and corporate political groups at the local level, the factions organize and channel political conflict in [a community]. In the attempt to gain power, which involves an attempt to defeat and sometimes do serious damage to each other, factional rivals also perform certain necessary political tasks.... The factional rivalry goads opponents

into what may be called goal-directed activity...that, almost incidentally, benefits the entire community. (1969, 1099)

In West Papuan politics, factions, which are divided along strategic and generational lines, have helped keep the West Papuan resistance struggle alive and have contributed to the attainment of the various achievements gained over the last five decades. In internal West Papuan politics, the result of the conflict over strategy among three generations of leaders has been a strategic, dynamic, and shifting unity in which opposing ideas and tactics work side by side, sometimes complementarily, toward the same goal, *merdeka*. As a West Papuan refugee in PNG informed me, "We are solid. We are different but we are solid. This [factionalism is the] Melanesian type of democracy."

Intermittent unity among factions in West Papuan politics at key moments in the struggle has been far more important than maintaining consensual or factionless unity. Bujra observes: "No real community exists in a state of perfect political unity, since economic resources of various kinds are always in short supply and competition for control over them is inevitable. But there may be periods when a temporary unity is achieved, and there may be others when public opinion is divided but unorganised. A community may be divided by factions at some periods, while at others it is more or less united....A period of unity may thus occur as part of the cyclical process of factionalism" (1973, 143–144).

An example of the brief unity in 2010 between leaders of rival factions, Otto Ondawame (who until his death in 2014 was vice chair of the West Papua National Coalition for Liberation [WPNCL] faction) and Jacob Rumbiak (who is foreign affairs minister for the West Papua National Authority [WPNA] faction), is illustrative. Ondawame and Rumbiak (see figure 5) were reacquainted at the International Peace Research Association Conference in July 2010 in Sydney, Australia, after a period of several years marked by political tension between them. Their respective Second Generation factions each considered itself to be the sole representative body of West Papuans striving for independence at that time. And each faction had achieved significant political successes in the preceding month. The WPNA, according to Rumbiak, had been instrumental in mobilizing major demonstrations in West Papua against Special Autonomy, which had captured global attention. According to Ondawame, the WPNCL had played an important role in the passing of the Wantok Blong Yumi Bill in Vanuatu's Parliament, which enshrined in Vanuatu law the goal of challenging West Papua's legal status as part of Indonesia. The WPNCL, in general, has focused on the international dimensions of the struggle, while the WPNA has tended to work on political advances within West Papua.

When they met at the conference (to which each leader had been invited to present a paper on West Papuan political strategy), I was surprised to

FIGURE 5. Jacob Rumbiak and Otto Ondawame "unite" at the International Peace Research Association Conference, Sydney, July 2010. Photograph by Wendy Lambourne.

witness what appeared to be a sincerely friendly reunion between the two rivals. Over dinner, each rejoiced in the other's political achievements of the previous month. They remarked that each faction, although operating in different arenas, was working complementarily toward the common goal of decolonization. Rumbiak and Ondawame decided at that conference that their factions would conjointly represent West Papua at the Pacific Islands Forum meeting in Vanuatu the following month. The brief period of unity served its purpose. The two factional leaders, following a temporary reunion building on the momentum of their respective factional achievements, were able to present a united face at the forum, a regional meeting at which the show of political solidarity was strategically important for the movement, even though they fell out again shortly thereafter. This example demonstrated that in the West Papuan context, the "'unity' that matters is a linkage between [the] articulated discourse [of decolonization] and the social forces with which it can, under certain historical conditions, but need not necessarily, be connected" (Grossberg 1986, 53).

WEST PAPUAN FACTIONS

Just as the schema of generations outlined above is imprecise, developed to decipher patterns rather than focus on detail, so, too, is this chapter's definition of West Papuan factions. For the purposes of this analysis, a faction is defined as any West Papuan group carrying out decolonization-oriented political functions that for a range of reasons and at different times is in contention with groups with similar goals. Because of their highly political nature, I categorize as factions the various West Papuan cultural decolonization groups as well as the strictly political bodies that are concerned with independence. I include in this grouping the Dewan Adat Papua (DAP; Papua Customary Council), which has acquired a degree of central Indonesian government recognition, even though it was formed in 2002 by West Papuans concerned with defending West Papuan indigenous rights; the Presidium Dewan Papua (PDP; Papua Presidium Council), which was charged with the responsibility of working peacefully for West Papuan independence during the Second Papuan Kongres in 2000; and the Majelis Rakyat Papua (MRP; Papuan People's Assembly), which was created under the Special Autonomy Law and is a Papuan Upper House tasked with protecting Papuan cultures.

These groupings and the array of others explored in the remainder of this chapter are oriented, to a greater or lesser degree, around various strategic choices of action for realizing the common goal of decolonization. It is important to note that many West Papuan decolonization leaders belong to more than one faction—factions are not mutually exclusive. Many leaders from the First Generation, for example, have been members of the OPM-TPN since their early years but more recently have joined factions favoring alternative strategies to armed resistance while retaining OPM allegiance. In the West Papuan context, multiple simultaneous and changing factional allegiances are a form of political articulation, a tactical "connection that can make a unity of two different elements, under certain conditions" (Grossberg 1986, 53). Historian and cultural studies theorist James Clifford writes that the term "articulation" "suggests discourse or speech. . . . Meaningful discourse is a cutting up and combining of linguistic elements, always a selection from a vastly greater repertoire of semiotic possibilities. So an articulated tradition [of factions, in West Papua's case] is a kind of collective 'voice,' but always in this constructed, contingent sense" (2001, 474–478).

Because of the articulated nature of factions in West Papua, "there's a lot of middle ground; and crucial political and cultural positions are not firmly anchored on one side or the other but are contested and up for grabs" (Clifford 2001, 477). A desire to end Indonesian occupation is the middle ground in West Papuan factional politics and is what constitutes the movement as a polycentric one in which "believers [do not necessarily] agree about [all of] the essentials of their creed, its interpretation and application" but achieve progress through "strengthening the centrifugal trends" (Laqueur 1962, 1, 5).

OPM (Organisasi Papua Merdeka). Most First Generation West Papuan leaders started their Indonesian-resistance activities as members of the

OPM-TPN. The OPM is perhaps the most difficult faction to define, given its huge symbolic significance to West Papuans (at a certain level, the OPM is representative of the entire independence struggle: most West Papuans identify at least loosely as part of the OPM) and its own internal factional divides. The OPM has lost its strategic and political monopoly on the struggle as its founders, mostly members of the First Generation, have aged, moved overseas, or died. For example, in October 2010 Seth Rumkorem passed away, and Jacob Prai has resided in Sweden since 1979. Many OPM members of the Second Generation have channeled their energies into alternative factions practicing nonviolence. Prai maintains an OPM office in Malmö, Sweden, but its significance (beyond the symbolic) for those resisting on the ground in West Papua is difficult to ascertain (although Otto Ondawame, OPM international spokesperson, maintained that Prai retained credibility and influence among freedom fighters within West Papua; interview, 2009). The OPM itself has restructured many times and features a military wing of very limited physical power,[2] the TPN, with its own command structure, and a political wing (of which a large number of its constituents now compose the leadership of the WPNCL).

Traditionally, the OPM, through the TPN, practiced armed resistance against Indonesian forces as its strategy for achieving independence. Since at least 2004, though, a number of OPM members have committed (publicly at an August 2004 meeting in Wewak, PNG) to nonviolent resistance (Balmain 2004). Although some TPN leaders also agreed to a laying down of arms, according to Otto Ondawame, there is no "effective communication or control [between] each [command] to coordinate activities, so... commander[s] from Merauke or Timika area[s] do activities in their own region[s]" (Interview, 2009). In other words, not all TPN commands have refrained from violent methods since then. The OPM and TPN have, historically, consisted of a number of internal factions, but many of their most influential members now also represent other highly proactive and organized factions.

ULMWP (United Liberation Movement for West Papua). The ULMWP formed in December 2014 in Port Vila, Vanuatu. It is a coalition of West Papua's three most significant contemporary factions, the Federal Republic of West Papua, the WPNCL, and the National Parliament of West Papua. As such, it is composed of members of all three generations but has a heavy Second and Third Generation contingent. Its origins can be traced to the previous year at the 2013 meeting of the Melanesian Spearhead Group (MSG), where members of the WPNCL, the most internationally recognized West Papuan independence group, put in a bid for MSG membership at the same time as did two lesser-known but influential factions claiming to be the legitimate and most suitable representatives of West Papuans: the WPNA and the recently declared Federal Republic of West Papua. According to Vanuatu

Foreign Affairs Minister Ralph Regenvanu, this contention around "true" representativeness was disconcerting to MSG leaders, and it weakened West Papua's MSG support base. They advised West Papuan leaders to return to the MSG the following year with a united front to be reconsidered for membership.

In 2014, representatives of West Papua's key independence factions—the WPNCL (First and Second Generation leaders), the Federal Republic of West Papua (Second Generation leaders), and the West Papua National Parliament (Third Generation leaders) gathered in Vanuatu and undertook to act for the purposes of international diplomacy as one united body, the United Liberation Movement for West Papua. Benny Wenda (Third Generation, based in the UK) is the current ULMWP chair, while Rex Rumakiek (First Generation, based in Australia), Octo Mote (Second Generation, based in the US), Paula Makabory (Second Generation, based in Australia), and Jacob Rumbiak (Second Generation, based in Australia) sit on the Executive Committee. Edison Waromi (Second Generation, based in West Papua) and Buchtar Tabuni (Third Generation, also in West Papua) provide support for the ULMWP from within West Papua, and up until his death in 2020, Andy Ajamiseba (First Generation, based in Vanuatu), former manager of the West Papuan reggae band the Black Brothers, supported the ULMWP from Vanuatu, the ULMWP's headquarters. In 2015 the MSG granted the ULMWP observer status, a sure step forward in regional recognition of West Papua's political unity and the legitimacy of its decolonization struggle (although Indonesia was simultaneously elevated from MSG observer to associate member).

The next decision facing the MSG of whether to appoint West Papua as a full member, however, has politically crippled the organization, and it has not been able to make a pronouncement on West Papua's status since 2015. In July 2019 the ULMWP received a boost in international stature via the recognition of its chair, Benny Wenda, with the prestigious Oxford Honorary Freedom of the City Award for his human rights work on behalf of West Papua. Previously given to well-known human rights heroes such as Nelson Mandela and Aung San Suu Kyi, the award bestowed on Wenda infuriated Indonesia, which had previously put out an Interpol red notice for his arrest. The award demonstrates the growing seriousness with which the West Papuan conflict is being considered on the world stage and places the ULMWP in a favorable position for making international progress.

WPNCL (West Papua National Coalition for Liberation). Before the formation of the ULMWP, the WPNCL, which still exists and has its headquarters at the West Papua People's Representative Office in Port Vila, Vanuatu, was perhaps the most significant contemporary faction. When it formed, it had at its head three OPM-TPN leaders who retained their OPM allegiance: the group's chairperson, Richard Yoweni (who died in 2015), onetime supreme commander of the TPN; Rex Rumakiek, who remains the secretary-general; and Otto Ondawame, who (before his death in 2014) was the vice chair. Despite this, not all OPM members have supported the coalition. OPM-TPN founders Jacob Prai and Seth Rumkorem both indicated to me that they did not belong to the WPNCL, that the founding of the faction was not an OPM undertaking (notwithstanding its heavy OPM contingent), that they did not consider the group's openness to dialogue with Indonesia a viable strategy, and that the group contains too many political novices (J. Prai, interview, 2008; S. Rumkorem, interview, 2008). The coalition, as it is also known, was founded in April 2008 in Port Vila, Vanuatu, and is an umbrella group that claims to represent twenty-nine organizations working for West Papuan independence. Its aim, until relatively recently, was to lobby for peaceful dialogue with Indonesia through a united national front representative of all proindependence groups in West Papua and the diaspora (although several key factions refused to join forces for various personal and political reasons). In late 2017, Rex Rumakiek announced that the coalition no longer sought dialogue with Indonesia but instead had decided to pursue decolonization through the UN.

Prior to the formation of the ULMWP, the WPNCL represented West Papua's decolonization movement at most regional and international events. The coalition mainly comprises First and Second Generation leaders. Some Third Generation leaders were invited to the inaugural meeting, but according to Third Generation activist Victor Yeimo, they have felt largely excluded since then (Interview, 2010). Third Generation leader Herman Wainggai, from the WPNA, offers a possible explanation for this perceived exclusion, describing the coalition as a group of mainly older leaders keen to hold on to power: "Our senior leaders . . . want their leadership . . . for themselves; they don't want to promote the young people. [They] need to show [the] international community they have power in Papua" (Interview, 2009).

WPNA (West Papua National Authority). The WPNA, one of West Papua's self-proclaimed provisional governments, has been the WPNCL's chief rival. It was formed in August 2004 and is headed by Edison Waromi in West Papua. It shares several members with the coalition inside West Papua but has chosen not to officially become part of the coalition. WPNA members have cited as reasons for its nonaligned stance its inability to see the value in a provisional government submitting to an umbrella group of nongovernment organizations and its belief that the WPNA has far greater "people power" within West Papua than the coalition (J. Rumbiak, interview, 2009). The WPNA has clashed in the past with the WPNCL, both vying for recognition as West Papua's peak representative body. The WPNA is also composed of mainly Second Generation members but works closely with Third

Generation leaders from student and youth movements in West Papua. The WPNA is lobbying for international recognition of West Papua's right to self-determination and a referendum.

KNPB (West Papua National Committee). A key factional member of the ULMWP, the WPNA, and perhaps, to a lesser extent, of the WPNCL, the KNPB continues to grow in popularity. Student and youth movements exercise remarkable power within West Papuan politics and the KNPB is no exception, comprising primarily student leaders or former student activists from all over West Papua. The International Crisis Group has described the group as "radical" (2010); it has certainly been strident in its mobilization for independence efforts. It is led by Buchtar Tabuni and Victor Yeimo, who have each spent significant periods in jail as political prisoners in Jayapura, and is composed of primarily Third Generation members. However, it works closely with the WPNA, as well as the OPM, throughout West Papua. The KNPB was formed in 2008 to support the London launch of an international solidarity group for West Papua, the International Lawyers for West Papua (V. Yeimo, interview, 2010). It considers itself a media clearinghouse for all independence-related activities, and it advocates a referendum for independence.

National Parliament of West Papua. The National Parliament of West Papua was established by the KNPB in 2012 as an organization of West Papuan regional bodies, with political representatives elected by constituencies in the twenty-three West Papuan regions: including Biak, Manokwari, Sorong, Fak Fak, Kaimana, Timika, Paniai, Hubula, Numbay, Tabi, Yahukimo, Puncak Jaya, Yalimo, Baliem, Nabire, Intan Jaya, Star Mountains Dogiyai, Deiyai, Yamo, Nduga, Ilaga, and Tolikara (National Parliament of West Papua, n.d). The National Parliament is made up of smaller parliaments from each of these regions that were formed to bring together all rival factions. The chair of the Parliament is Buchtar Tabuni. National Parliament leaders, primarily belonging to the Third Generation (with some Second Generation members), state on their website that the creation of the Parliament "does not mean that we do not respect the elders in the struggle and some organizations are under way, or also not to blame and justify this idea. But it is actually an invitation for us to understand how creating a leadership that stood with the power of the people [*sic*]" (National Parliament of West Papua, n.d.). This appears to be a veiled criticism of factions created by the First and Second Generations that have not been as democratic in their leadership structures or, being headquartered outside of West Papua, have not been as connected to West Papuans "inside" as the younger generations may have hoped. The Parliament recognizes the UK-based Free West Papua Campaign as the primary body for carrying out international diplomacy and raising awareness for the struggle (National Parliament of West Papua, n.d.).

Free West Papua Campaign. The Free West Papua Campaign is to international mobilization for West Papuan decolonization what the KNPB is to domestic West Papuan mobilization. The UK-based campaign operates out of the Office of Benny Wenda, maintaining a constantly up-to-date website and multiple social media accounts, liaising with mainstream media, hosting international awareness-raising events and speaking tours for Wenda, and conducting up-to-the-minute political analysis of events affecting West Papuan politics. It is a faction insofar as it exists to promote West Papua's independence movement as presented through the music and oratory of Benny Wenda, above others. It derives its credibility from Wenda's popularity both within and outside of West Papua and is responsible, through conscientization campaigns around the world, for much of the international awareness of West Papua in recent years. Its (and Benny Wenda's) impact is certainly being felt by the campaign's enemies: in April 2018, a massive distributed denial-of-service (DDoS) attack brought down the campaign's website and those of the ULMWP, the International Parliamentarians for West Papua, and the International Lawyers for West Papua—all organizations closely associated with Wenda—for over one week.

NRFPB (Federal Republic of West Papua). The NRFPB describes itself as "a sovereign nation-state," a status claimed in 2011 at the Third Papuan National Congress in Jayapura. It is largely a Second Generation–membered faction. The NRFPB's president, Forkorus Yaboisembut, is also chair of the DAP; its prime minister, Edison Waromi, is president of the WPNA; and its foreign affairs minister, Jacob Rumbiak, is director of foreign affairs for the WPNA. The NRFPB website reported in 2011 that moments after the declaration of independence by the federal republic on October 19, 2011, Indonesian security forces commenced firing into the crowd of five thousand gathered for the occasion, arrested Yaboisembut and Waromi for subversion, and imprisoned them for three years. The republic recognizes seven traditional, or adat, Papuan provinces: Mamta Province, Saireri Province, Doberai Province, Bomberai Province, Animha Province, Lapago Province, and Mepago Province (F. Yaboisembut, interview, 2008).

POLYCENTRIC FACTIONS

Countless other West Papuan decolonization factions have waxed and waned in importance over the course of the struggle. Key factions are mentioned in the following section on factional strategies. Some of these have formed on the basis of geographical location—for example, DEMMAK and AMPTPI, which represent West Papuan highlanders—but for the most part factions such as these do not rival, in terms of political influence on the struggle, the larger, more powerful factions comprising members from all around West Papua. The leaders of most prominent factions and some minor factions are well educated. Most have attended college—some in Indonesia, others in Australia and Europe—and a significant number have earned PhDs (for example, Benny Giay, Neles Tebay, Otto Ondawame, Thom Wainggai, and Jacob Rumbiak). What appears to drive factional affiliation most significantly is generational membership and a closely related phenomenon—strategic orientation. I am not able to gauge the extent to which religious faith and denomination affect factional affiliation. While the Catholic and Protestant Churches have their own human rights–seeking organizations, factions such as the PDP, for example, bring together Muslims and Catholic, Protestant, and Kingmi Indigenous Church members involved in decolonizing West Papua.

The previous overview of factions and affiliations throws up various inconsistencies, however. For example, how do the members of the WPNGC who also hold WPNCL membership reconcile the two when the WPNGC condemns attempts at dialogue with Indonesia and the WPNCL has previously pursued it? How is it that so many West Papuan factions have been led by OPM-TPN affiliates, yet those factions reject violence as a decolonization strategy? How are Third Generation–led factions, such as the KNPB, the West Papua National Parliament, the Free West Papua Campaign, and now the ULMWP, able to take the movement forward without leaving the First and Second Generations behind? These apparent contradictions are difficult to understand unless the overall movement is viewed as a polycentric one and West Papuan factions as articulated parts of a greater whole.

The points that members of different factions disagree about are of less importance than the centrifugal trends, the middle ground, on which they agree. The boundaries that define each faction produce a friction that pushes different factions' members in diverse strategic directions—to pursue armed conflict, or dialogue, or a referendum, for example. The movement's unity is made up of factions hinged together by members with multiple allegiances who retain pride in their original factional affiliation but see the wisdom of other factions following different strategies (for example, OPM-TPN members who have joined nonviolent factions, such as the WPNCL).

The movement's increasing unity is being facilitated by younger generations who can examine the past and see what has not worked yet who respect their elders and seek their blessing as they push forward with different strategies. For example, in 2018 leaders of the ULMWP welcomed, with great ceremony, a declaration from Jacob Prai endorsing the ULMWP that stated: "I as the leader of OPM and the founder of the struggle of free Papua, fully support and give full mandate to Mr. Benny Wenda as the leader of ULMWP and the political wing of OPM, to carry out the task as the leader of the nation of Papua" (Garae 2018). While many leaders have tended to group together with other leaders of their generation to pursue specific strategies, the presence of factions, whether defined by generation units or composed of multiple generations, represents opportunity. In West Papuan decolonization politics, the impermanent boundaries of the movement's polymorphous factions provide temporary protected spaces in which to engage in processes of strategic contestation, experimentation, and collaboration in pursuit of a common goal.

Strategies

ARMED RESISTANCE

"In its bare reality, decolonization reeks of red-hot cannonballs and bloody knives," wrote Fanon (1963, 3), his observation a fitting description of the resistance movement that had begun to mobilize in West Papua in 1965 with the OPM's first uprising in Manokwari (Osborne 1985, 35). Guerrilla warfare was (and is) a common strategy of national liberation/decolonization wars (Higgins 2004, 2) and also of the proxy wars fought in the Cold War, particularly during the 1960s when West Papuan armed resistance became organized. Revolutionary guerrilla warfare assumed the dimensions of a Marxist, anti-imperialist liberation ideology in the 1960s, taken up by some of the world's colonized to wage their national and social revolutions (Kraemer 1971, 138). Once diplomatic efforts to work with the Dutch for eventual independence were thwarted, the OPM took up arms. Some of that First Generation's independence advocates left with the Dutch but were roundly criticized for "abdicating responsibility" by the so-called Generation of '69 (those who fought in various ways against the sham Act of Free Choice) who stayed behind (Ondawame 2010, 48–49).

As war critic Joseph Kraemer observed, however, "Guerrilla warfare as a means to a revolutionary triumph [is] an act of faith which is very often without foundation in the socio-political context in which the guerrilla campaign has to be waged" (1971, 138). At the beginning of the struggle, West Papuan guerrillas were not aware just how futile their militarism would be in terms of having an impact on Indonesia's occupation and attracting global sympathy. They were, however, aware of the risks to their lives inherent in their David and Goliath battle, reflected in a conversation between OPM-TPN (and now WPNCL and ULMWP) member Rex Rumakiek and the late West Papuan OPM-TPN fighter Kelly Kwalik, which Rumakiek related to me. Kwalik, Rumakiek told me, had warned Rumakiek:

> "Don't forget . . . we OPM have the same kind of philosophy. The moment you take up membership with OPM you are already dead, only not buried yet. . . . I am not afraid of [being] dead, I'm already dead, I'm already dead anyway, but while I am still here I will be useful for the struggle so [long as] I am doing my job." So I [Rumakiek] said [to Kwalik]: "You don't forget this

> one" (something I learned...from my trips overseas, the liberation movements in Latin America). I said, "The first duty of a revolutionary is to stay alive, so you [can] continue tomorrow." (Interview, 2010)

Kwalik, sadly, was summarily killed by Indonesian police in Timika, West Papua, on December 16, 2009.

Although armed resistance has not brought West Papua significantly closer to independence, the strategy has achieved some more minor victories. An early OPM-TPN triumph, for example, was the attack on the Freeport mine on June 22, 1977, in which "trucks, bridges, factories and the airport were destroyed and pipelines, which transferred tons of partly processed minerals...were dynamited. The Amungme, Moni, Ekagi, Nduga and Dani peoples who worked for Freeport joined the guerrillas and blockaded important installations....The company was estimated to have lost at least $US11 million per week during the attack" (Ondawame 2010, 105–106). Inside West Papua, the TPN, with recruits from all generations, is still active around mining towns and in rural areas (although it is likely that some if not many of the instances of violence attributed in local media to the TPN are acts of subterfuge by Indonesian security forces hoping to justify their presence in West Papua; see Elmslie, Webb-Gannon, and King 2011).

But those who have traditionally advocated armed resistance as a decolonization strategy for West Papua, and still do, are primarily First Generation OPM-TPN members. Jacob Prai, for example, believes that armed struggle is the only way to deliver West Papua out of Indonesian hands. He described, from Malmö, Sweden, in 2004, the weaknesses and strengths of the contemporary OPM-TPN, making clear his ongoing belief in its viability:

> The OPM has been fighting for more than four decades without any help from the outside world, using arms left from World War Two and our ancestral weapons such as bows and arrows, spears, javelins, stone axes, bush knives, [and] cassowary bones, and they have been effective against the modern Indonesian weapons because we have been fighting on our own terrain. We have also ambushed the Indonesian troops and taken their weapons and ammunition and [then we] fight them back again, and they are afraid to go into the jungle and fight the OPM guerrillas. The OPM thus controls the jungles and its major lack is modern automatic weapons. (2004, n.p.)

Regardless of the accuracy of Prai's assessment in terms of the extent to which the OPM controls the West Papuan jungles, what is certain is, to apply Memmi's words to the West Papuan context, that "the meaning of [armed resistance is] so much greater than [its] arithmetical weight!" (1965, 95).

However, most other factions, the Second and Third Generations (and, increasingly, even many of the First Generation), maintain that the West Papua struggle is primarily nonviolent now, that the international community no longer (if it ever did) supports revolutionary wars out of principle, and, in the words of Otto Ondawame, that "any military attempt [at] struggle [that] you try to lead, it will not help" (Interview, 2009). Even Seth Rumkorem acknowledged in 2008 that there was no hope for West Papuan independence if it depended solely on armed struggle: "Military means is just sort of [a] stimulus," he explained. "You cannot solve political conflict... totally by military means" (Interview, 2008).

Nevertheless, many West Papuans from all generations and factions hold fast to the option of armed struggle as a last resort. For example, Second Generation leader from the WPNA Jacob Rumbiak explained: "We must have four wings of struggle: political, diplomatic, military and intelligence. But [the] military [wing] we cannot use until [there is] deadlock [at the] UN, not deadlock in Jakarta. [It is a] last resort, this" (Interview, 2009). Nearly all West Papuan leaders that I interviewed (with some exceptions, such as Catholic priest Neles Tebay) agree on the symbolic and morale-boosting significance of the TPN to the overall struggle. Herman Wainggai, a Third Generation member, explained the WPNA's position toward the TPN: "Forget about military as our weapon for today. [It is] a symbol. [It] stay[s] in the bush but does [not] make any noise" (Interview, 2009). The potency of the OPM-TPN's symbolism for West Papuans is captured in the following observation made of the indigenous North American context by Taiaiake Alfred: "While it is clear that guerrilla and terrorist strategies are futile—certainly so from within the centre of industrial capitalist countries—[they represent] the spirit of the ancestors who went to war against the invaders [which] is compelling and honourable" (2005, 26).

SPECIAL AUTONOMY

Following the 1998 deposing of Indonesian president Suharto, his successor, B. J. Habibie, struggled to cope with the demands for decentralization coming from across the Indonesian archipelago, including demands for independence from West Papua, East Timor, and Aceh (McGibbon 2006, 13). Because of the pressures on Jakarta from these secessionist struggles and the 1997 economic crisis, the special autonomy laws in Aceh and in Papua were, in political analyst Rod McGibbon's words, "a product of an opportune moment in Indonesia's democratic transition" (2006, 14). While the leaders of most West Papuan factions remained intent on pursuing independence, other leaders recognized Indonesia's offer to Papuans to draft their own autonomy bill as an opportunity to decolonize in increments. The drafting team, formed by Papuan governor Jaap Salossa, and a technical assistance team from Cenderawasih University (UNCEN) in Jayapura, produced a comprehensive draft calling for a referendum after three years of Special Autonomy (McGibbon 2006, 19). The referendum clause, along with the other "471 'problems'" that the Indonesian Home Ministry Affairs approval body found in the draft, did not find its way into the 2001 version of the bill that was eventually passed by the central government in Jakarta (McGibbon 2006, 19). Political scientist Akihisa Matsuno argues that after East Timor's referendum, Megawati Sukarnoputri (whose regime was responsible for implementing the West Papuan Special Autonomy Law) had "learned that any genuine popular consultation should be avoided because if given such a chance Papuans would almost certainly choose independence" (Matsuno 2010, 1).

Nevertheless, significant concessions (few of which were ultimately implemented) were made for West Papuans in the law itself, which was why some West Papuan leaders hoped that it might open up a path to independence. For example, the law legislated the following: a name change for the province from Irian Jaya to Papua; the use of Papuan cultural symbols, such as the Morning Star flag; that the governor of Papua must be an indigenous Papuan (a clause known as SK14); that a generous reallocation of resource revenues must be channeled back into Papua; and that provincial police security forces would be "coordinated" between the national government and the governor (King 2004, 86–87).

The late First Generation leader Viktor Kaisiepo, member of the DAP, was an ardent supporter of the Special Autonomy Law up until his death in 2009, saying that the law

> simply says: the neglect of West Papuans as an indigenous part of Indonesia for the last thirty-eight years requires a different type of approach. . . . That [law] is going to look after the indigenous heritage of the West Papuans irrespective of whether they are under Indonesian control, Australian control, US control, or whoever's control. (Interview, 2008)

Kaisiepo believed Special Autonomy was a practical solution that would lead to independence, primarily because it promised change for West Papua in a form supported by the international community:

> This is a process. This is not a product, this is a process. And the more people [who] are engaged in it, the better. . . . In order to get Indonesia to come to some kind of understanding, autonomy is vital you see. Because the European Union, the United Nations, the Pacific Islands Forum, they all agree with autonomy, from the political perspective that they don't want to recognize an independent state of West Papua in that part of the world. I mean,

> it's of course obvious [that] West Papua is not in the backyard of Europe. Would we have been Kosovo, or... Georgia, we would be independent because we [would be] part of the ball game. For the moment, we are not. But things are changing. (Interview, 2008)

When in 2008 I interviewed the now deceased Erna Mahuze, a Second Generation leader of the MRP, she, too, expressed hope that Special Autonomy, the law that brought the MRP into existence (after a lengthy delay), might protect West Papuan culture and independence aspirations.

Support for Special Autonomy as a strategy for independence, though, was sparse and, in most cases, short-lived. Its detractors were many. Despite Erna Mahuze's 2008 defense of Special Autonomy, in June 2010 the MRP put out a list of recommendations that, at its top, stated: "The Special Autonomy Law should be handed back to Government of the Republic of Indonesia" (Papuan People's Consultative Assembly and Indigenous People of Papua 2010). In January and February 2011, having had very little response from Jakarta regarding their list of eleven recommendations on June 9, 2010 (which included the rejection of Special Autonomy), and in anticipation of new MRP elections, some MRP members and other high-profile opponents of Special Autonomy (including the reverend Socrates Sofyan Yoman of the Baptist Church Association in West Papua and human rights lawyer Yan Christian Warinussy of the West Papuan legal foundation LP3BH) urged all current and potential MRP members not to stand for reelection as a protest against the Special Autonomy Law that had created the body. This demand, backed by the massive popular demonstrations in West Papua in June and July, did not emerge from a vacuum. For years, West Papuan leaders had expressed deep dissatisfaction with the Indonesian government's overall failure to implement the Special Autonomy Law.

In 2009 the West Papuan Consensus team, a group of primarily Second and Third Generation "leaders of the Papuan Nation from various positions within the struggle for Papuan nationhood," made up of the DAP, the PDP, and the WPNA, issued a joint statement that "the implementation of the Special Autonomy Law from 2001 to the present day has not resulted in any significant changes in the lives of Papuans," and they listed fifteen ways West Papuans had suffered under the law at the hands of the Indonesian government and military (Papua National Consensus 2009). Political scientist Marcus Mietzner noted the general dissatisfaction of the West Papuan public surrounding the delayed establishment of the MRP until 2005. Under the Special Autonomy Law, the MRP was imbued with the power to approve or veto administrative division within West Papua. Nevertheless, in January 2003, Megawati's government overrode this legality (the MRP had not yet been established and so could not decree otherwise) and created the province of West Irian Jaya (later, Papua Barat, or West Papua), a move seen by many in West Papua as a blatant divide-and-rule tactic (Mietzner 2007, 4–7).

Far from having decolonizing potential, Jacob Rumbiak maintains that "Special Autonomy is [the] strategy used by Jakarta to break West Papuan independence" (Interview, 2009). To protests from Jakarta and its international supporters that Special Autonomy has potential, that it has only failed thus far in its implementation, Rumbiak retorts that since it has "failed in implementation, this . . . means the Special Autonomy is not [the] solution" (Interview, 2009). Because it holds no potential for advancing West Papuan independence, Rumbiak told me in 2009, the WPNA is committed to stopping Special Autonomy. Andy Ajamiseba suggested that even if Special Autonomy was to be "properly implemented," it was not an acceptable solution for West Papuans: "The issue here is not about social betterment," he argued, but rather about "our identity . . . we are not Indonesian" (Interview, 2009). Ajamiseba's position on Special Autonomy and identity forms an interesting contrast to the views of Kaisiepo and Mahuze: the latter two had hoped that Special Autonomy might provide a safeguard for West Papuans as indigenous peoples in Indonesia, but Ajamiseba's focus was on national rather than indigenous identity (Interview, 2009). A First Generation West Papuan church minister in PNG succinctly summed up, in 2009, many West Papuans' views of Special Autonomy: "Special Autonomy is all bullshit. We never knew the date of its start or [its] finish; there was never any date set. So we don't believe in the thing called Special Autonomy. It is not like in Bougainville—Bougainville has a date set [for a referendum]—that is true autonomy" (Interviewee A, 2009).

Since the introduction of the 2001 Special Autonomy Law, there has been increased militarization in West Papua, assassination of leaders, the creation of a new province without MRP approval, political imprisonment and intimidation, "sweeping" and terror operations, impunity of security forces, and torture (Papua National Consensus 2009). In its defense of the law, the Indonesian government focused almost singularly on its financial component, boasting about the money sent back into the provinces (which ultimately found its way into corrupt pockets, rather than to the intended recipients; Widjojo et al. 2008, 18). The massive demonstrations against Special Autonomy as the solution to the major social and political problems in West Papua in June and July 2010 represented, as far as many West Papuans were concerned, the final rejection of a law never properly implemented and of any potential it may have ever held as an avenue to independence.

DIALOGUE

Dialogue is an established tool of peaceful conflict transformation (Galtung 2000, 4). A couple of reasons might explain the commitment of First and Second Generation West Papuans to peaceful dialogue as a strategy for transforming their conflict. It is possible that the leaders of the peaceful dialogue movement were influenced by a Christian "turn the other cheek" doctrine:

the West Papuan champion of the movement, Father Neles Tebay of the Second Generation, was a leading Catholic intellectual. In addition, many Papuans believe that peaceful dialogue is very similar to Melanesian and traditional methods of resolving interpersonal, intervillage and intertribal disputes (O. Ondawame, interview, 2009; C. Runawery, interview, 2009; N. Tebay, interview, 2008). Among the Mee people, to which Neles Tebay belonged, disputes are worked out through dialogue. Tebay described the process: "Both the perpetrators and the victims should be there... there must be an arbitrator, and then [other community] people. So when... Papuans and myself think about dialogue, [we] think [about it] in this way. The Indonesians should be there, the Papuans should be there, arbitrators should be there, and then people should be there. I think this is very culturally easy to understand" (Interview, 2008).

In 2008 Tebay, in partnership with a group of Indonesian scholars at the Indonesian Institute of Sciences (LIPI), headed by the late Muridan Widjojo, initiated the strongest push yet for dialogue between West Papuans and "Jakarta." In 2009 he published "Dialogue between Jakarta and Papua," detailing his vision of what such a dialogue might entail. Tebay underscored the "importance of... Jakarta-Papua dialogue as a means for the peaceful resolution of the Papua conflict" and detected "a will for dialogue among both parties to the conflict" (2009, 3). However, and this is where he differs from many First and Third Generation decolonization leaders, he argued that "Papuans need to make clear that the issue of Papuan independence will not be on the agenda for dialogue" (3). The objective of dialogue, in his view, is solely to discuss how to establish "Papua [as a] Land of Peace" (22).

Tebay's publication followed LIPI's *Papua Road Map: Negotiating the Past, Improving the Present and Securing the Future,* which also outlined a comprehensive vision for Papua-Jakarta dialogue (Widjojo et al. 2008). LIPI's *Road Map* was especially significant given its Indonesian genesis, and it demonstrated the increasing desire of Indonesian civil society to find a way of making peace with West Papua. It was possibly this publication that gave Tebay hope that there was a will for dialogue on the Indonesian side of the conflict. The LIPI team wrote that it felt "optimistic that the atmosphere of reform and democratic advances has provided the space to break the vicious circle of the Papuan Conflict" and recalled President Yudhuyono's unfulfilled 2005 promise to resolve the conflict "peacefully, justly and with dignity by stressing the approach of dialogue and persuasion" (Widjojo et al. 2008, 3–4). *Road Map* proposed four areas of conflict that needed addressing: the effects of transmigration and ethnic discrimination; the failure of development for West Papuans; divergent versions of history and political identity between Papua and Jakarta; and accountability for past and ongoing human rights abuses (Widjojo et al. 2008, 2). Both Tebay and the LIPI authors emphasized the importance of involving a third-party mediator, with the latter arguing that third-party involvement contributed to the success of the Aceh dialogue (Widjojo et al. 2008, 26) and Tebay writing, "As a Papuan, I can also draw inspiration from the role of neutral and independent third parties in assisting conflict mediation in the cultural practices of a number of tribes in Papua. In Papuan cultures, resolution of conflict between two people or families or groups in conflict involves a third party" (2009, 34).

The WPNCL, largely comprising First and Second Generation leaders, has been the strongest factional supporter of dialogue as a solution to the Papuan conflict (O. Ondawame, interview, 2009). In fact, in 2009 the late WPNCL member Clemens Runawery, with Tebay, envisaged the WPNCL as the group that would represent the West Papuan position in a dialogue process (C. Runawery, interview, 2009). However, the coalition leadership took exception to the explicit exclusion of independence from Tebay's proposed dialogue agenda. In Rex Rumakiek's view, "If dialogue [precludes] independence, there is no use for dialogue" (Interview, 2010). The coalition felt that the utility of dialogue lay in its potential to create a "bridge between the hardliners in Indonesia [and the] hardliners [like] us, [because with] both hardliners continuing as we are at the moment, there can never be any communication," but independence could not be left out of the equation (R. Rumakiek, interview, 2010).

Other West Papuan factions either do not believe that dialogue is feasible (according to Jacob Rumbiak, "We already know that dialogue—Jakarta can't do it"; interview, 2009) or are philosophically opposed to the idea. For example, as Third Generation Victor Yeimo of the KNPB contends, the point of dialogue is finding a win/win solution, and when it comes to West Papuan independence, only one side can win (Interview, 2010). Despite the momentum that the dialogue initiative had built in 2009 as Tebay, with financial and facilitation support from the Centre for Humanitarian Dialogue, traveled with a team across West Papua to prepare the nation for dialogue (HDC 2010), the notable lack of interest from high-ranking officials within the Indonesian government saw the push for dialogue fall flat. In 2010, in the wake of the multigeneration, multifaction rejection of Special Autonomy, the dialogue campaign was also decidedly overshadowed by energetic calls from the Third Generation for a referendum. With these calls catching on across West Papua and being heard around the world via social media, an offer from the current Indonesian president Joko Widodo for dialogue with West Papua was finally extended in September 2017 (Radio New Zealand 2017b). The ULMWP, however, views the offer as too little, too late—an attempt by Indonesia to undermine the powerful push for a referendum with what was designed (in the assessment of the then ULMWP chair, Octo Mote) to look like an Indonesian peace offering immediately prior to the 2017 Pacific Islands Forum and UN General Assembly meetings (Radio New Zealand 2017b). The ULMWP has its sights firmly set on "getting the members of the countries at the UN to put West Papua back on the UN agenda" and no longer "pay[s] attention to dialogue" (Mote, quoted in Radio New Zealand 2017a).

INTERNATIONAL INTERVENTION AND THE PUSH FOR A REFERENDUM

There are cracks in Jakarta's apparently monolithic oppressive power over West Papuans that were not visible in the heyday of Papuan armed resistance, and it is through the harnessing of the technologies and networks afforded by increasing globalization that West Papuans are forcing these cracks to expand. West Papuans are becoming increasingly adept at accessing and using their limited share of power in more effective ways—in particular, through international and national lobbies calling for a referendum on independence. A referendum is by far the most popular current demand being made by (especially Third Generation) West Papuans through their civil resistance tactics at home and internationally.

West Papuans frequently compare their political situation to that of East Timor, believing that their treatment at the hands of the Indonesian administration, and their colonial history, resonate with those of the Timorese. Both were colonies (East Timor was Portuguese and West Papua, Dutch) that became recolonized by Indonesia when the former colonial powers withdrew (in East Timor in 1975, in West Papua in 1963). West Papuans dismiss the relevance of the dictum of *uti possidetis juris* (which is commonly put forward to support the argument that differentiates East Timor's legal colonial history from that of West Papua) to their case (see the introduction), claiming that West Papua is still a colony that has never had the chance to exercise its right to self-determination (see Ondawame 2010, 4). Legal scholar Thomas Musgrave explains the reasoning behind this—Indonesia undermined its claim to *uti possidetis juris* by holding the Act of Free Choice for Papuans (regardless of the act's shortcomings), thereby conceding that West Papua was not part of Indonesia but a separate territory possessing the right to choose integration or independence (2015, 223).

Many West Papuans from the Third Generation who witnessed East Timor's independence during the years in which they were politically coming of age argue that a similar outcome, a referendum leading to independence, is the logical—indeed, the only—solution to their struggle (H. Wainggai, interview, 2009; V. Yeimo, interview, 2010). Others, including the more conservative Second Generation activist Neles Tebay, doubt Indonesia will ever allow a referendum. Tebay contended: "The Indonesians are traumatized by the East Timor experience... they allow[ed] the people, the East Timorese, to decide, and then many voted not for Indonesia but for independence.... I think they will not follow the same way" (Interview, 2008). First Generation leader of the WPNCL Rex Rumakiek also expressed reticence early on about the wisdom of calling internationally for a referendum, claiming that such a strategy is confusing for outsiders considering that West Papua, according to the OPM, has been independent since 1971; that the WPNA has already set up a provisional government; and that the West Papua New Guinea National Congress (WPNGNC) declared independence anew in 1997.

This last declaration made by the president of the WPNGNC, Michael Kareth, a Second Generation leader, to capitalize on international support and networks and bypass another referendum, occurred in the act of a proclamation of the independence of "West Papua New Guinea" in the European Parliament in Brussels, Belgium, on November 27. In making the declaration, Kareth claimed that West Papua New Guinea had territory, a people, a sovereign government, and international recognition, and he hoped that the proclamation would act "as [a legal guarantee] to bring [West Papua's status] up in the United Nations, [and] likewise [in] international institutions and state forums." The WPNGNC's proclamation did not have the intended results at the UN, and the WPNGNC lost much of its momentum thereafter (there have also been major problems in resecuring initial church funding, and with Kareth in exile in the Netherlands, the PNG civil society support the Congress had enjoyed when Kareth lived in PNG has waned; M. Kareth, interview, 2008). Finally, the Federal Republic of West Papua declared independence once again at the Third Papuan Congress in Jayapura in 2011.

Against this pushback from First and Second Generation leaders, members of the Third Generation, for the most part, are busy developing international networks that will aid their demand for a referendum. If the international community refused to recognize West Papuans' previous declarations of independence, the Third Generation reasons, what is needed now is a call for a referendum supported from the outset by the international community. The International Parliamentarians for West Papua (IPWP; launched at the Houses of Parliament in London in October 2008) and the International Lawyers for West Papua (ILWP; launched in Guyana in April 2009) are two campaigns drawing on extensive international professional and political networks, with grassroots support in West Papua, that recommend a referendum. These organizations were founded by Third Generation leader Benny Wenda in Oxford, together with UK parliamentarians and international human rights lawyers. Politicians and lawyers from around the world have pledged their support for a referendum via these organizations' websites (IPWP 2008; ILWP 2009), which host open letters explaining West Papua's legal right to self-determination and appealing for global legal and political solidarity for West Papua.

The very act of establishing these two organizations proved successful in raising international awareness about rights abuses in West Papua. For example, when prominent student activist Buchtar Tabuni of the KNPB and West Papua National Parliament was arrested for taking a lead in the demonstration held in Jayapura in support of the IPWP, he subsequently served a three-year prison sentence for "provocation" (Flassy 2009). Tabuni's treatment prompted Human Rights Watch (2010, 34) to take up his case as a prisoner of conscience. Tabuni's imprisonment and Human Rights Watch's response were, according to Third Generation activists Herman Wainggai and Victor Yeimo, a tactical success. One of the ways in which Third Generation activists work together to raise international awareness of the need for a referendum, they explain, is by publicizing the political imprisonment of Papuan activists (H. Wainggai, interview, 2009; V. Yeimo, interview, 2010).

In September and November of 2010, two significant West Papua–focused events capitalized on US support for West Papua, but the impact of the first was compromised by intergenerational and factional friction. The first was a US Congress hearing on human rights in West Papua, chaired by the late Congressman Eni Faleomavaega of American Samoa. Several human rights advocates and academics from the United States and from the Netherlands, alongside primarily First Generation and some Second Generation West Papuans, were invited to testify about their experience of human rights abuses in West Papua. All of the West Papuans present (excluding First Generation Nick Messet from the Independent Group Supporting Special Autonomous Region of Papua in the Republic of Indonesia [IGSSARPRI]) expressed a rejection of Special Autonomy. However, the event's potential to effect change was lost due to the lack of unified strategic recommendations from the West Papuan speakers on alternative ways to decolonize (Federal News Service 2010).

One significant West Papuan faction that felt its perspective was not seriously heard in the hearing was the WPNA, which had sent its Third Generation representative, Herman Wainggai, to attend. Offended, but still determined to make the most of the international attention given to the West Papua issue at the hearing, the WPNA, led by Wainggai, initiated another event at George Mason University in Virginia that November, which they called the "Washington Solution." In ways that the US Congress hearing could not (due to its focus on "human rights" rather than independence and the presence of the IGSSARPRI), the Washington Solution discussed practical solutions for West Papua's future, primarily a referendum on self-determination (Department of Foreign Affairs, Immigration and Trade 2010).

By 2014, united by the ULMWP, all major factions had decided to back the call for an internationally supervised referendum, seeking first for West Papua to be reinstated to the UN Decolonization Committee. To this end, one of the most remarkable feats of the ULMWP so far took place when Benny Wenda presented a petition to the UN General Assembly during its 72nd session. The petition demanded a referendum on independence for West Papua and contained, Wenda alleges (although it is difficult to confirm), the signatures of 1.8 million West Papuans—a staggering 70 percent of the Papuan population (Doherty and Lamb 2017). Signatures had been collected over the course of the year, with many West Papuans facing arrest and torture as they signed or facilitated the petition's circulation (Doherty and Lamb 2017). The initiative gained global media attention, with observers realizing that the signing of the petition was itself a referendum act, a free expression of the will of the West Papuan people for independence.

Significantly, the facilitation of this referendum-by-petition was supported by members from within all three generations and factions included in the ULMWP. Intergenerational and interfactional disagreements ensued about when, how, and to whom the petition should have been presented. Controversy surrounded whether or not the petition was accepted: the chair of the UN Decolonization Committee announced that he could not receive the petition because West Papua was not part of the committee's mandate. In 2019, Wenda took the petition to the UN again, this time presenting it to the UN High Commissioner for Refugees Michelle Bachelet (Wright 2019).

Anonymous sources inside the ULMWP indicated to me that conflict arose among leaders within the ULWMP regarding the method of petition handover at the UN. Some considered Benny Wenda a hero, while others thought he was acting unilaterally when he delivered the petition in 2017 prior to executive leadership agreement on the process to be followed. This conflict may have played some role in the change of leadership later that year when Wenda was made chair of the ULMWP and Octo Mote, who had been chair, was demoted to deputy chair. However, the collection of signatures for a petition of this magnitude marks the first time in the history of the struggle that West Papuans from all generations and factions have been united behind a particular decolonization strategy, if not the way it was executed. Whereas the First Generation may have allowed leadership style, ideological differences, personal differences, and place of origin/location to create unproductive friction in the movement, the following generations appear to be increasingly less afflicted by political factionalism during critical political moments, having learned hard lessons from previous generations about the importance of the appearance, at least, of unity. The first two generations are, for the first time, following the direction of a Third Generation leader, Benny Wenda, current chair of the ULMWP. Not only is the movement more generationally and strategically unified than in past times, in July 2019 Benny Wenda's office issued a press release claiming that in an unprecedented move, West Papua's armed forces had agreed to come under another faction's leadership—that of the ULMWP (2019). Practically speaking, given the dispersal of the armed forces throughout the West Papuan jungles, it will be difficult for the ULMWP to maintain command of the West Papuan guerrilla forces. Symbolically, however, this coming together of the military and political branches of the decolonization movement is significant.

It announces to the world that West Papua is a "legitimate unified military and political state-in-waiting" (Wenda, quoted in ULMWP 2019a) and that should West Papua gain independence, its politicians will not be beholden to rogue military elements.

The revolutionary urge that drove the West Papuan First Generation independence leaders to advocate guerrilla tactics has come full circle to the Third Generation, albeit this time with an insistence on using peaceful means to achieve independence. Both the taking up of arms and the call for a referendum are demands for an immediately decolonized West Papua and are radical compared to the "decolonization as a long-term process" perspective held by (primarily) Second Generation advocates of Special Autonomy and dialogue. The reoccurrence of West Papuan revolutionary zeal adds weight to the theory that important ideas, especially those intimately linked with liberation, will be revisited time and again, even if the particular strategies associated with their epochs dissipate (Trompf 1979).

An analysis of the four main strategies employed by three generations of West Papuan freedom fighters has demonstrated that choice of strategy is highly contingent upon leaders' political and social milieux. Thus, once leaders of the First Generation realized they had been abandoned by the Dutch, the ones who remained in West Papua engaged in guerrilla warfare, given its strategic prevalence during the postwar decolonization era and its revolutionary philosophical underpinnings. As time progressed and international support for decolonization wore thin, some First and many Second Generation leaders searched for other ways to acquire international support for West Papuan freedom. Some pragmatists chose to work with Jakarta's offer of Special Autonomy, believing that an increasingly democratizing Indonesia should be given a chance to display its new colors. Others decided to pursue peaceful dialogue, with the hope that independence might eventually be put on the dialogue agenda. Recently, however, as the world faces challenges requiring immediate and radical social and political action (for example, climate change), the revolutionary appeal to the international community to sponsor a fair referendum for West Papua, instigated initially by Third Generation leaders but taken up from 2010 onward by those from the First and Second Generations too, appears to be the strategy that currently enjoys the most traction.

This chapter has shown that factional membership loosely follows generation membership and dictates, to a degree, strategic preference. Hence, factions of the OPM, particularly those with OPM-TPN affiliations, are proud of their guerrilla backgrounds, even if they have renounced guerrilla strategies and have joined new factions. Few have given up OPM allegiance, preferring instead to join other groups as well, including the WPNCL, the WPNGNC, the WPNA, and the ULMWP. Until his death, prominent member of the DAP

Viktor Kaisiepo considered Special Autonomy the best strategy for working toward West Papuan independence. He was in the minority within the DAP, however, which has become increasingly referendum focused. Until 2010, the MRP also supported Special Autonomy, the law to which the MRP owed its existence. The WPNCL is primarily composed of Second Generation members, with some First Generation supporters as well, and until joining the ULMWP it pursued strategic, peaceful dialogue with Indonesia. The WPNA and the Federal Republic of West Papua comprise mainly Second and some First Generation leaders. Both reject dialogue and seek international recognition of West Papua's independence, the former seeking a referendum. Third Generation youth and student instigated groups, the most prominent of which are the KNPB and the West Papua National Parliament, also reject dialogue and seek an internationally monitored referendum for West Papua.

Of course, cultural background and diasporic location play a role in factional and strategic choice as well. And conflict between generations persists, with resentment among some young leaders that older leaders are outstaying their welcome and among some older leaders that the younger ones have too little strategic discretion. However, for the most part, each generation has built, and continues to build, on the strategic strengths and ideas of the others. This pertains to factions also. While interpersonal feuds between leaders of different factions are at times destructive and a waste of energy, they are by no means uncommon in any political conflict situation in any country in the world. Instead, this chapter has argued that strategic interfactional conflict has played a constructive role in West Papuan politics, with each faction promoting its own strategies and chasing strategic achievements, expanding the reach of the movement. A bigger-picture unity of spirit and of ambition, as West Papuans build a more enhanced international profile, is thus emerging.

In light of this overall picture, perhaps Prai and Rumkorem's jungle feud in 1976 was not the beginning of the end, as has been claimed. They had worked well together for an extended period of time, teaching unity when they needed to and collaborating to declare an independent West Papua. When they went their separate ways, the next generation came to realize that the struggle could not depend solely on guerrilla warfare. New leaders came into their own. Otto Ondawame even described the Prai/Rumkorem conflict as a breath of life for the struggle, having "the positive effect of opening up alternatives in approach, and increased areas of control and mass participation" (2010, 123). Although Rumkorem has passed away and Prai resides in Sweden, both remain central to the legacy of the struggle, representing the beginning of its genealogy. When Prai's endorsement of the ULMWP was welcomed by the Third Generation–led faction in 2017, the occasion proved that the struggle's elders and their achievements are symbolically ever present, even as the movement forges ahead, led by the younger generations.

5

STARS ALIGNING

West Papua in the Black Pacific and Beyond

One tribe
Melanesian
From Sorong to Samarai
One skin, one tradition, one culture
Full freedom!

—*Airileke and Benny Wenda*

Beginning around 2010, Melanesian musicians started to release an outpouring of songs on social media in support of West Papuan independence, building to a quantity of more than fifty by 2017 (Webb-Gannon and Webb 2019). The lyrics in the epigraph are excerpted from one of these songs coproduced by the Papua New Guinean artist Airileke, expressing solidarity with fellow Melanesians living under occupation in West Papua. The song declares that West Papuans (identified through Sorong, located on the Doberai Peninsula) and Papua New Guinean Melanesians (identified through Samarai, lying off the easternmost tip of the New Guinea mainland) are of the same "tribe," phenotype, and origin (tradition) and share the same cultural practices. Moreover, it demands for West Papua the political independence ("full freedom") that the eastern half of the island achieved in 1975.

This musical phenomenon is indicative of a surge of support in Melanesian civil society for decolonization in West Papua (Webb-Gannon and Elmslie 2014), which in turn is the focal point of a developing indigenous

Melanesian "black Pacific" (a loose association of subaltern ideas and identities in the Pacific espousing pride in nonwhite skin color and Pacific cultures; Webb-Gannon, Webb, and Solis 2018). Such a notion resonates with Paul Gilroy's (1993) *Black Atlantic,* which concentrates on historical and contemporary identifications and articulations between African and Atlantic Rim African diasporic peoples, cultures, and politics, based upon shared Otherness to colonial occupiers. Having struggled for decades to attract mainstream backing for their movement, West Papuans have started reconstructing and rebuilding black and indigenous political alliances in Melanesia and even further afield in the Pacific and Africa.[1] These recent alliances, reformulated or newly forged, supersede in strength and reach the intermittent Pacific-based expressions of support from previous decades. As such, these identity affiliations have fortified the leadership of West Papua's decolonization movement in its quest for international support, contributing to an unprecedented degree of West Papuan strategic unity.

Understanding the current alignment of West Papua's decolonization politics with Melanesian and other black and indigenous identity politics requires uncovering a historical narrative of popularly articulated negritude (defined by one of its founders, Leopold Sedar Senghor, as "the right of Blacks to work in an independent state for the renaissance and development of their values of civilization"; quoted in Swan 2018, 71) and *indigènitude* (indigenous identity politics; Clifford 2013) in Melanesia. This chapter will articulate this narrative that is "largely lost in the historiography of the decolonization of Melanesia" (Gardner and Waters 2013, 115). In the 1960s and 1970s, when Melanesian elites' countercolonial politics were drawing inspiration from the black consciousness politics of negritude,[2] barring a few exceptions, the leaders of each colony were concerned more with their own future independence than with the independence of their fellow Melanesian colonies. This was despite their common experiences of degradation at the hands of their colonizers on account of being labeled the "black islanders" (*mela* = black; *nesia* = islands). By 1980, when Fiji, Papua New Guinea (PNG), the Solomon Islands, and Vanuatu had won political independence, the politics of countercolonial negritude espoused by the elites of those new countries waned. With the exception of Vanuatu, all avoided the issue of West Papua's recolonization. West Papuan elites still pursued allegiance with African countries along black identity lines, but conflict within the West Papuan independence movement and a lack of support from Melanesia prompted African allies to withdraw from the West Papua cause until Papuans could demonstrate Pacific solidarity for their movement.

For decades, West Papuans struggled to solicit international *state* support. It was, however, *grassroots* solidarity in Melanesia, rather than support from Melanesian state elites, that began to turn the tide for West Papuans. Pacific artists, poets, and activists have reformulated the intellectual Pacific negritude movement of the postwar decolonization era into a countercolonial indigenous negritude movement (that is, *indigènitude*) for contemporary times, taking advantage of the mass connectivity afforded by digital media, which relies on visual (and to some extent, aural) communication as much as it does text. Melanesian *indigènitude* is expansive in its purview, building on a shared history of colonial discrimination to address region-wide concerns such as nuclear weapons testing, climate change, and West Papuan occupation. With the calibration of West Papua's decolonization aims to Melanesian *indigènitude,* West Papua's struggle, bolstered regionally and unified like never before, has finally found itself in a position to reach out once more to black allies beyond the Pacific.

This chapter traces West Papua's decolonization movement from the rise of negritude in Melanesia to its subsequent convergence with a regional *indigènitude.* These "performed" modes of identity developed as a means to ameliorate the impact of colonialism. The chapter's first section provides context and explores the relationship between colonialism and the label "black" in West Papua and elsewhere in Melanesia. The second section, spanning the late 1700s to World War II, surveys preconditions in the formation of Melanesian "black" identity. These two sections are concerned with Melanesia-wide encounters and events, demonstrating the ways black consciousness developed in various parts of Melanesia at different times. An outline of the evolution of black consciousness in Melanesia outside of West Papua is essential for understanding the roots of the post-2010 swell of Melanesian support for West Papua.

The third section charts the articulation of black and indigenous empowerment across Melanesia or, in scholar Quito Swan's words, "how the ideas of Black Power, African American freedom struggles, Pan-Africanism, *Négritude,* and African/Caribbean nationalism streamed across Melanesia" (2017–2018, n.p.). It identifies what are discernably two waves of decolonization consciousness—namely, the period of the 1960s to the 1980s and the renewed movement that dates from approximately 2010. It was during this latter period in particular that Melanesian negritude began to coalesce around and merge with the struggle for decolonization in West Papua, resulting in a distinctly Melanesian, anticolonial *indigènitude* that in 2014 gave birth to the United Liberation Movement for West Papua (ULMWP). This organization unites West Papua's three most prominent independence-seeking groups as they attempt to secure Melanesian, African, and European support. The fourth section examines the impact of these indigenous black alignments on the unification of West Papua's decolonization movement.

Colonialism and Melanesian Blackness

Since Paul Gilroy published *The Black Atlantic* in 1993, a number of scholars have taken up his framework, tracing connections between Atlantic-oriented cultures of marginality and movement in order to map out, for example, a "Black and Green Atlantic" (O'Neill and Lloyd 2009) and a "Red Atlantic" (Weaver 2014). Paul Lyons notes that a shift is underway toward regarding the Pacific "as an understudied counterpart" to such "Atlantic Ocean–focused discourse" (2016). While scholars have begun to use the term "black Pacific" (see Shilliam 2015; Solis 2014, 2015; Swan 2018; Webb-Gannon, Webb, and Solis 2018), historians and anthropologists documenting incidences of black Atlantic culture in the Pacific is well established (see, for example, Banivanua Mar 2016; Boxill 1996; Carr 2014; Chappell 2005; Fullagar 2012; and Sharrad 2001). Teresia Teaiwa (2006), David Chappell (2005), and Donald Denoon (1999) have each critiqued the phenomenon of European-drawn analogies between Africa and the Pacific. At least since the early 1800s, these analogies have turned on observations of shared skin color (in European racial hierarchies, the darkest-skinned peoples ranked lowest; Reynolds 2005, 85), racist cultural stereotypes of primitiveness, and the association of both regions' landscapes and cultures with tropes of "heaven" and "hell." From the 1960s onward, problems with decolonization and state building in the Pacific have been compared to those in Africa (see Doumenge 2002; Reilly 2000), despite the lack of clear cultural-political similarities. With a throwaway reference to sub-Saharan Africa, one scholar has even queried whether an independent West Papua, being a Melanesian territory, would result in a failed state (Stott 2011, 6). Misleading and derogatory references to "the Africanization of the South Pacific" (Reilly 2000) have led Teaiwa, Chappell, and Denoon to plead caution in the application of such analogies that obscure more than they reveal (the practice of which Denoon [1999], referencing Evelyn Waugh, labels "Black Mischief").

Nowhere in the Pacific has this analogy been so historically demoralizing as in Melanesia, the group of islands named for the dark skin color of its peoples (see Rokolekutu 2016). Europeans saw Melanesians as "Oceanic Negroes" (Kabutaulaka 2015, 113); in fact, the island of New Guinea was so named by the Spanish maritime explorer Ortiz Retez in 1545, who, on his way from the Maluku Islands to Panama, sailed via the northwestern coast of New Guinea and remarked that the people he saw resembled the Guineans of Africa (Osborne 1985, 7). Europeans' racism, which centered on the "fulcrum of blackness" (Nakagawa 2012), shaped Polynesian attitudes toward Melanesians too (Lawson 2013, 6–7). French explorer Dumont d'Urville, who popularized the tripartite classification of the Pacific, judged Melanesians to be "hideous" in appearance, "limited" in languages and institutions, and "generally very inferior" to the copper-colored race (Polynesians) in dispositions and intelligence, except where they had been improved by frequent communications and racial intermixture with Polynesians, as in Fiji (Douglas 2008, 123). This assessment was to influence later Polynesian political interactions with Melanesians, particularly in the Polynesian articulation of a "Pacific Way" that set itself up as superior to Melanesian cultural and political values (Lawson 2013, 10).

Having suffered from such racism since first encounters with Europeans and later as a result of Indonesian occupation as well, Melanesian identification with political blackness holds deep resonances. Melanesians are not only politically black in terms of their subalternness; they have also experienced two centuries of abject racism on the basis of phenotype and so identify as "Melanesian black," as distinct from both "African black" (N. Jouwe, interview, 2015) and *non*-Melanesian politically black (for example, the politically black Polynesians of the Polynesian Panthers movement).

In keeping with European perceptions of black people and their cultures elsewhere in Melanesia, West Papua's Dutch colonizers thought of the territory's population as existing in a "miserable and depraved condition" (Rutherford 2012, 41). The Dutch resident of Ternate in the nearby Maluku Islands, P. van der Crab, described Papuans in 1888 as "crude in their manners, cruel to one another, treacherous with foreigners and traders, little subordinated to their own chiefs and more than frank with Europeans" (quoted in Rutherford 2012, 57). Since colonizing West Papua in 1962, Indonesia has perpetuated the European characterization of that territory and its population as dark, dangerous, and animalistic. Tanah Merah, the Dutch penal camp used to exile Indonesian prisoners in West Papua, was described by descendants of the prisoners as the "land beyond the moon" (Osborne 1985, 9)—that is, a dark wasteland. Ambonese working in West Papua as teachers and administrators believed they were bringing Papuans "from darkness to light," indicating the low esteem in which the Ambonese held the Papuans (Pouwer 1999, 162). Indonesia, Viktor Kaisiepo argued, has continually portrayed West Papuans as a people who "are black, curly, lazy" and, according to Otto Ondawame, as "a primitive people, a lazy and inferior race who are living in an unenlightened dark age" (2010, 6). "When it comes to Natives," Trask writes, "negative statements are eagerly believed, with but the thinnest evidence or none at all, because of the general racist belief in Native cultural and physical inferiority" (1993, 171).

This attitude persists with regard to West Papua today, even outside of Indonesia. For example, in 2006 a story about a West Papuan child known as Wawa aired on an Australian television network and alleged that Wawa was in imminent danger of being cannibalized for witchcraft. Despite there being no factual basis to this sensationalist tale (see Stasch 2014), it appeared sufficiently believable to network producers to make prime-time television. This is but one example supporting Fanon's observation of how "the colonist [or its sympathizers] turns the colonized into a kind of quintessential evil... the enemy of values. In other words, absolute evil. A corrosive element, destroying everything within his reach, a corrupting element, distorting everything which involves aesthetics or morals" (1963, 6). In the words of the late West Papuan politician Erna Mahuze, Indonesian "soldiers shoot . . . the black and curly-haired [Papuans] . . . so casually as if they are shooting a deer or a kangaroo" (Interview, 2008).

In the struggle against the colonial racism associated with being labeled the "black islanders," West Papuans and other Melanesians absorbed and modified the cultural resources of others through acts of mimesis, making use of them "as a conscious attempt to seize the power of the person or thing being mimicked" (Carr 2014, 10). Negritude is only one example, but in Melanesian decolonization politics, it has been an influential one, and in West Papua it is experiencing a revival. This tendency toward mimesis is not to be read as a lack of agency among Melanesians. There are multiple examples of autochthonous uprisings and revolt against colonialism in Melanesian history, demonstrating Melanesian initiative and persistence. In a well-known example, in 1939 Angganita Manufandu, prophet of Koreri (see the introduction and chapter 1), advocated resistance to Dutch missionaries and colonialism. She claimed that the Utrecht Society, a missionary organization, had "stolen the last page of the Bible before giving it to locals, thus depriving them of the knowledge with which the Europeans had achieved so much material wealth and power" and organized protests against Dutch authority (Osborne 1985, 11). Although her movement was not ultimately successful in ousting the Dutch, her agitation was influential, and she remains a Papuan hero.

Mimesis neither implies that West Papuans are unimaginative in their resistance nor suggests the rote application by West Papuans of others' ideas. Mimesis of black power in West Papua, "with its underlying ethic of transnational unity as the basis for building independence," has been an umbrella that has "connect[ed] disparate movements and interests" (Banivanua Mar 2016, 178), assisting rather than leading the task of decolonizing West Papuan identity. It is worth noting that even in Manufandu's early nationalist movement, the significance of skin color emerges. In the Koreri myth upon which Angganita's resistance was founded, the protagonist, an old man named Manarmakeri whose skin was covered in itchy scabs, built a fire and stepped into it. Already endowed with the power to bring a utopian future to Biak Islanders, during his fiery baptism Manarmakeri was also able to shed his afflicted skin. As he emerged from the fire, he noticed that "he was whiteskinned like a European. This did not please him, so he leapt into the fire once more until he was burnt a brown color. He looked into the mirror again and liked it this way" (Kamma 1972, 34). Manarmakeri clearly considered blackness, as a contrast to white Europeanness, a source of pride and distinction.

Melanesian cultures are well known for their porosity (Douglas 2007); for their valorization of outsider-inspired knowledge and incorporation of foreign cultural elements into their own (Harrison 1993; Lindstrom 1990;

Rutherford 2003). As such, incorporating elements of black consciousness politics from Africa, Europe, the Caribbean, and the United States into Melanesian decolonization struggles—including West Papua's—has been an empowering act of boundary-breaking mimesis (Carr 2014, 10). It has enabled the production and inhabitation of a Melanesian political blackness—a black Pacific—that is "not derivative but syncretic" (Chappell 2010, 61–62). Black diasporic cultural politics have helped unify West Papuans in their politico-cultural positioning as black and Melanesian, not Malay, and strengthened their black Pacific and international alignments.

Early Beginnings of Melanesian Negritude

The history of cultural exchange between Pacific Islanders and African Americans began in the late 1700s when Hawaiians, African Americans, and other African-descended peoples labored together in the whaling industry and contributed to the development of sea shanty singing (Carr 2014, 56). Following the American Civil War and the abolition of slavery in the United States, which were critical events in the evolution of black consciousness in the black Atlantic,[3] African American performance troupes including former slaves and their direct descendants began touring the Pacific.

Frederick J. Loudin's Fisk Jubilee Singers (FJS) stand out among these with their performances of jubilee songs (spirituals) in the 1880s in Australia and New Zealand. The FJS, who sang about slavery and emancipation, were popular in Australia, in spite of the racism with which Australians treated the indigenous black peoples of their own country (Bellanta 2014; Seroff and Abbott 2002). The FJS announced plans in *The Queenslander* (October 22, 1887) to perform in Melanesia—in Fiji, Vanuatu, and PNG—but for reasons unknown did not end up doing so. At this time, some Melanesians at least, including those who were disparaged for their phenotypic blackness, became aware of the existence of other black peoples and possibly also the comparative freedom the latter enjoyed, which would later become a source of considerable empowerment for West Papuans in their struggle for decolonization and the basis of solidarity between West Papuans and other Melanesians after 2010.

West Papuans first became widely aware of the existence and cultures of black people from the Atlantic in World War II, during which time approximately two hundred thousand African American military personnel served in East Asia and the South Pacific from 1942 to 1945 (Lindstrom and White 1990, 27). Seeing black and white servicemen working in cooperation was consciousness-raising for Melanesians (Banivanua Mar 2016, 128; Chappell 2005, 303). In the words of Solomon Islander Jonathan Fifi'i, who in 1942 was a sergeant in the Solomon Islands Labour Corps, "We saw from the way other black people lived, when they came during the war, that we were being treated like dirt. They were being treated as equals" (1989, 136).

According to West Papuan independence leader Nicolaas Jouwe, now deceased, during World War II in West Papua, "There were black Americans and under them there were white Americans serving. That was a surprise. That opened the eyes of the Papuans. Then, at once, the national feelings came out. We're not Indonesians. Before that, we had very few Dutch. The entire administration was run in the colonial period by the Indonesians. And the Indonesians treated the Papuans like slaves" (quoted in Farhadian and Babuljak 2007, 157–158).[4]

Jouwe identifies this encounter with black Americans as the beginning of West Papuan anti-Indonesian nationalism, the "moment all the Papuans didn't want to be with Indonesia" (quoted in Farhadian and Babuljak 2007, 158). Similarly, the late Zachi Sawor said of the war, "We saw that... [the] black Americans like us... became sergeants, lieutenants and captains.... This was a revolutionary way of thinking in the minds of many young Papuans.... They thought... that what these black Americans can [do], we too can do it!" (Interview, 2008).

Bonding between islanders and African American military personnel was facilitated through cultural exchange. One image in the photographic study *Island Encounters: Black and White Memories of the Pacific War* shows Solomon Islanders teaching African American Seabees how to make thatch shading (Lindstrom and White 1990, 21) while another depicts African American soldiers bartering with Solomon Islanders for betel nut (1990, 22). In turn, Americans, including black personnel, introduced new music genres to Melanesians, such as blues, jive, and swing (Webb 2005, 289). "The most important thing that happened [during World War II] in our part of New Guinea," Nicolaas Jouwe states, "was the presence of the black Americans, the Negros" (quoted in Farhadian and Babuljak 2007, 157). Through the sharing of music, dance, philosophy, food, betel nut, survival skills, and friendship, Melanesians and African Americans enriched each other culturally. Mimesis of Atlantic blackness prepared the way for the development of a Melanesian negritude and later, *indigènitude,* locating West Papua's self-determination struggle and the Melanesian solidarity it later attracted within an emerging black Pacific identity.

Melanesian Black Empowerment and West Papua

THE FIRST WAVE—MELANESIAN NEGRITUDE

The German scholar Ulli Beier and his English-born artist wife, Georgina Beier, encouraged creative indigenous expression among aspiring artists and politicians in PNG. Having encountered African anticolonialist ideologies while teaching at the University of Ibadan in Nigeria, the Beiers subsequently nurtured a negritude-focused arts movement at the University of Papua New

Guinea (UPNG; Dawrs 2009, 10–20) and as a result were key figures in the development of a black Pacific in Melanesia in the 1960s. Developed in France in the 1930s by African and Antillean students in Paris who opposed colonialism, the negritude movement both drew from and inspired black consciousness movements around the world. Scholar of postcolonial literature Paul Sharrad recalls the visit of Kenyan nationalist leader Tom Mboya to Port Moresby in the 1960s and identifies a number of connections between colonial rule in Africa and in PNG relating to governance and plantation and education systems dating back to the beginning of the twentieth century (2001, 723–725). He also points out similarities between African and PNG decolonization literature produced in the 1960s, resulting, in part, from the circulation of staff between universities in African and Pacific countries (2001, 723–725).

Melanesian students and elites in territories slated for independence embraced the movement in the 1960s as a philosophy compatible with the decolonization processes taking place in their own region, one that celebrated the blackness of Melanesia's indigenous peoples *and* the connections they were able to forge with other decolonized black peoples and cultures around the world. Negritude highlighted for Melanesians possible avenues for asserting agency by bringing awareness of the ways in which other black people had fought for political independence and decolonization of the mind. It allowed them to join what scholar Chandra Mohanty calls an international "communit[y] of resistance," a political rather than essentialist community "not based on any ahistorical notion of the inherent resistance and resilience of Third World peoples [but] on a historical, material analysis of the concrete disenfranchising effects" of colonialism (2003, 47).

As the Beiers taught negritude ideas to students at the UPNG, keen to connect with the "global ferment of the late 1960s" (Banivanua Mar 2016, 185), Melanesian leaders were being drawn toward expressions of black consciousness as a result of their own black Atlantic (and East Africa) travels and reading of black consciousness philosophy. In 1974 Walter Lini, who became Vanuatu's founding prime minister and whose left-leaning views were influenced by the political philosophies of the African American visionary Frederick Douglass and the African socialist Julius Nyerere (Premdas 1987, 109–111), stopped over at the United Nations (UN) in New York when returning home from the sixth Pan African Congress in Tanzania. There he met Pauulu Brown, a black power activist and engineer from Bermuda. On Lini's invitation, Brown came to Vanuatu and advised on independence policies (Banivanua Mar 2016, 198–199). Ni-Vanuatu was receptive to Brown's black power politics, which the people related to their ancestors' mistreatment in the South Sea Island labor trade era from 1848 to 1904. At a well-attended talk at Lelepa during this visit, Brown specifically linked "Islanders' history of Blackbirding in the Pacific to the enslavement of Africans, connecting deep local memories to an international story" (Banivanua Mar 2008, 200).

New Caledonians also found negritude compelling (Chappell 2005, 310). Through his leadership of the Kanak independence movement and his role in forming the Palika proindependence party, the Kanak activist, politician, and intellectual Nidoish Naisseline aimed to dismantle the colonial system that "animalizes the colonized [so that] the latter accepts his inferiority and hates himself" (quoted in Chappell 2010, 51). To combat this internalized racism, Naisseline "drew inspiration from Aimé Césaire's *Négritude* poetry and the Black Panthers' demands" (Chappell 2010, 52; see also Topping 1977, 8).

Michael Somare, who in 1975 became PNG's first prime minister, visited decolonized Ghana in the late 1960s and commented: "Many of the African politicians, civil servants and academics we met clearly thought that we had not been fighting hard enough for our independence.... I made up my mind that, next time, Papua New Guinea would show a more progressive face to our African friends" (quoted in Chappell 2005, 204). Papua New Guinean civil servant and intellectual Albert Maori Kiki was also inspired by community development initiatives in Nigeria (Chappell 2005, 306) and during travels to Australia in 1969 became aware of the black consciousness spirit prevalent among black Aboriginal activists (Banivanua Mar 2016, 183).

Melanesian negritude coincided in the 1970s with a regional solidarity movement for West Papua, advocated within Narokobi's Melanesian Way and fostered by Melanesian university students at UPNG (R. Regenvanu and J. Simmo, interview, 2009). For example, in 1970 a student at UPNG, Leo Hannet, formed the "Niugini Black Power Group—a Frantz Fanon-inspired 'African Negritude' movement" to support decolonization in West Papua (Swan 2018, 73). Zachi Sawor recalled talking with Somare in Port Moresby during that era about the future possibility of a combined PNG–West Papua nation-state and believed that Somare was "very sympathetic... I think... because we are the same people, Melanesians, and black people" (Interview, 2008).

This perspective was not shared, however, by all black power advocates in the region. Kiki, who in 1974 was serving as PNG's minister for defense, foreign relations, and trade and was conscious of not aggravating PNG's powerful neighbor to the west, Indonesia, cautioned "a substantial toughening up of the attitude towards border crossers [from West Papua]... [and] the weeding out of officials, including police, who may in any way be sympathetic to the dissident movement" (quoted in Osborne 1985, 60). Kiki's insensitivity to the West Papua issue was shared by other Melanesian elites until shortly into the new millennium, when grassroots Melanesians' calls for justice for West Papuans began to challenge their politicians' realpolitik stance.

Between 1962 and 1969, an elite group of West Papuan nationalists focused their energies on letting the world know about the "Act of Free Choice" they faced, in which they were supposedly to choose between final integration with Indonesia or independence. Even the vote's lead-up showed strong signs that it would be unrepresentative and coercive. Although supervised by the UN, the Act of Free Choice was a sham: as detailed in earlier chapters, it bore no resemblance to a plebiscite but involved a traditional Indonesian decision-making process known as *musyawarah* (collective consultation), in which less than 1 percent of the West Papuan population was selected by the Indonesian administration to take part and then threatened with violence by the military if they did not opt for Indonesian rule. Not surprisingly, the result favored Indonesia. It was subsequently "taken note" of by the UN General Assembly.

"The manipulation of the Act of Free Choice to annex West Papua shocked the world community," writes Ondawame (2010, 57). Particularly aghast were newly independent countries in Asia, Latin America, and Africa who had attended the Non-Aligned Movement conference in Bandung, Indonesia, in 1955, at which all countries present had pledged not to meddle militarily in other countries' affairs (Ondawame 2010, 57). Anticolonial leaders in Africa feared that the acceptance of *musyawarah* as a legitimate form of consultation could threaten the decolonization efforts of African countries with white minorities who might exercise undue influence under such a process (Osborne 1985, 48). A group of decolonized African countries known as the Brazzaville Group, which included Ghana, Burkina Faso, Chad, Senegal, Niger, Mauritania, Madagascar, Congo, Cameroon, Benin, the Central African Republic, Gabon, and the Ivory Coast, declared themselves in support of West Papua's decolonization movement, identifying with its "Black people in the Pacific" (Jouwe, quoted in Farhadian and Babuljak 2007, 169), who "with their Negroid features seemed like... them" (Drooglever 2009, 430).

Expressions of solidarity were extended from leaders of the Brazzaville Group during the 1960s, 1970s, and 1980s. The first president of Senegal, Leopold Senghor, provided an office and diplomatic immunity to West Papuan political representatives to campaign throughout Africa for independence (Swan 2018, 74). Although the effect of the office in terms of making the West Papuan cause known internationally was limited, its presence "in Black Africa was psychologically important" to West Papuans, according to Ondawame (2010, 118). In 1962 diplomats invited by the Dutch government from Burkina Faso and Benin, Frederic Guirma and Maxime Zollner, visited West Papua, encouraging West Papuans to send missions to African countries but not to expect independence to be delivered on a "silver platter," referencing "the fierce struggle they themselves had been forced to wage to this end" (Drooglever 2009, 580). Much as Somare's earlier-mentioned trip to Africa had inspired him to present a more "progressive" side to Papua New Guinean decolonization, this advice from Guirma and Zollner to vigorously pursue independence was "carefully noted" by West Papuans (Drooglever 2009, 580).

When the UN General Assembly held a vote on whether to accept the results of the Act of Free Choice, eighty-four countries voted in favor and thirty abstained. Of the abstentions, twenty-seven were black African and Caribbean states (Farhadian and Banuljak 2007, 169). Ondawame attributes the felt affinities between African nations and that of West Papua to "the effects of racism, the painfulness of colonial experiences, and strong feelings of the unity of black people" (2010, 162–163). Black solidarity with West Papuans was also forthcoming outside of Africa in the 1960s, with the National Association for the Advancement of Colored People (NAACP) in the United States expressing support for West Papua's independence struggle in 1962 (Farhadian and Babuljak 2007, 169) and again in 1972 (Swan 2018, 70).

Back in West Papua, black consciousness during that period was being expressed at a popular level by that territory's iconic rock reggae fusion band,[5] the Black Brothers, formed in 1974. In PNG around that time, cultural nationalism was also giving rise to an arts movement that contributed to the creation of a negritude- and nascent *indigènitude*-inspired Melanesian regionalism from which West Papuans were gaining inspiration and to which they were contributing. Artists of this movement include, for example, the pan-traditional fusion band Sanguma (Crowdy 2016, 16–19), playwright William Takaku, and author John Kasaipwaolva.

The Black Brothers, exiled to PNG and later Vanuatu because of their opposition to Indonesia's occupation of West Papua, expressed their anticolonial black power politics in a range of ways. Their hugely popular songs appealed for West Papuan independence, the music genre they played was Afro-American and Caribbean-derived, the band's name was a "direct reference to racial pride and political solidarity of the seventies Afro-American tradition [that] to Jakarta . . . might as well have been 'Black Panthers' " (Pickell 2002, 225), and the band members' Black Panthers style included Afro hairstyles, berets, black leather jackets, sunglasses, and poses with fists raised.

Another West Papuan band formed in the 1980s, Black Sweet, some of whose members came from the Melanesian Kei Islands of Maluku, also became popular in West Papua. Wearing similar black power and indigenous-inspired attire to the Black Brothers (both bands incorporated indigenous body decorations into their "black power dressing"), the band was composed of members who had previously belonged to the Black Brothers and to another formerly popular political band, the Black Papas. "Papas" is an acronym for Papua Pasifik Selatan (South Pacific Papua), a phrase linking Papua to the Pacific rather than Indonesia and thus rendering the band conspicuously anticolonial (Pickell 2002, 225). That the Black Brothers, the Black Papas, and Black Sweet each projected a black power image and anticolonial message was evidence that black consciousness had by then become a major inspiration in the arts-inspired Melanesian decolonization movements of the day, particularly in relation to West Papua. The abstract basis of negritude as a product of the surrealist arts movement made it an attractive and sufficiently flexible philosophy for uptake around the world, providing

Melanesian artists early on with "a lens and inspiration for a complete revaluation of the current racial hierarchy" (Kohn and McBride 2011, 29).

ABATEMENT OF MELANESIAN NEGRITUDE

While colonization has been deeply felt and resented in Melanesia, for many people in Melanesia, politics at the nation-state level are considered a "relatively insignificant abstraction" (Solis 2012, 87). Ideas such as Bernard Narokobi's Melanesian Way, distributed via literary form (for example, newspapers) "to the majority of people... meant little or nothing" (Kabutaulaka 1994, 71). The negritude movement taken up by Melanesian politicians, travelers, and writers from the 1960s to the 1980s connected Melanesians to many other important figures in global black consciousness and decolonization movements elsewhere. But, other than through music (one of the primary affective and communicative media in Melanesia), it was seldom able to reach those of Melanesia who could not read or had no access to newspapers but were nonetheless deeply affected by colonialism.

Following the denouement of black power movements globally and the political independence of Fiji in 1970, PNG in 1975, the Solomon Islands in 1978, and Vanuatu in 1980, there was a lull in the negritude movement throughout much of Melanesia. Negritude was primarily a movement of the intelligentsia in these countries, and many of its Melanesian proponents gained leadership roles in the newly independent governments and supporting institutions. As a philosophy embraced by those who traveled internationally, who rubbed shoulders with foreign visitors, and who were university educated, negritude could only go so far in alleviating the effects of racism introduced by colonization among nonelite Melanesians. Consequently, the defiant declarations of negritude stilled in much of Melanesia as the world's focus on decolonization in the postwar era moved on to new global concerns. The battles against colonial occupation in West Papua, as well as in New Caledonia, continued internally to those colonies and were elsewhere little observed.

"Looking back at the history of decolonisation in the 20th century, it is clear enough that it was all about bringing about an end to *European* colonisation," writes Stephanie Lawson (2017, 151). "There was obviously good reason for this, but the rush to do so created new forms of colonialism and ignored the fact that Europeans were not the only ones capable of exploiting imperialist opportunities. The UN played a key role in creating a situation in which non-European powers such as Indonesia could take advantage of such opportunities" (151). Thus, recolonization of West Papua by postcolonial Indonesia went largely unnoticed by Pacific Island countries while the latter were simultaneously decolonizing (Gardner and Waters 2013, 114). Jakarta had made use of the "anti-Western colonial card" to pressure the Dutch to relinquish their vision for West Papuan independence (Ondawame 2010, 46), prompting the

Australian Labor Party's Charles Jones to comment in Parliament at the time, "Nobody seems concerned that there should be independence for coloured people from other coloured people" (Osborne 1985, 49).

Some of the key West Papuan independence leaders who felt "dependent on external help" left West Papua to reside in the Netherlands following the exodus of the Dutch (Ondawame 2010, 48). They faced criticism from within West Papua from the remaining leaders who felt abandoned (Ondawame 2010, 49) and who, in turn, were castigated by Nicolaas Jouwe for being parochial, "act[ing] as though we don't need help from outside. That is not true. Badly we need help!" (quoted in Farhadian and Babuljak 2007, 170). African support for West Papua dissipated following the internal West Papuan independence leadership clashes of 1976 (Ondawame 2010, 63), leading to the closure of the West Papuan Bureau in Senegal and an instruction from West African countries to "find support in your own region from Melanesian countries. If you have the support of your own region, please inform us. Then you can come and ask for our support" (ULMWP 2015, 31; Ondawame 2010, 163).

THE NEXT WAVE: MELANESIAN *INDIGÈNITUDE*

With the West Papuan decolonization struggle now passed over as a political priority by Melanesian and African countries, its political and cultural leaders had to focus internally on eradicating colonialism. As a result, the philosophy of negritude, so influential in the Melanesian independence politics of the 1960s and 1970s, started in the 1980s in West Papua to merge into what James Clifford identified as *indigènitude* (2013, 16):

> Like *négritude, indigènitude* is a vision of liberation and cultural difference that challenges, or at least redirects, the modernizing agendas of nation-states and transnational capitalism.... *Indigènitude* is less a coherent ideology than a concatenation of sources and projects. It operates at multiple scales: local traditions (kinship, language renewal, subsistence hunting, protection of sacred sites); national agendas and symbols (Hawaiian sovereignty, Mayan politics in Guatemala, Maori mobilizations in Aotearoa/New Zealand); and transnational activism ("Red Power" from the global sixties, or today's social movements around cultural values, the environment, and identity, movements often allied with NGOs). (2013, 16)

It is evident in the music examples of the Black Brothers and Black Sweet above that these bands were already concerned with blending indigenous culture with black power politics, adding locally sourced traditional body adornments to their Black Panthers–inspired aesthetics and, in so doing, pioneering at a very early stage a Melanesian *indigènitude.*

The global rise of *indigènitude* in the 1980s and 1990s has been associated with the neoliberal reforms of the day that "compromised the viability of indigenous communities and undermined their relationship with the state" (M. Anderson 2009, 107). But in West Papua, the shift from negritude toward *indigènitude* may also have been influenced by a desire to find a decolonization rhetoric and strategy that did not rely on ideas and support from outside the territory—experience showed this was ineffective overall—but that drew on internal strengths. Perhaps, too, West Papuans identified with Albert Memmi's colonized "man," who, upon discovering he cannot ultimately assimilate into foreign cultures, realizes that "what makes him different from other men has been sought out and hardened to the point of substantiation. He has been haughtily shown that he could never assimilate with others; he has been scornfully thrown back toward what is in him which could not be assimilated by others. Very well, then! He is, he shall be, that man. The same passion which made him admire and absorb Europe [and perhaps in this case even the negritude philosophy] shall make him assert his differences; since those differences, after all, are within him and correctly constitute his true self" (Memmi 1965, 132).

Negritude in Melanesia in the 1960s and 1970s, although concerned with positively reorienting constructions of blackness that had been central to colonizers' racist treatment of Melanesians, was still oriented to other cultures and hinged on connections to outsiders—to black political activists, philosophers, and artists in the black Atlantic and Francophone and East Africa. More so than the negritude of previous decades, West Papuan indigenous empowerment (*indigènitude*) of the 1980s onward focused on looking internally rather than further afield to solve the problems of ongoing colonialism and neocolonialism—to indigenous heritage and customs, resources West Papuans could draw on in the absence of global black support for their plight.

For Clifford, *indigènitude* is "performed" (2013, 16). Arnold Ap, the West Papuan independence leader and ethnologist, performed *indigènitude* in the early 1980s by gathering songs and dances from indigenous cultures around West Papua in order to preserve them from Indonesian cultural genocide (see chapter 3) and assert West Papuan cultural agency and vitality. In the absence of weapons, West Papuans resisted with culture (Glazebrook 2004). Tragically, Ap was assassinated in 1984 by the Indonesian military. The independence struggle carried on over the next few decades by indigenous West Papuans without attracting a great deal of international interest.

The Pacific Renaissance and Wansolwara *Movements for West Papua as* Indigènitude

The power behind the post-2010 surge in *indigènitude* and negritude in the Pacific appears to derive from a combination of grassroots

Melanesian—especially West Papuan—empowerment enabled by digital networking and a reengagement with the symbolism of the postwar black power movement, as well as continued engagement with the "symbolic repertoire" of *indigènitude* (the sacred, Mother Earth, shamanism, sovereignty, the wisdom of elders, stewardship of the land; Clifford 2013, 16). Examples include Facebook groups, such as "Black Pacific" (n.d.) and "We Bleed Black and Red" (n.d.), moderated by supporters of West Papuan self-determination and the framing of experiences in terms such as those used by Nancy Jouwe, daughter of Nicolaas Jouwe, who, after growing up in the Netherlands, visited West Papua and reported "feeling very safe, like my ancestors were protecting me somehow" (Interview, 2008). Identifying Jouwe's account as one evincing *indigènitude*—that is, as an experience that in its description draws on a common indigenous trope—is not to question its authenticity but rather to draw attention to the symbolic and strategic importance that such tropes carry in decolonization struggles (see Tuhiwai Smith 1999, 73).

In Melanesia in the 1980s, negritude intermingled with an inchoate *indigènitude* in the music and style of the Black Brothers. In the second wave of Pacific anticolonial sentiment (2010 onward), the Black Sistaz, a vocal trio comprising the daughters of the Black Brothers' vocalist and guitarist August Rumwaropen, Petra, Lea, and Rosa, are maintaining their father's vision for a free West Papua. They cite as a source of inspiration women leaders of the black power movement of the 1970s, including the former US Black Panther Elaine Brown (Heine 2017). In an Internet image, they appear dressed in black and prominently display pig's tusk necklaces while posing with their fists raised Black Panther style (Heine 2017). The Black Sistaz' repertoire includes traditional songs from West Papua, such as those collected by Arnold Ap.

It is worth mentioning that several groups committed to keeping Ap's archive in circulation label themselves "black": Black Paradise, based in Jayapura, West Papua, and Black Orchid in Melbourne, Australia. Powes Parkop, governor of PNG's National Capital District, brought the surviving members of the Black Brothers and also the Black Sistaz to Port Moresby in 2016 for the forty-first anniversary of national independence celebrations. At a press conference for the event, manager Andy Ajamiseba stated: "Black Brothers is more than a music, it's a movement" (EMTV 2016). Through their performances, the Black Brothers and Black Sistaz came to represent black and indigenous power and identity as they progressed the cause of decolonization in West Papua.

As West Papuan cultural activism was being oriented toward Melanesia and the Pacific along black and Melanesian indigenous countercolonial lines, Pacific *indigènitude* embraced West Papua. From around 2010, Pacific *indigènitude,* concerned with climate change and ongoing colonialism in the Pacific and communicated largely via social media, has combined with a reinspired Pacific negritude. The latter draws on the revival of black consciousness in the US, particularly as it has underpinned movements such as Black Lives Matter, which originated as a social media response to police brutality against African Americans in 2013 and, more recently, the removal of monuments commemorating supporters of slavery in the American South. Following the intense controversy in 2017 in the American South surrounding the removal of these monuments, Australian South Sea Islanders, the Australian descendants of blackbirded Melanesians in the Australian labor trade (1848 to 1904), sparked a similar conversation in Australia proposing that statues of prominent figures in the labor trade, after whom Australians towns have been named (for example, Robert Towns and John Mackay), be accompanied by plaques describing their dubious role in Australian labor history. This new wave of countercolonial Pacific sentiment, a "Pacific Renaissance" (Mackley-Crump 2015; Newton Cain 2016; Radio New Zealand 2016), has taken on decolonization in West Papua as an important focus of its energy, raising the issue's status to a top Pacific politicocultural priority.

Politically, the issue of human rights and/or self-determination in West Papua was taken up in the 2015–2019 Pacific Islands Forum meetings, at the 2016 Asia-Pacific Economic Cooperation meeting in Peru, and at the 2017 African, Caribbean and Pacific Group of States meeting. In the cultural realm, since 2010 a surge of at least fifty songs advocating a "Free West Papua," mentioned at the start of this chapter, have been produced by non–West Papuan Melanesians as a symbol of solidarity and circulated via YouTube, Facebook, and SoundCloud. The majority of these songs are in the black Atlantic genres of reggae and hip-hop, but the focus of the songs is "thoroughly Melanesian, relying on tropes such as *wantok* (Melanesian pidgin for 'one talk,' referring to speakers of the same language or, more colloquially, to friends) and *wansolwara* to unite Melanesians in support of West Papua" (Webb and Webb-Gannon 2016). Indeed, the indigenous Melanesian concept of *wansolwara* has become the call rallying the entire Pacific behind West Papua as a new black power movement and has cast the black Pacific not just as a black Atlantic counterpoint but also as an endogenous movement with long-standing black transnationalist articulations.

In 2014 the late Pacific poet and scholar Teresia Teaiwa attended a gathering of artists, academics, and activists in PNG called the Madang Wansolwara Dance 2014. The point of the event, according to Teaiwa, was to "re-ignite a movement of solidarity across the Pacific," particularly in relation to decolonization issues such as West Papuan occupation (Fightback 2014). One year later, the idea of an Oceanic *wansolwara* united around West Papua's decolonization movement was taken up by a group of artists and academics at the University of Hawai'i who gathered to present (and later publish) a book of poems and artworks titled *Wansolwara: Voices for West Papua* (*Hawai'i Review* 2015).

Fijian and Tongan writer Tagi Qolouvaki, who was involved in organizing the *wansolwara* event, later reflected, in a creative writing piece titled "Dreaming Black Love," on where West Papua fits into the new wave of black consciousness sparked by the Black Lives Matter movement: "Anti-black racism and colonialism permits with impunity Indonesia's 50-year occupation . . . of Indigenous peoples in West Papua. For true Oceanic unity in kinship, we must commit to loving Blackness" (2015, n.p.). Such love, Qolouvaki asserts, is demonstrated through the *wansolwara* network of pan-Pacific unity for West Papua, a movement that "utilize[s] Pacific arts/stories and kinship (most recently we witness a turn to Melanesian unity and pride in the campaign to free West Papua) for mana-full resistance and an Oceanic imaginary that is decolonial, contagious and muscled" (Qolouvaki 2015, n.p.). Pacific organizers of various *wansolwara* events have linked the idea of *wansolwara* to black consciousness, decrying the international racism against the blackest Pacific Islanders (Melanesians) that has assisted in enabling Indonesia's occupation of West Papua. But *wansolwara* is also a concept imbued with *indigènitude*, paying homage to the language, agency, and indigenousness of Melanesians through its pidgin name.

West Papuan Indigènitude

Although their movement is increasingly Melanesia/Pacific oriented, West Papuans still draw inspiration from the black Atlantic. The ULMWP's eponymous booklet published in 2015 quotes in its preface former African American US president Barack Obama: "Change will not come if we wait for some other person or some other time. We are the ones we've been waiting for. We are the change we seek" (xii). And West Papuans have welcomed slowly reemerging gestures of solidarity from the black Atlantic, such as the late American Samoan Congressman Eni Faleomavaega of the Congressional Black Caucus writing to former UN secretary general Kofi Annan and the African American US ambassador to the UN, Susan Rice, requesting a review of the Act of Free Choice (Kirksey 2012, 203, 209).

But while links between the Pacific Renaissance, the black Atlantic, and West Papuan decolonization are apparent, they are no longer dominant in its unfolding. Robbie Shilliam's statement concerning Aotearoa/New Zealand applies more widely, including to Melanesia. He writes that we have "witnessed a subtle shift from identifying with Blackness to inhabiting Blackness on indigenous grounds" (2015, 107). The most successful black-power-informed initiatives performed by West Papuans themselves have started to hinge more on *indigènitude*—pride in black West Papuan cultures—than on foreign ideas of negritude. *Indigènitude* in West Papua focuses less on distinctive West Papuan ethnic identities or international networking with other indigenous lobby groups and more on pan-Papuan indigenous nationalism. As Jacques Bertrand has observed, "Papuans [have] played the 'indigenous' card ambiguously, as they also maintained demands as a nation" (2011, 852). Beginning in 1980, West Papuan activist Viktor Kaisiepo pursued the issue of indigenous rights for West Papuans at the UN Permanent Forum on Indigenous Issues and was accused by other Papuans of forsaking the independence dream (Interview, 2008). At the 2017 conference I hosted with the West Papua Project at the University of Sydney (September 1), various ULMWP leaders present stated that indigenous issues are only important insofar as they further the cause of independence/decolonization. They are not, however, considered the most straightforward way to influence independence politics and therefore the decolonization leadership gives them little attention at present.

Even the pan-Papuan Customary Council (Dewan Adat Papua), tasked with preserving West Papuan traditional heritage, is a West Papuan nationalist (rather than ethnic-group-focused) initiative, pursuing West Papuan independence. This is because, as the leader of the Dewan Adat Papua explained to me in 2008, experience has demonstrated that even the promotion of indigenous West Papuan rights, cultures, and traditions is considered a separatist activity under Indonesian colonialism—therefore, the pursuit of independence must precede the pursuit of indigenous rights (F. Yaboisembut, interview, 2008).

In 2016 West Papuan activist John Anari was invited by the UN Permanent Forum on Indigenous Issues to present at its fifteenth session on the theme of "Indigenous Peoples: Conflict, Peace and Resolution." After discussing various localized sovereignty conflicts in West Papua, such as exploitative resource extraction at Freeport mine, for example, Anari then linked these to colonial occupation in his recounting of West Papuan history, declared West Papuans' right to independence, and concluded by asking for the forum's support for decolonization (unpublished data). For many West Papuans, focusing on indigenous issues is a means of furthering the nationalist independence movement as much as it is an attempt to safeguard indigenous rights. Ultimately, it is not thought that the second can be achieved before the first.

This is in contrast to approaches taken by some other indigenous peoples to ideas of indigeneity, self-determination, and sovereignty. Cherokee scholar Jeff Corntassel, for example, argues that self-determination cannot be granted by an external power; sovereignty must be asserted by an indigenous nation. "Acts of state-building," he contends, "are also actions of Indigenous nation-destroying" and thus indigenous attempts to pursue self-determination on the terms of organizations such as the UN are antithetical to the goal of achieving indigenous sovereignty (Corntassel, quoted in Waziyatawin and Yellow Bird 2012, 7). This variance in perspective provides different views on what lends legitimacy to indigenous sovereignty and how self-determination processes are best enacted but may also reflect the perceived opportunities for pursuing sovereignty available to different indigenous groups. For example, Native Americans make up approximately 1.6 percent of the United States' population, whereas indigenous West Papuans compose close to half of the West Papuan population. This goes some way toward explaining the efforts West Papuans invest in making their nationalist cause known in the halls of supranational politicolegal institutions compared to the efforts of less statistically dominant indigenous peoples, whether utilizing the terms of and fora for indigenous rights or those of decolonization.

The indigenous nationalism expressed through West Papuan *indigènitude* centers on being Melanesian, black, and *not Indonesian*. Hence, West Papuan *indigènitude* is evinced through signifiers such as body adornments worn by activists, politicians, and musicians that are immediately recognizable as Melanesian, such as highlands headdresses made of feathers and shells and pig tusk necklaces. These are not intended to symbolize the West Papuan highlands or the locales from which the tusks and shells were sourced so much as to signify to outside observers a sense of "Melanesianness" more generally. While incorporating symbols of Melanesian identity, *indigènitude* in West Papua is often also accompanied by activism pointing geopolitically to the black Atlantic—raising fists in photographs, incorporating the word "black" in a name, singing in reggae or hip-hop style, or referencing the Black Lives Matter campaign. West Papuan *indigènitude* combines international inspiration with an emphasis on Melanesian, non-Malay blackness.

This is evident, for example, in the ways UK-based West Papuan leader in exile Benny Wenda carries out political activism for West Papua. Wenda's authority as a leader of West Papua's independence movement comes from his role as an indigenous West Papuan leader; he is secretary-general of DeMMak (roughly translated as Penis Gourd Tribal Assembly), and to represent his West Papuan indigenousness (that is, distinctiveness from Indonesians), he sings traditional West Papuan songs with his band, the Lani Singers, and frequently appears for public presentations wearing a traditional highlander headdress and jewelry. While performing *indigènitude* in the pursuit of decolonization for West Papua, Wenda also leverages the power of black identity politics. In March 2017 he took advantage of a visit by popular black Atlantic artists the Wailers (Bob Marley's band) for a photo opportunity in which he gave the Wailers the West Papuan Morning Star flag to hold. As a result of Wenda's lobbying, the Wailers' lead singer, Joshua David Barrett, saluted from stage all those fighting for West Papuan independence, declaring "from Ethiopia to West Papua people are fighting for freedom" (Free West Papua 2017a).

This event was shared on Wenda's Free West Papua Campaign website. His Free West Papua Campaign has also seen potential in tapping into the Black Lives Matter movement. In a 2014 tweet, the Free West Papua Campaign wrote: "Black lives matter. The people of West Papua are crying out for help. When will the world take notice?" (Free West Papua 2014). Just as Twitter has served as an expedient conduit for the resurgence of black activism in the US, it is also being put to political use by West Papuans. Social media has enhanced Melanesian black agency. In the past it has been extremely difficult for West Papuans to disseminate news of the atrocities being carried out against them because of Indonesia's media blackout in the territory. Facebook, YouTube, and Twitter have effectively undercut Indonesia's ban on international media and enabled West Papuans to join a revived global black consciousness movement that links closely to their own indigenous circumstances.

Unity and Alignments

West Papuans have heard the message loud and clear that unless they can unify internally and gain the support of their Melanesian and other Pacific neighbors, they will not be able to rely upon black solidarity further afield. In 2014, Melanesia's regional political bloc, the Melanesian Spearhead Group (MSG), rejected an application for MSG membership for West Papua from one of West Papua's primary independence-seeking bodies, the West Papua National Coalition for Liberation (WPNCL). Ostensibly, this was on account of it not being representative of all West Papuan independence groups and because West Papua was not yet a state (and so needed Indonesian approval to join the organization; Special MSG Leaders' Summit 2014). West Papuans were, however, advised by the MSG to reapply after addressing these issues. The Kanak and Socialist National Liberation Front (FLNKS) had been a full member of the MSG since its inception without the approval of France, so West Papuan leaders were confident they could argue that a representative West Papuan political body should not need Indonesia's consent to join.

However, the factionalism that had characterized West Papuan politics for decades was being held up by the MSG as a reason for withholding membership from West Papuans, and countering this was more difficult for West Papuan leaders. (The fact that Indonesia was applying heavy diplomatic pressure on MSG members was not mentioned as a third and highly persuasive reason for refusing West Papua full membership.) Three of the major West Papuan independence organizations—the WPNCL (an umbrella initiative for all West Papuan independence groups inside and outside of West Papua), the Federal Republic of West Papua (the self-proclaimed national government of West Papua since 2011), and the National Parliament of West Papua (an internal West Papua body representing activists working toward a referendum for West Papua) all claimed to be most representative of West Papua's body politic. Recognizing the urgency of responding to the MSG's unprecedented receptiveness to West Papua—a consequence of the widespread Melanesian *indigènitude* that placed West Papuan decolonization high on its agenda (Webb-Gannon, Webb, and Solis 2018)—West Papuan independence leaders met in Vanuatu in 2014 to decide how to proceed. After one week of negotiations and unification ceremonies (ULMWP 2016), the three groups emerged as one in focus and function—the ULMWP, a child of Melanesian *indigènitude,* was born, and concerted lobbying of the MSG and individual Pacific countries recommenced.

While much of the credit for the unification of the West Papuan decolonization movement in recent years can be attributed to the efforts of the ULMWP leadership and the extensive support they have within West Papua (including a highly effective leadership support team in-country), a nexus of factors and a long history of belonging to the "black islands" have contributed to the post-2010 outpouring of grassroots support from the Pacific. Together, these factors can be viewed as composing a Pacific-wide *indigènitude* that has "democratized" Melanesia's historically elite-led and externally focused negritude using digital media and indigenous creative expressions. It has also tapped into the power of the new-negritude activism gaining ground in the United States in particular and has highlighted West Papua's struggle as the apotheosis of the broader effects of colonialism and neocolonialism in the region.

The Future of Black Unity for West Papuans

Through the examples provided in this chapter, it is evident that indigenous and black identification in the Pacific Renaissance gain strength in connection with each other. Melanesian *indigènitude* turns on a Melanesianized negritude. The outward-oriented negritude of the 1960s and 1970s embraced by Melanesian (including West Papuan) leaders was not a sufficiently powerful movement to bring about the decolonization of West Papua and Kanaky and to counter neocolonial issues such as the natural resource depletion threatening the Pacific. The elite nature of the negritude of the 1960s and 1970s saw the movement diminish with the efforts of the elites who had promulgated it. Following the emergent Melanesian "indigenous turn," negritude has newfound relevance.

Nancie Gonzales makes the point that taking on a black identity can potentially cause one to be perceived as "neoteric"—that is, too cosmopolitan, part of an amorphous global diaspora stemming from the Atlantic slave trade and therefore rootless, without tradition, inherently placeless (M. Anderson 2009, 11). Identifying as black *and* indigenous, on the other hand, "involves drawing on models of culture and identity that have their own past" (M. Anderson 2009, 13). West Papuans need to demonstrate a cultural past that differentiates them from Indonesians. For West Papuans, identifying as politically black alone is not enough to prove that they do not belong with Indonesia since, from a subaltern point of view, Indonesia can also claim blackness. Indonesians *and* West Papuans were both black (in the sense of being subaltern and nonwhite) colonial subjects of the Dutch. Hence, identifying as both black *and* Melanesian indigenous is critical for West Papuans. If West Papuans might be considered subalternly black along with Indonesians, then performance of their Melanesian indigenous blackness (*indigènitude*) sets them apart from Indonesians as a culturally distinctive people of the Pacific and not Asia. Negritude and *indigènitude* are not just inspirational philosophies for West Papuans—they are ontologies, core to their political survival.

Indonesia has become wise to the ways the wind of indigenous, black Melanesian identification is filling the sails of West Papuans' decolonization movement. Oridek Ap, the West Papuan activist son of Arnold Ap based in the Netherlands, worries that soon

> you will not talk about the indigenous people of West Papua, you will not talk about the Papuan culture, but you will talk about the Indonesian Melanesian people.... That is what [Indonesia is] now promoting. Papua is... their Melanesian part of Indonesia. But five years ago, they did not talk like that. Since they've heard we are [be]coming Melanesian, we are raising awareness, they started to talk about [it].... This is the Indonesian campaign. I think they know they should fight us back with the same weapon we are using because it is our weapon to save ourselves, our culture, our identity. You know when people say we are Melanesian, they say we are not Indonesian. But now Indonesia is saying that you are Melanesian, you are the Melanesian part of Indonesia. (Interview, 2008)

In other words, Indonesia is attempting to skew the bearings of West Papua's strengthening alignments with Melanesian indigenousness by claiming that Indonesia is Melanesian too and that there is no reason why West Papuans cannot be Melanesian *and* Indonesian.

Unfortunately for West Papuans, at least two members of the MSG appeared to have been swayed by Indonesia's diplomacy, as in 2015 the MSG granted Indonesia associate membership status to the regional body and observer status only to the ULMWP. PNG, which shares a border with Indonesia, and Fiji, which substantially benefits economically from Indonesian diplomatic largesse, are reluctant to offend Indonesia over West Papua. The leaders of Vanuatu, the FLNKS, and the Solomon Islands are more critical of Indonesia and supportive of West Papua's decolonization aims than are PNG and Fiji. In a public address in 2017 to the Lowy Institute in Sydney, Solomon Islands prime minister Manessah Sogavare commented in answer to my question from the floor about Indonesia and the MSG:

> Indonesia has a duty to ensure that it respects the right of Indigenous Melanesians.... There is of course an appropriate venue at the United Nations to handle that, but we are trying... to get the support and we are actively doing that now; we have expanded the coalition [of countries supporting West Papua], the group, beyond Melanesia to also include Polynesia and Micronesia. And we are actively now working as well in Africa and South America. If we can get that support we should be able to try to push that thing through to C24 [the UN decolonization committee] as the appropriate... venue to address issues of self-determination. So, the fight against [Indonesia] continues. (Sogavare 2017)

The "coalition" to which Sogavare refers is the Pacific Coalition on West Papua (PCWP), formed in 2016 at his initiative, the membership of which includes Tuvalu, Nauru, Vanuatu, FLNKS, the ULMWP, the Solomon Islands, and the Pacific Islands Alliance of Non-Governmental Organisations (PIANGO), while Tonga and the Marshall Islands express support for the group too. The aim of the PCWP is to shore up Pacific support for taking West Papua's case to the UN for intervention. Following the formation of the PCWP, in 2016 seven Pacific Island countries (Nauru, Marshall Islands, Tuvalu, Vanuatu, Solomon Islands, Tonga, and Palau) raised concerns about human rights violations in West Papua at the seventy-first session of the UN General Assembly and, in 2017, at the UN Human Rights Council. These were landmark occasions since previously few of these countries had been willing to take a public stand at all on the West Papuan conflict. Momentum from the PCWP also prompted Benny Wenda to travel to New Zealand in 2017, where he met with members of its Parliament and lobbied them to support putting West Papua back on the UN Decolonization Committee agenda (Radio New Zealand 2017a). There, he was able to gain Maori and Pasifika activist backing. Whereas in 2013 Wenda was barred from addressing New Zealand's Parliament by the speaker of the house for fear of upsetting Indonesia, he was welcomed in 2017, a change that indicates the increasing perceived legitimacy of West Papua's struggle throughout the Pacific (Free West Papua 2017a).

Support from West Papua's "backyard" (ULMWP 2015, 21), the Pacific, has for the first time (besides the long-term backing of Vanuatu) begun to mount. As a result, West Papuans are confident in once more reaching out to their former African allies. On May 3, 2017, members of the PCWP addressed the seventy-nine member states of the Africa Caribbean Pacific Group of States (ACP), calling for the ACP's Council of Ministers to uphold West Papua's right to self-determination. The PCWP spokesperson, Vanuatu's Johnny Koanapo, stated that "the ACP was the right place to seek further support for the plight of West Papua because African and Caribbean [*sic*] are 'the oldest defenders of West Papua's right to self-determination'" (Ariane 2017). Ambassador Alfredo Lopez Cabral from Guinea-Bissau responded by saying "there was no reason why the ACP shouldn't take up the issue and help" West Papua achieve a referendum similar to that allowed East Timor in 1999 (Ariane 2017).

It is important to remember that although many Melanesian, Pacific, and, more recently, African and Caribbean states are helping to raise awareness of West Papua's decolonization movement, perhaps the most important reason this negritude-inspired activism is able to progress in such a unified fashion is because Pacific Island grassroots populations identify with West Papua's black, indigenous struggle. Pacific Island governments have woken up to West Papua's plight as a result of the ways their citizens have embraced identity politics in relation to Papua. For the most part, it is a grassroots music, arts, and activism-driven movement that the region's elites have been pressured to advance through statecraft. This is how *indigènitude* is distinguishable from the negritude of the 1960s and 1970s that failed West Papua. Nancy Jouwe, for example, points to the music of the Black Brothers as a catalyst for building black consciousness (and black pride, perhaps) among West Papuans and identification with other black peoples: "We all listened as kids to the Black Brothers.... Because music I think is very important [for] building identity.... The Black Brothers, just the name already was, I think, enough, and for Papuans, being Melanesian automatically means you're black.... Papuan, I think, very much goes together with black.... So [the Black Brothers] really helped shape that collective identity" (Interview, 2015).

In fostering confidence in West Papuan black Melanesian identity, the Black Brothers also prepared West Papuans for a cultural-political positioning that has again attracted black solidarity from beyond the Pacific. In 2017 an office for West Papuan decolonization was reestablished in Africa, this time in Uganda, by executive member of the ULMWP Jacob Rumbiak. Rumbiak reports from this recent experience that "Africans" consider West Papua their "child" (2017). Finally confident that West Papua is sufficiently unified with its Pacific siblings, African countries are now prepared to offer guidance to West Papua as the latter navigates the newly receptive seas embracing its decolonization voyage.

CONCLUSION

A New Day Dawning

Covering substantial ground, this book has analyzed five of the major issues affecting West Papua's struggle for decolonization, treating each as a "point" of the pentagram West Papuans call their Morning Star, the nation's prevailing symbol of freedom. The issues that have been under examination comprise, in turn, the various components of West Papua's decolonization goal, *merdeka;* West Papuan visions for what an independent West Papuan state might look like; the significance of West Papuan cultural identity for maintaining the fight at home and in the diaspora; the impact of factionalism on the strategic progress of the struggle; and the importance of international black alliances to the decolonization process. Each chapter took up one of these issues, looking in detail at the tension existing within the movement in relation to individual issues (the pointy end of each "arm") and the areas of consensus on each issue (the broad bases of each arm).

The argument developed over the course of the book has run thus—that despite the considerable conflict that has existed within West Papua's decolonization movement over the previous half century, the strategic political and cultural unity that continues to build over the course of the battle has enabled it not only to survive but, in recent years, to thrive. Against all odds, including decades of a seeming lack of interest from global powers and Indonesia's relentless, brutal occupation, West Papuans continue to take decolonization into their own hands. What is more, the evidence presented shows that at certain points throughout the history of the struggle, conflict within the movement has sparked productive friction. To sustain the Morning Star analogy, the sparks of friction are the luster emanating from the tips, or contentious points, of the Morning Star. As a result, the West Papuan decolonization movement today is an internationally networked, culturally nuanced, politically dynamic, and (when it needs to be) unified force to be reckoned with, a glowing light in the darkness of ongoing colonialism.

The reader may, however, have lingering questions. For example, how does West Papua's decolonization approach fit within broader Melanesian perspectives on decolonization? West Papuan leaders might have plans for a postindependence period, but is the West Papuan body politic sufficiently prepared for it? What are the implications for the region if West Papuan independence is continually delayed? And, finally, how realistic is West Papuans' belief that they will, eventually, be granted independence? Each of these important questions is worthy of further, comprehensive investigation. The remainder of this book sets out some of the dimensions of these issues. It is my hope that this discussion might inspire readers to take these up through further research.

Decolonization: Some Perspectives from the Melanesian Pacific

A critical argument in the West Papuan campaign for decolonization is that its history, geography, and Melanesian cultures and the ethnicity of its peoples combine to designate West Papua as part of an Oceanic world that is very different from the Asian region to which it has been geopolitically assigned under Indonesia. Oceania has a rich canon of decolonization literature, and many of these authors have been leaders of decolonization movements in their nations and/or of the broader region. Might it be argued, then, that there is a distinctive Melanesian Pacific perspective on decolonization, and if so, how does West Papua's approach to decolonization fit into this? Is West Papua's situation unique to the region, or are there important similarities between the decolonization experiences of West Papua and those of other Melanesian nations? To address these questions, I have attempted to extract themes from the thinking of some of Melanesia's leading decolonization theorists, including Walter Lini and Grace Mera Molisa from Vanuatu, Dewe Gorode and Jean-Marie Tjibaou from New Caledonia, Bernard Narokobi from Papua New Guinea (PNG), and Epeli Hau'ofa, whose parents were Tongan but who grew up in PNG and later lived and worked in Fiji.

Many of these theorists have been concerned with similar issues to those that West Papuan leaders are dealing with in their own independence trials, including decolonizing in a "Melanesian Way," reconciling the role of God and Christianity in the region's national politics, centering culture and custom in politics, working out "the role" of women in Melanesian politics, balancing independence and interdependence, defining a regional identity, and prioritizing land as part of national well-being. As West Papua and New Caledonia are the two remaining colonies in Melanesia, there are perhaps lessons (on what to do and what not to do) for each of these nations to learn from the decolonization aspirations and critiques offered by several of the region's seminal leaders—lessons to draw out in future research.

Writing after PNG's independence in 1975, Papua New Guinean politician and jurist Bernard Narokobi, who widely popularized the concept of the Melanesian Way among literate Papua New Guineans through newspaper articles and his 1983 eponymous book, was nonetheless critical of the lingering colonial influences on the new nation-state. He envisioned a Papua New Guinean state and a Melanesian region that was open to innovation and change (this was part of the Melanesian Way) but that prioritized Melanesian customary and traditional rather than foreign ways of doing things (Otto 1997, 38). Narokobi et al. identified three pillars of Papua New Guinean culture, a respect for which represented the Melanesian Way: the centrality of the village as the place for learning how "to be" (1980, 85), the consumption of betel nut (1980, 79), and the practice of silence (1980, 68; see also Otto 1997, 51–53). In West Papua, perhaps the centrality of *lawan* (struggle) to survival; music as a means of enjoying collective, temporary freedom; and the consumption of *papeda* (sago, a staple food symbolic to Papuans, in contrast to rice, the equivalent Indonesian staple) might be the counterparts to Narokobi et al.'s village, betel nut, and silence in PNG. (It should be noted that sago is also consumed in many parts of eastern Indonesia as well and that there is an antirice discourse in Maluku, Nusa Tenggara Timor, and parts of Sulawesi. So when Papuans celebrate sago eating, they, along with other disaffected Indonesian populations, are resisting the Java-centric influence of the Indonesian state.)

In New Caledonia, the performance of *la coutume* (a customary greeting involving the exchange of fabric, money, and an expression of humility upon entering another group's environment) and the symbolism of yams might hold similar significance. Narokobi admits that there are probably many Melanesian ways and "that diversity or pluralism is in itself a Melanesian way" (1983, 20). Working out a distinctive national narrative is foundational to the formation of new nation-states, and this is something that West Papuan visionaries are in the process of doing. But do they need a specifically West Papuan narrative, or is participation in the ongoing narration of a broader Melanesian identity sufficient for a nation (West Papua) that perceives, at this point in its endeavor, its Melanesian identity to be as significant as its independence from Indonesia?

The importance of steeping the policies and practices of newly independent Melanesian states in some form of a Melanesian Way was recognized by the priest and first prime minister of Vanuatu, Father Walter Lini. Prior to Vanuatu's independence in 1980, Lini attended theological school in New Zealand, where he began to realize that "most of the teaching materials in books on philosophy and theology were all foreign. They were either European or American ideas. . . . I [Lini] began to grow uneasy about the way New Zealanders and Pacific Islanders were forced to learn the theology, ethical principals [*sic*], philosophies, and ideas which were completely foreign to us" (1980, 15). In response, he determined to ensure that in his leadership of the Anglican church in Vanuatu, and later of the country itself, that "Pacific principles [were] not lost and the heritage of our forefathers continue[d] into the future" (1980, 11).

The eschewing of violence for political ends is part of the Melanesian Way, according to Lini, who condemned political militancy, even as a response to colonial violence (1980, 53). This is a point of contention among Melanesian leaders, however, including those of the West Papuan Organisasi Papua Merdeka (OPM)–TPN who form West Papua's military resistance wing and others such as Kanak (indigenous New Caledonian) politician and author Dewe Gorode. In 1974 Gorode and a colleague formed "the Groupe 1878, in memory of the Kanak revolt of that year under chief Atai," and she was later imprisoned on charges of "inciting violence and armed revolt through the publication of a tract written in the wake of the death of a young Kanak protestor" (Brown 2004, xx). It could be that territories suffering heavier colonial violence are more accepting of such as a form of resistance, or it could be a matter of individual philosophy (after all, most West Papuan leaders outside of the OPM-TPN, for example, are committed to achieving independence via peaceful means). Whatever its internal philosophical contradictions may be, the idea of a Melanesian Way has political utility, according to anthropologist Ton Otto, and, accordingly, is used to "give a legitimate basis to intergovernmental co-operation such as in the Melanesian Spearhead Group or to render support to opposition movements such as the OPM [in West Papua] and the Kanak FLNKS in New Caledonia" (1997, 58).

As much as Christian missionaries may have contributed to colonization in Melanesia, Christianity has been and continues to be equally as important in the region's later decolonization movements. "Of all things first foreign" to the Pacific, anthropologist Margaret Jolly writes, Christianity "has been the most thoroughly indigenized" (2005, 139–140). "Christianity is [often] seen as inherently local, as fundamental to the Pacific way and as foundational to the imagination of most Pacific nations" (140). On the cusp of Vanuatu's independence, Walter Lini asked, in a short publication, "Should the Church play politics?" (1980, 19). His answer? "Yes. The Church must play politics because the Church and politics are two sides of one thing: man's existence" (19). "The Church," he explains, "is a body which should uphold moral standards of justice. Politics is the way in which moral judgements…are channelled so that every man is protected from being exploited or robbed of his rights as a human being or as a nation among other nations" (19). The relationship between church and politics is perhaps even more pronounced in West Papua than in many other Pacific nations because in Papua, Christianity has the added significance of differentiating the indigenous (mostly) Christian population from the settler (mostly) Muslim population. A faith that God recognizes the inherent moral righteousness of their trials has sustained West Papuans in their decolonization efforts over the *longue durée*. In its prioritization of Christianity, West Papua's decolonization struggle is very much a Melanesian one, and it is likely that a future independent West Papua would weave a strong Christian perspective into its foundational documents, such as its constitution (as have PNG, the Solomon Islands, and Vanuatu), and in its national narrative.

Also of note in the way decolonization has played out throughout Melanesia is the central place of cultural heritage and creativity in the unfolding of the region's resistance movements. Author, academic, and visionary Epeli Hau'ofa claimed that in Oceania, "we aim to harness creativity to our practical struggle for survival" (2008, 87). In New Caledonia, Jean-Marie Tjibaou, the former leader of the Kanak independence party, the FLNKS, was "convinced that the way to independence was through an overhaul of tradition and its image [, which would give] a cultural dimension to the struggle" (Bensa and Wittersheim 2005, xix–xx). This in turn would help Kanak people rediscover "dignity and pride in a cultural heritage which is part of the experience and the wealth of humanity" (Tjibaou 2005, 4). Without this, Tjibaou warned, Kanaks would continue to experience "personal feelings of shame and self-contempt," which would augur poorly for an independent Kanak state (2005, 4). To this end, he organized the 1975 Melanesia 2000 cultural festival in Noumea, intended to unite and showcase the different cultural traditions of each of the territory's various indigenous peoples.

Although she characterized the Melanesia 2000 festival as a "folklorisation and trivialisation of Kanak culture and a distraction from more serious forms of political action" (Brown 2004, xxxvii), Gorode nonetheless also believed that "cultural and political" activities were "twin aspects of one drive" and as part of her decolonization efforts in Kanaky pursued cultural heritage projects that included collecting and transcribing Melanesian stories to use in schools (Brown 2004, xxi). As Kanak leaders have done, so, too, have West Papuan leaders, making use of their cultural heritage and expressive cultures to progress their decolonization effort, especially in diaspora. The performance of West Papuan music and dance, as this book has shown, has been an important method of maintaining morale among Papuans, preserving threatened culture for posterity, demonstrating opposition to the more hegemonic settler cultures in the territory, and shoring up support from outsiders.

The role of women in a decolonized Melanesia has been a particularly fraught topic, with some of the leading male decolonization leaders disavowing the "Women's Lib" movements sometimes championed by proponents of decolonization, which the former view as a Western imposition. Narokobi considered "traditional" Melanesian women of the village to be far more liberated than "modern" urban Western or Papua New Guinean women because of the "freedom" life in the village afforded them (1983, 74). At the same time, he "dread[ed] the situation that men and women, even husband and wife, become competitors for the same jobs," fearing that child rearing and family life would suffer (Otto 1997, 44). He thus, in Ton Otto's words, "reveal[ed] his basically conservative male point of view: ultimately [a] woman's place in society is determined by her 'natural' task of rearing the children" (Otto 1997, 44). Objecting to his "conservative male point of view," one Papua New Guinean woman responded in the *Post-Courier* newspaper to Narokobi's comments on "liberated" village women: "You know what men are like. Sitting all day long chewing betel nut, smoking, eating, drinking and fornicating from woman to woman. What else do they need? Of course bride price for their daughters so the money and food can last long. Oh, what a lovely Melanesian life! And what a hell of a life for us women!" (quoted in Narokobi 1983, 248).

Like Narokobi, Lini "portrayed himself as a supporter of women's rights," but also like Narokobi, he "defined women's affairs as family affairs" (Zimmer-Tamakoshi 1995, 122). As a result of the conservative view of gender roles held by many Melanesian male politicians, women have been, and continue to be, considerably underrepresented at the top levels of Melanesian politics, with some notable exceptions. (For example, Walter Lini's sister, Hilda Lini, was Vanuatu's first female member of Parliament. She was, however, scorned by Ni-Vanuatu men for her political efforts on behalf of Ni-Vanuatu women and the nation, according to fellow female Ni-Vanuatu politician and author Grace Mera Molisa [1987, 26–27].)

Anthropologist Laura Zimmer-Tamakoshi points out that Melanesian women writers and thinkers have been "less likely than male writers to suggest that all or most problems facing their nations are the result of colonialism, Westernization or rural-urban differences" (1995, 117). Molisa was strident in her condemnation of the "masculinism of the new nation-state" (Zimmer-Tamakoshi 1995, 123)—for example, calling out many of Vanuatu's "customs" as traditions invented by male leaders to oppress women (Zimmer-Tamakoshi 1995, 123). Later to become political advisor to Walter Lini, she argued in 1980 that Vanuatu's independence would only be a "half-victory if Vanuatu's women did not achieve political equality with their men" (Zimmer-Tamakoshi 1995, 123), and in 1987 she maintained that Ni-Vanuatu women were still colonized by Ni-Vanuatu men (Jolly 2005, 14).

Like Molisa in Vanuatu, much of Gorode's writing on decolonization in New Caledonia focused on the "double dispossession" of Kanak women

(Brown 2004, xxx), following "the tragic events that punctuate the lives of women [and] serve to underscore the misery that is their daily lot, their destiny to serve men during their life" (Brown 2004, xxvi). Her writing, according to literature scholar Peter Brown, "is made more complex by the fact that Kanak pro-independence discourse is projected on to the situation of women through the metaphor of land, thereby transforming, by analogy, Kanak men into colonisers of women" (2004, xxv).

The male West Papuan leaders I have interviewed have indicated that a decolonized West Papua promises independence for women as well as men and that women will hold prominent political positions in the yearned-for state. They hold up the appointment of female politician Tokoro Hanasby to the 1961 New Guinea Council, and of female activists Leonie Tanghama and Paula Makabory to the contemporary United Liberation Movement for West Papua (ULMWP), as evidence of West Papuans' ongoing commitment to female political representation. Yet the report above of Hilda Lini's treatment in Vanuatu's Parliament is a red flag that although women might be elected to political positions, their work is also liable to be undermined by sexism once there. Another warning comes in the form of Papua New Guinean academic Anne Dickson-Waiko's criticism of the "great abundance of male rhetoric about the importance of women to nation-building" at the time of PNG independence, which in the following decades has largely amounted to naught (2003, 101).

Although I was able to interview many women involved in daily decolonization activism and organization (for example, women's rights activist Frederika Korain and cultural activist Erna Mahuze in Jayapura), I found it more difficult to find women in prominent positions within the leadership of the independence movement who were willing to speak, on the record, about women's roles in the movement. This may have been partly because few women hold high political positions in the independence movement, but it could also have been that women at this level of representation are reluctant to highlight problems for fear it could detract from the movement's international support. It is sometimes the case, in certain colonial situations and at certain points in time (particularly when decolonization appears to be gaining momentum, as is the case in West Papua), that national solidarity is the paramount concern of a decolonization movement, even as it papers over other fundamental oppressions, such as gender inequality. Haunani-Kay Trask, for example, explained her perspective on this issue in Hawaiʻi: "Our sovereignty struggle requires working with our own people, including our own men. This is preferable to working with white people including feminists. Struggle with our men, occurs laterally across and within our movement. It does not occur vertically between white women and indigenous women on one side and white men and Hawaiian men on the opposing side. . . . Culture is a larger reality than women's rights" (quoted in Jolly 2005,

142–143). Dickson-Waiko suggests that in the case of PNG, the reluctance of women to denounce their unequal status in nation-state politics may also have to do with the "fear of being labelled elitist and Westernized, the reluctance to identify as feminist, and a genuine concern not to antagonize men and be accused of destabilizing family, clan, and community solidarity" (2003, 99).

Questions about the meaning of independence within the broader struggle for decolonization, too, have preoccupied other Melanesian leaders, just as they have West Papuan decolonization leaders. When he was leader of the FLNKS, Tjibaou believed, as many West Papuans do, that his nation was on an "irreversible march towards independence" (2005, xxxix) and that even if France sent "riot police . . . the atomic bomb, helicopters and the rest . . . all that won't wipe out the claim for Kanak independence" (2005, 113). "Indigenous legitimacy," he stated, "is in the belly of the Kanak land," and he was certain it would "emerge in independence" (Tjibaou 2005, 113). While Tjibaou viewed political independence as necessary for decolonization, he did not consider it "an end in itself": it was the day after the referendum, rather, that really counted (Bensa and Wittersheim 2005, xvii). He knew that no nation-state is truly independent—all such entities operate in a system. What was important was working out a position of interdependence in which a decolonized New Caledonian nation-state was neither exploited nor exploiter but a dignified, respected, contributing, and benefiting member of the world community (Bensa and Wittersheim 2005, xx). The FLNKS continues to wrestle with how to achieve this balance as it prepares for a series of future referenda on New Caledonian independence (Goa 2018), and West Papuans are watching closely to see what the eventual outcome will be and how interdependence might be brokered (R. Rumakiek, interview, 2018).

Connection to land and place continues as a strong theme in the ongoing decolonization of Melanesia. Narokobi identified, in an interview with Ton Otto, "the [Melanesian] vision of life in nature, in stones, in rocks, in trees and the environment" as being critical to postcolonial PNG's survival in a modern world obsessed with money and technological power (Otto 1997, 42). Hauʻofa linked landmarks to Oceanic memory and history and argued that the destruction of the first leads to the erasure of the second two (2008, 73). Tjibaou identified a deep sense of belonging to a specific place/land and group in New Caledonia, a connection that functions like a "rubber band": "When we live in town . . . every time there is an event, the rubber band takes us back to the tribe, and it is hard. You are there [in town], but always under tension, and it is the tribe which pulls on you" (2005, 87).

Yet, to Hauʻofa (and his philosophy is shared by other Melanesian decolonization thinkers), "the whole of Oceania is connected" despite indigenous attachments to specific groups, places, and landmarks (White 2008, xv). The sea has acted as a highway between Oceanic places and peoples, facilitating the exchange of thoughts as well as things (White 2008, xv). Perhaps it is this Oceanic connection that has prompted decolonization theorists throughout Melanesia to think of their nations, in past decades, as firmly embedded in a cultural-political region. Like many West Papuans, Tjibaou was interested in "developing federations of Melanesian countries" of which New Caledonia could be a part (2005, 92). Narokobi viewed Melanesian regionalism as pre-colonial, even: "Melanesians of PNG, West Irian, the Solomon Islands and Torres Strait Islands, New Hebrides, New Caledonia and Fiji had been living and working through unity long before they encountered Europeans and Asians," he asserted (1983, 37).

The strategic benefits of pooling sovereignty as a region have been recognized by the region's decolonization theorists. Hau'ofa contended, for example, that by "acting together as a region, for the interests of the region as a whole, and above those of our individual countries, we would enhance our chances for a reasonable survival" (2008, 42). While West Papuans (like the leaders of contemporary Melanesian states) seem, for the most part, to have abandoned earlier aspirations of Melanesian federalism for now, they have certainly continued to cling to their identity as a Melanesian nation and work to leverage any support offered to them as a result of membership in the Melanesian cultural and political community.

Are West Papuans "Ready" for Independence?

It is evident from the discussion above that although West Papuans are pursuing independence in a different era to that of many of their Melanesian neighbors, they hold cognizant concerns and values to those espoused by the leading Melanesian decolonization thinkers in some of those states, as well as New Caledonia. In other words, the West Papuan decolonization effort could be said to be unfolding in a Melanesian Way. To many outsiders (and nationals), however, Melanesian decolonization has not been a straightforward success. PNG and the Solomon Islands have been afflicted with internecine warfare, Fiji has experienced coups and a dictatorship, and multinational mining and logging companies continue to plunder PNG's natural resources and economy. That West Papua aspires to attain sovereignty like its Melanesian neighbors has prompted some observers to question whether West Papuans are ready for independence and, similarly, whether an independent West Papuan state would be a "failed" or "failing" state (see, for example, Stott 2011).

I argue, however, that these are the wrong questions to be asking in the so-called postcolonial era. They are paternalistic and patronizing. West Papuans hold the right to self-determination, and it is the business of West Papuans alone to question their preparedness to exercise that right. Instead, the more ethical, as well as practical, questions to ask might be: What strengths does the West Papuan body politic already possess that can be built upon? How might West Papua's vast resource wealth, strong national identity forged over more than half a century, committed politicians, well-connected diaspora, and strong culture of civil resistance be best utilized to forge a functional nation-state? What structures, policies, and institutions are already in place that will help smooth the way to independent governance, and how might these be strengthened and supported? What are the primary causes of the problems that challenge the independent Melanesian states (and newly independent states around the world), and what mechanisms and processes might West Papuans put in place to prevent encountering or to overcome these?

Benny Wenda has described how difficult it is for West Papuan leaders to gather for a sufficient length of time in a safe place to draft, as a body politic, a constitution for the hoped-for state. Leaders are still discussing among themselves, and with their constituents, what type of governance system would best suit an independent West Papua. West Papuan researchers are investigating options, but Wenda willingly shared with me that he and the ULMWP are open to suggestions from non-Papuan experts. This is certainly an issue worthy of further exploration in partnership with West Papuans. It is also one to which research resources could be put to good use if they permitted Papuan leaders and other governance experts to find time and an adequate environment in which to collaboratively explore appropriate governance structures suitable to West Papua's specific historical, political, and cultural context.

Many problems facing Melanesian states today are as much a result of underdevelopment (in the Walter Rodney [1972] sense), the signature of colonialism and neocolonialism, as they are of any Melanesian cultural or political pathology. Rather than ask "Can West Papuans succeed?," we should ask, "What can we, as a global community of states that has passively watched and even participated in the exploitation of West Papuans for decades, do to enable West Papuans to succeed"? Many states have been complicit in Indonesia's occupation of West Papua. External assistance, whether financial or advisory, ought to be considered reparation rather than aid.

Regional Implications of Indefinitely Delayed Independence

This book has looked in detail at what is likely to happen to West Papuans if independence is indefinitely delayed. Cultural genocide is taking its toll on the indigenous population, and without independence there is little chance of meaningful decolonization taking place. With the destruction of indigenous cultures and the environment, research indicates that the long-term survival of an indigenous population as a people is jeopardized (Alfred 2005, 30; see also Barber and Moiwend 2011, 45–49). The picture is grim for West Papuans.

But what are the implications for the region surrounding West Papua? West Papuans have demonstrated that they do not intend to give up their fight for decolonization, no matter what the consequences may be. What does this mean for Indonesia, then, as the occupying power of the territory? For PNG, the country sharing a border with West Papua? And for Australia, a country playing reluctant host to a number of West Papuan refugees?

In Indonesia there is growing civil society support for West Papuan decolonization. A number of solidarity groups (including Papua Itu Kita, or Papua Is Us) are raising awareness throughout Indonesia about the injustice of colonialism in Papua (see Koman 2016) and now regularly organize in protest at the Indonesian occupation (Associated Press 2016). In at least one such protest, "Indonesians who joined the protest knelt on their knees and apologized to West Papuans for their government's rule of [the] region" (Associated Press 2016). Pressure on Indonesia from the UN and various nongovernmental organization (NGO) lobby groups to clean up their human rights record in West Papua is mounting as the conflict stretches on. The Geneva for Human Rights' (2018) Working Group on Human Rights in West Papua has compiled a compendium of official actions that have taken place at the UN in support of West Papua since 2008. As West Papuans up the ante, organizing bigger protests, becoming bolder in their demands (for example, the ULMWP no longer requests dialogue with Indonesia but insists that an internationally supervised referendum is the only solution to the conflict), we can anticipate that Indonesia's crackdowns will become bloodier to counter the resistance. As a result, Indonesia risks undoing its developing reputation as a democratic power. Similarly, as West Papuans gain more influence in the Pacific and at international fora, Indonesia is having to invest more in expensive and aggressive foreign diplomacy to counterbalance West Papuan political traction in the Melanesian Spearhead Group and at the United Nations (UN).

If West Papuans are continually denied independence and the conflict, as a result, grows ever more heated, PNG will be at the receiving end of a protracted refugee crisis. This will be expensive for the government in terms of resettling West Papuan refugee populations and will also exacerbate preexisting tensions between PNG nationals and West Papuan refugees along the border as the latter rely upon the gardens, lands, and other resources of the former for survival. Tension will also increase between the PNG and Indonesian governments as the porous border, notoriously difficult to monitor, becomes an ever more militarized zone. Indonesian forces will increase border patrols to prevent West Papuans from crossing, and PNG forces will become more vigilant against Indonesian military border incursions. Additionally, PNG and the other Melanesian countries face the implosion of their regional political body, the Melanesian Spearhead Group, which is already locked in a stalemate over whether West Papua should be granted full membership to the group. West Papua currently holds observer status, while Indonesia has been granted associate group membership. The question of West Papuan membership has so immobilized the Melanesian Spearhead Group, with Vanuatu, the Solomon Islands, and the FLNKS in support of West Papuan full membership and Fiji and PNG siding with Indonesia against it, that Vanuatu's foreign minister Ralph Regenvanu announced in July 2018 that "the MSG was failing because of a lack of political engagement" on the issue (Radio New Zealand 2018).

Unfulfilled independence in West Papua can only spell trouble for Australia, too, as civil society groups within the country continue to put pressure on the Australian government to intervene in the conflict, as it did in East Timor in 1999, and the mainstream news media increasingly shines a light on human rights abuses in the territory. This, in turn, puts Australian relations with Indonesia on shaky ground despite Australian diplomats' best attempts to reassure the Indonesian government that the Australian government has no intention of becoming involved. Indonesia appears to harbor "lingering grievances" over Australia's role in East Timor's independence, with new events concerning West Papua and Australia often interpreted by the Indonesian government in "the light of old shadows" (Parameswaran 2017).

If the conflict escalates, which is likely if independence continues to be withheld from West Papua, Australia can expect to receive more asylum seekers from West Papua and can then look forward to further diplomatic disputes with Indonesia, similar to the breakdown in relations between the two countries when Australia granted refugee status to forty-three West Papuan asylum seekers in 2006. Resettlement will be costly for Australia and so will an ongoing strained political relationship with Indonesia. The best-case scenario, in terms of bilateral diplomacy, would be if Australia encouraged Indonesia to engage in steps toward self-determination for its colony sooner, rather than later. Relations between the two countries will be difficult whether Australia promotes the decolonization of West Papua now or is forced to intervene because of escalating violence later. The former scenario would be far preferable if it led to the prevention of violence in the long term. With the overwhelmingly negative effects for the region, as well as for West Papuans, from continually delayed independence, the following question begs further research: How can regional players be convinced it is in their national interest to work with Indonesia and West Papuans toward Papuan self-determination, and what steps can to be taken to encourage this?

How Realistic Is West Papuans' Hope for Independence?

When on a winning streak, the unpredictability of politics is potentially unnerving. But if you have been an underdog for a substantial period of your political life, as West Papuans have been in their fight for decolonization from Indonesia, unpredictability provides hope. The hope West Papuans find in the unpredictability of politics is sustained by faith in an international system that enabled the political independence of East Timor (in 2002), Kosovo (in 2008), and South Sudan (in 2011) against international trends in the so-called postcolonial era. How realistic is this hope, one might ask?[1] Are the conditions that enabled independence in these three countries also in place in West Papua?

The self-determination movements that preceded East Timorese and South Sudanese independence were products of the nations' respective colonial histories. The Timorese had been occupied first by the Portuguese (1702–1975) and then by Indonesia (1975–1999), and the southern Sudanese population, following the end of British Egyptian condominium rule, had been grouped together into the state of Sudan with northerners who "often bore a greater resemblance to colonizers than fellow citizens" (de Waal 2015, 194). Jonathan Charney observes that nations that have experienced colonial occupation have a greater chance of their right to self-determination being internationally acknowledged than nations without a colonial background (2001, 456). This is because the right to self-determination is, under international law, largely perceived to be a decolonization doctrine (Charney 2001, 456). Because it can be clearly argued that West Papua is an Indonesian colony, West Papuans stand on strong moral and legal ground when they claim their right to self-determination.

A factor that may have influenced international opinion to favor the right of Kosovars (who were not victims of colonialism, as such) to self-determination, and which was also present in preindependence East Timor and South Sudan, was the extensive violence that the populations of these territories experienced at the hands of the occupying forces. Albanian Kosovars had been subject to "ethnic cleansing" under the regime of Slobodan Milošević. The Timorese were victims of (what many analysts have called) "genocide" under Indonesia (see Saul 2001). And the South Sudanese were brutalized and experienced land and natural resource theft by an Arab Islamic elite in Khartoum (de Waal 2015, 194). In the first two cases, it was the severity of the violence being carried out by state operators against their "own" citizens that prompted international humanitarian intervention. In 1999, the International Force East Timor (INTERFET), a non-UN intervention comprising mainly Australian Defence Force troops, was deployed to restore peace to East Timor in the wake of the Indonesian army massacre in the territory. The UN Interim Mission in Kosovo (UNMIK) and the North Atlantic Treaty Organization (NATO) intervened in the terrible Serbian offensive against Kosovo in 1999. International actors (Egypt and Libya) attempted to broker peace between the North and South Sudanese, and the referendum itself was monitored by international observers, including representatives from the African Union, the European Union, and the League of Arab States while a UN Secretary-General's Panel on the Referenda was established.

West Papuans currently enjoy the support of Vanuatu, the Solomon Islands, the FLNKS, the Pacific Islands Alliance of Non-Governmental Organisations (PIANGO), Tuvalu, Nauru, Tonga, and the Marshall Islands in their battle for self-determination. However, these supporting countries would not be able to intervene militarily, either unilaterally or in alliance, to stop the conflict in West Papua, nor do they have sufficient international clout at present to influence international intervention on a greater scale. Unfortunately, it is likely to take an atrocity with immediately evident monumental consequences in West Papua (rather than the "slow motion" catastrophe that is the current Indonesian occupation) to mobilize the international community behind any kind of military action in West Papua.

The international reputation of the aggressor may play a role in the willingness of the international community to acknowledge an oppressed minority people's right to secession (Charney 2001, 459). For example, the International Criminal Tribunal for the Former Yugoslavia had already indicted Milošević for international crimes (Charney 2001, 459); in 2009, President Omar al-Bashir of Sudan was indicted by the International Criminal Court for war crimes in Darfur. These days, Indonesia has come a long way in convincing the world that it is a democracy, with four rounds of democratic elections since 1999, a decentralized government, and the implementation of military reform (with varying degrees of success). Indonesia's democratic turn since 1999 might work against efforts to encourage international intervention in favor of West Papuan decolonization, as democracies are reluctant to infringe upon the "sovereignty" of other democracies. On the other hand, Indonesia's poor human rights record, particularly in East Timor and West Papua, undermines its democratic claims and give West Papuans leverage when discussing their case at international fora (see Blades 2017, for example).

The "exhaustion of peaceful methods of resolution" may also be a factor in attracting international support for secession claims (Charney 2001, 466), a condition met by the Timorese and Albanian Kosovars prior to international intervention, although possibly not by South Sudanese independence leaders who utilized "the strategy of militarizing tribes as instruments of control" to resist the North (de Waal 2015, 194). In West Papua, although an armed resistance movement has been in operation since the early 1960s, the official leadership of the decolonization movement is committed to struggling nonviolently. To this end, they have sought dialogue with the Indonesian government and have attempted to make Indonesia's Special Autonomy package work, but to no avail. Up until recently, the Indonesian government has repeatedly ignored requests for dialogue and has never committed to implementing Special Autonomy in a way that is meaningful to a majority of West Papuans. The ULMWP has now moved beyond attempts to establish dialogue with Jakarta, applying its diplomacy efforts to engaging UN mechanisms for justice. If they are unsuccessful at this level—in other words, when peaceful methods of resolution have been exhausted—there is no telling what methods the West Papuan population may resort to in its struggle for survival.

Finally, the support of international civil society was critical in keeping the battle for political independence alive in East Timor, Kosovo, and South Sudan. International audiences had been aware of the atrocities taking place in East Timor for several decades with the murder of five Australian journalists (the Balibo Five) by the Indonesian military in 1975 and the military massacre of 250 Timorese citizens (the Santa Cruz Massacre) in 1991. Media coverage of the violence in Kosovo and the controversial NATO intervention in 1999 brought the plight of civilians in Kosovo into living rooms around the world. And Hollywood actor George Clooney's attention to the conflict in Sudan made the process of South Sudanese independence a widely known phenomenon (Notley and Webb-Gannon 2016). As part of Melanesia, a region often ignored by the world, West Papua and its conflict have largely escaped international attention over the past nearly six decades. Due to a combination of increased strategic unity within the West Papuan decolonization movement, the advent of social media, and a resurgence in political activism in the Pacific, West Papuans have recently experienced increasing success in placing their struggle more firmly on the international agenda.

So how realistic, then, is West Papuans' anticipation that their efforts will yield political independence? Many of the conditions present during the secession of East Timor, Kosovo, and South Sudan also exist in West Papua. Like the Timorese and the South Sudanese, West Papuans have been colonized. As in Timor, Kosovo, and South Sudan, West Papuans have seen the occupying power carry out horrific violence in their territory. Like the Timorese and the Kosovars, West Papuans have all but exhausted peaceful methods of conflict resolution. But whereas Timor, Kosovo, and Sudan were ruled by regimes of dubious democratic acclaim, West Papua is under the grips of a "reformed" Indonesia that enjoys relatively stable relations with democratic neighbors reluctant to jeopardize them. And while the conflicts in East Timor, Kosovo, and South Sudan were fairly well known internationally, West Papua's quest for decolonization is still clawing its way into the international spotlight. Nevertheless, not all of the favorable conditions for self-determination were present in Timor, Kosovo, and South Sudan. The South Sudanese had not potentially exhausted peaceful methods for conflict resolution in their territory. The Albanian Kosovars were not "colonized" by Yugoslavia. And Indonesia was already a budding democracy when its army wreaked havoc in East Timor in 1999. Despite the former's democratic status, a coalition of other democratic powers was nonetheless willing to intervene to assist the East Timorese. Politics, especially in international relations, are infinitely complex and as such are not always predictable. So while we might conclude, then, that independence in West Papua is not probable, it is certainly possible. And it is on this glimmering possibility that West Papuans are hanging their hopes.

Increasingly united around a common goal, a future vision, a cultural-political identity, a strategic direction, and an alliance with black solidarity movements around the world, West Papuans' hope in the possibility of independence is reinforced by a faith in the righteousness of their struggle. They take heart in the knowledge that similar battles have prevailed in the face of just as great odds and that they are doing everything they can to heighten their chances of success. West Papuans are looking outward from within their long night of strife to the light spilling over the horizon, a promise that the Morning Star of decolonization is moving ever closer. This is largely due to the determination and indefatigable efforts of the West Papuan body politic, a constellation of strategically articulated actors that, in the words of Benny Wenda (Interview, 2008), shines ever brighter as "one in spirit under the Morning Star."

Notes

INTRODUCTION

1. The territory located on the western half of the island of New Guinea has undergone several name changes with its different colonial occupiers. In this book I use the term "West Papua," in solidarity with West Papuans who chose this name in 1961, to denote the entire territory of what has now been divided into Papua and Papua Barat provinces. (For more on the history of the territory's names, including West New Guinea, West Irian, and Irian Jaya, see King 2004, 19–20.)
2. For example, the Dutch administered West Papua via a treaty with the Dutch vassal state of Tidore rather than as part of the Dutch East Indies (Indonesia), treating West New Guinea and the Dutch East Indies as separate colonies; the United Nations General Assembly "took note" of rather than "endorsed" the results of the 1969 sham referendum through which West Papua was formally annexed to Indonesia (Pouwer 1999, 171), displaying a less than wholehearted acceptance of the forced outcome.
3. For more detail on the litany of human rights abuses and deprivations that West Papuans have suffered under Indonesian occupation, see AwasMIFEE 2013; Brundige et al. 2004; Dabbagh 2016; Harsono 2018; Human Rights Watch 2014; International Coalition for Papua 2017; Kirksey and Grimston 2003; Munro 2016; Papuans Behind Bars 2011.

4. Given that the leaders of West Papua's decolonization movement are struggling not only "for civil rights but . . . against [what they believe is their] planned disappearance" (Trask 1993, 33), it is perhaps not surprising that this gives way to a sense of urgency and degree of conflict within the movement. Albert Memmi wrote in 1965: "What is clear is that colonization weakens the colonized and that all those weaknesses contribute to one another" (1965, 115).

CHAPTER 1: WISH UPON A STAR

An earlier version of this chapter appeared in Webb-Gannon (2014, 355–369).

1. Timmer's analysis here echoes that of the Indonesian human rights lawyer and democracy advocate Todung Mulya Lubis on the meanings of *merdeka* in East Timor. In *Tempo* magazine on November 23, 1991, Lubis vastly underestimated the East Timorese desire for independence, writing:

   > The problem of self-determination is not the major problem anymore. The government's effective presence and its process of economic development must be able to make silent the normative interpretation of self-determination. . . . The common understanding of independence is more simple and practical. It leaves political questions aside and asks how far can one realise one's social and economic aspirations. Corlea, a *temukung* (traditional leader) in a village, proudly and frankly stated that he had become a free (*merdeka*) person. His reason was simple enough. He had been able to replace his house of straw thatch (a symbol of a colonised people) with a house with cement walls, a manifestation of freedom (*kemerdekaan*). (Quoted in Matsuno 1998, 204–205)

   This limited definition of *merdeka* did not turn out to be widely representative in East Timor, as demonstrated by the results of the 1999 referendum for independence.
2. The desire for independence is not just an elite one: Papuans in both towns and villages, with money and without, high ranking and not, have experienced the brutal oppression of Indonesian security forces and policies, have been forced to flee from burning houses and gardens, and yearn for a life not dominated by the security apparatus of the Indonesian state. Nonie Sharp argues that viewing West Papuan independence politics as a matter for elite West Papuans rather than a matter concerning the masses is "a peculiarly Western distortion which fails to perceive the close connection between certain Western-educated intelligentsia and the group of people to which they belong" (1994, 13). "The result of this blindness," Sharp continues, "is a thinning out of meaning in explanations of grass-roots movements for independence which tend to assume they had their beginnings in the neo-colonial occupation of Papua Barat by the state of Indonesia" (1994, 13) when indeed, as Sharp and others have demonstrated, West Papuan nationalism long precedes Indonesian intervention.
3. See, for example, the testimonies presented at the same hearing by Sophie Richardson

from Human Rights Watch and Salamon Yumame from the West Papuan NGO Forem Demokrasi (FORDEM; Federal News Service 2010).

CHAPTER 2: DREAMS

1. On West Papuan perceptions of HIV as a genocidal strategy in West Papua, see Butt (2008).
2. An acute interest in Israel and in the history of the Israelites can be found among other peoples in the Pacific who have been colonized and among followers of black liberation theology. Black liberation theologians in the United States, such as James Cone, have cast black people as God's "chosen people" (Spengler 2008); Martin Luther King Jr. (1968) orated that black people will reach the Promised Land; a book published in PNG in 2010, *Bina Mene: Connecting the Hebrews,* claims the Bine tribe of the Western Province of PNG has Hebrew heritage because of linguistic similarities (Were 2006); and there are stories among many (especially black and oppressed) groups around the world that trace connections—for example, through migration paths or various customs—between their own heritage and that of the lost tribes of Israel. Outsiders have also constructed similar but rather more exotic links between Pacific peoples and the lost tribes of Israel. For example, photographer Frank Hurley's celebrated documentary *Pearls and Savages* from 1921, filmed partly in PNG, was renamed *The Lost Tribe.* In it Hurley described a "'tribe of head hunters' as bearing 'a striking resemblance to the ancient Jews of Babylon'" (McNiven 2010).
3. There are some West Papuans, of course, who do not subscribe to this discourse, the most well known being Nicolas Messet and the late Franzalbert Joku, and who support Indonesian Special Autonomy in West Papua (for more on Joku and Messet, see chapter 1). However, their views are not the dominant ones. Other than in PNG, where they established a pro–Special Autonomy group (see chapter 4), Joku and Messet appear from my research to have limited credibility among West Papuans. There is another minority view that downplays the importance and inevitability of independence, championed by Papuan activist Viktor Kaisiepo until his death in 2010, that considers West Papuans' rights and future to be tied up with those of all indigenous peoples around the world. Because of this, state sovereignty for the Papuan nation is less of a concern to him than protecting the "cultural, social, [and] economic rights" of all indigenous peoples. If these rights cannot be ensured for West Papuans and other indigenous peoples, Kaisiepo argued, political independence is ultimately worthless (Interview, 2008).
4. Migrants' impact on the economy, land, and politics in West Papua, as well as their religious and cultural differences, has been a source of great resentment among indigenous West Papuans (Fernandes 2006, 113).
5. In nearly all of my interviews, West Papuans emphasize, however, that only indigenous West Papuans (meaning no so-called mixed-race Papuans, or those with a transmigrant background) will be allowed to vote in a referendum on self-determination. This is in the best interests of the latter two populations, according

to Jacob Rumbiak, as indigenous West Papuans cannot then blame them if the outcome of the referendum is in Indonesia's favor (J. Rumbiak, interview, 2009).

6. According to Jacob Rumbiak, these cultural regions are *adat* states represented by the seven blue stripes of the Morning Star flag (Pers. comm., 2011). Nancy Jouwe, whose father Nicolaas Jouwe designed the Morning Star (by some accounts), describes the seven blue stripes as having biblical significance as well, given the special status of the number seven throughout the Bible (Pers. comm., 2011).
7. PNG also has a treaty with Indonesia—the 1986 Treaty of Mutual Respect, Friendship and Cooperation—in which each side has agreed "not to cooperate with others in hostile or unlawful acts against each other or allow their territory to be used by others for such purposes" (May 2004, n.p.).

CHAPTER 3: CONSTELLATIONS

1. Although the "official" language in West Papua is Bahasa Indonesia, a number of West Papuans have emphatically informed me that the lingua franca of West Papua is not in fact Bahasa Indonesia but rather Bahasa Melayu, the major language of the Austronesian family. It is also one with a political distinction in this case, signaling opposition to the oppressor and incorporating words from West Papuan dialects. In this instance, to borrow Memmi's words, "the two worlds symbolized and conveyed by these two tongues are in conflict; they are those of the colonizer and the colonized" (1965, 107).

CHAPTER 4: WRESTLING IN THE DARK

1. The term *wantok* derives from the Melanesian pidgin for "one talk," people from the same language group. *Wantokism* refers to the Melanesian practice of looking after one's own people or friends. The term "Big Man" derives from the anglicized Melanesian pidgin phrase for *bikpela man,* meaning "prominent man" and used in ethnography to denote Melanesian men of wealth, influence, oratorical skills, and political standing (Shore 2014, 180).
2. Jason MacLeod writes that militarily the TPN, with few weapons and poor communication and coordination between commands, does not constitute a threat to the Indonesian military. However, the TPN functions as a morale booster for West Papuans, its existence a symbol that resistance to Indonesia has not disappeared (MacLeod 2009, 11).

CHAPTER 5: STARS ALIGNING

Epigraph: Airileke, "Full Freedom," from the album *Weapon of Choice,* 2012. Lyrics by Benny Wenda; music produced by Airileke and Dizzl.

1. Some of the content of chapter 5 originally appeared in Webb-Gannon, Webb, and Solis (2018, 217–246), doi:http://dx.doi.org/10.15286/jps.127.2.217-246.
2. In using the term "elite" when discussing certain Melanesian intellectuals and politicians, I am referring to the relatively small number of Melanesians in the 1960s,

1970s, and 1980s who were able to variously travel overseas, attend universities, have their literary works published, and/or work in positions of national/regional influence.

3. The "black Atlantic" refers to African diasporas and the cultures they have produced in Anglophone countries, with (in Paul Gilroy's [1993] work) a strong focus on Britain and the United States.
4. From the beginning of the twentieth century until the outbreak of World War II, Dutch colonizers handed over the day-to-day administration, education, and missionization of West Papua to Ambonese and Kai Islanders. This group of Malukan middle management "looked down on [what they thought of as] the less developed Papuans and treated them accordingly" (Drooglever 2009, 748). In the view of historian Pieter Drooglever, Papuans, who were already "suspicious of outsiders or 'amberi' who had, in earlier years, plundered their coasts as participants in [raids] from Ternate and Tidore, found their existing aversion deepening. . . . This anti-amberi sentiment was the negative form of the Papuans' own sense of identity" (2009, 748).
5. Identification with the theology and philosophy of resistance of Rastafarianism, the religion closely associated with reggae music, resonates with many oppressed black peoples globally, including West Papuans. While in West Papua, I witnessed the clever integration of Rasta and West Papuan cultures of political resistance through the incorporation of Rasta colors in West Papuan fashion, style (many Papuan men grow their hair into long dreadlocks, a Rasta symbol relating to the "Lion of Judah," or God, and encase them in West Papuan Rasta hats, which are often decorated with the colors and patterns of the Morning Star flag), technology (reggae ringtones), and music (the songs of Bob Marley, for example, are revered). Identifying as a "Rasta" is a unifying identity among West Papuans, and it also serves to unify West Papuans with black diaspora peoples struggling for justice throughout the world. The Rasta culture embraced by Papuans, and made their own, "combines the histories of the children of slaves in different societies. Within it are contained both the negative and the positive—the idealist and the ideological—responses of an exploited and racially-humiliated people" (Campbell 1980, 2). To West Papuans it would appear that Rastafarianism connotes a culture of black hope and defiance.

CONCLUSION

1. The success or otherwise of the intervening international missions in each of these territories and the stability of the resulting independent states is not under discussion here. Rather, I focus on the conditions present that may have facilitated the acts of self-determination in and international acceptance of claims to statehood by each territory. It should be noted that not all states recognize the independence of Kosovo—Russia and China, for example, do not.

References

INTERVIEWEES

Ajamiseba, Andy. Interview with the author, July 20, 2009, Port Vila, Vanuatu.
Al Hamid, Thaha. Interview with the author, translated by Rex Rumakiek, December 4, 2008, Jayapura.
Ap, Oridek. Interview with the author, September 10, 2008, The Hague.
Douw, Amatus, Allen Galilee, and Pirimapun Florentinus. Interview with the author, November 5, 2009, Melbourne, Australia.
Garu, Selwyn. Interview with the author, July 20, 2009, Port Vila, Vanuatu.
Giay, Benny. Interview with the author, December 5, 2008, Jayapura.
Haluk, Markus. Interview with the author, translated by Rex Rumakiek, December 1, 2008, Jayapura.
Interviewee A. Interview with the author (name withheld at interviewee's request), August 30, 2009, Port Moresby.
Interviewee B. Interview with the author (name withheld at interviewee's request), September 1, 2009, Port Moresby.
Interviewee C. Interview with the author (interpreter used but names of both withheld at author's discretion), November 12, 2008, Merauke, West Papua.
Jouwe, Nancy. Interview with the author, September 12, 2008, Utrecht, the Netherlands.

———. Interview with the author, April 23, 2015, via Skype from Sydney (author) to Utrecht, the Netherlands (Jouwe).
Kaisiepo, Viktor. Interview with the author, September 11, 2008, Amersfoort, the Netherlands.
Kareth, Michael. Interview with the author, September 24, 2008, Boekel, the Netherlands.
Karubaba, Sonny. Interview with the author, September 3, 2009, Port Moresby.
Korain, Frederika. Interview with the author, December 3, 2008, Jayapura.
Mahuze, Erna. Interview with the author, December 6, 2008, Jayapura.
Makanuey, Frank. Interview with the author, September 12, 2009, Port Moresby.
Mofu, Suriel. Interview with the author, August 26, 2008, Oxford.
Ondawame, Otto. Interview with the author, July 11, 2009, Sydney.
Prai, Jacob. Interview with the author, September 15, 2008, Malmö.
Prai, Joseph. Interview with the author, September 15, 2008, Malmö.
Regenvanu, Ralph, and Joel Simmo. Interview with the author, July 20, 2009, Port Vila, Vanuatu.
Rumakiek, Rex. Interview with the author, January 21, 2010, Sydney.
———. Interview with the author, June 29, 2018, via Facebook Messenger call from Sydney (author) to Canberra (Rumakiek).
Rumbiak, Jacob. Interview with the author, November 5, 2009, Melbourne.
Rumkorem, Seth. Interview with the author, September 19, 2008, The Hague.
Runawery, Clemens. Interview with the author, September 1, 2009, Port Moresby.
Saltford, John. Interview with the author, September 2, 2008, London.
Samuelson, Richard. Interview with the author, August 27, 2008, Oxford.
Sapioper, Opina. Interview with the author, September 19, 2008, The Hague.
Sapioper, Simon. Interview with the author, September 19, 2008, The Hague.
Sawor, Zachi. Interview with the author, September 25, 2008, Ede, the Netherlands.
Soei Liong, Liem. Interview with the author, September 3, 2008, Surrey.
Tebay, Neles. Interview with the author, December 6, 2008, Jayapura.
Tekwie, David. Interview with the author, September 2, 2009, Port Moresby.
Tekwie, John. Interview with the author, August 31, 2009, Port Moresby.
Wainggai, Herman. Interview with the author, November 4, 2009, Melbourne.
Waromi, Freddy. Interview with the author, September 6, 2009, Port Moresby.
Wenda, Benny. Interview with the author, August 27, 2008, Oxford.
———. Interview with the author, June 29, 2018, via Skype from Sydney (author) to Oxford (Wenda).
Yaboisembut, Forkorus. Interview with the author, December 2, 2008, Jayapura.
Yeimo, Victor. Interview with the author, June 1, 2010, via Skype from Sydney (author) to Jayapura (Yeimo).

OTHER SOURCES

All websites accessed February 20, 2020.

Alfred, Taiaiake. 2005. *Wasasé: Indigenous Pathways of Action and Freedom*. Toronto: Broadview Press.
Anderson, Benedict. 2006. *Imagined Communities*. Rev. ed. London: Verso.

Anderson, Kjell. 2015. “Colonialism and Cold Genocide: The Case of West Papua.” *Genocide Studies and Prevention* 9 (2): 9–25.

Anderson, Mark. 2009. *Black and Indigenous: Garifuna Activism and Consumer Culture in Honduras.* Minneapolis: University of Minnesota Press.

Ariane, Zely. 2017. “PICWP Push ACP to Draft Resolution of Support for West Papua Self-Determination.” *West Papua Daily,* May 7. http://tabloidjubi.com/eng/pcwp-push-acp-draft-resolution-support-west-papua-self-determination/.

Asian Human Rights Commission. 2010. “Indonesian Military Ill-Treat and Torture Indigenous Papuans.” YouTube video. http://material.ahrchk.net/video/AHRC-VID-012-2010-Indonesia.html.

Aspinall, Edward. 2005. *The Helsinki Agreement: A More Promising Basis for Peace in Aceh?* Policy Studies. Manoa: East-West Center, University of Hawai‘i.

———. 2006. “Violence and Identity Formation in Aceh under Indonesian Rule.” In *Veranda of Violence: The Background to the Aceh Problem,* edited by A. Reid, 149–176. Singapore: National University of Singapore Press.

Associated Press. 2016. “Indonesia Police Arrest Hundreds at West Papua Protests.” *Daily Mail Online,* December 19. http://www.dailymail.co.uk/wires/ap/article-4046928/Indonesian-police-arrest-dozens-ahead-West-Papua-protest.html.

Australian Broadcasting Corporation. 2010. “A West Papuan Story: Strange Birds in Paradise.” *Radio National, Late Night Live,* presented by Philip Adams. http://www.abc.net.au/radionational/programs/latenightlive/a-west-papuan-story-strange-birds-in-paradise/3043194.

AwasMIFEE. 2013. “Three years of MIFEE (Part 1): A Growing Movement against Plantations in West Papua.” https://awasmifee.potager.org/?p=650.

Ballard, Chris. 2006. “Seeds of Papuan Identity Born of Suffering: Opinion.” *Sydney Morning Herald,* May 22. http://www.smh.com.au/news/opinion/seeds-of-papuan-identity-born-of-suffering/2006/05/21/1148150120018.html.

Balmain, Anthony. 2004. “West Papuan Separatists Reject Armed Struggle.” *Sydney Morning Herald,* August 3. http://www.smh.com.au/articles/2004/08/02/1091432117925.html?from=storylhs.

Banivanua Mar, Tracey. 2008. “A Thousand Miles of Cannibal Lands: Imagining Away Genocide in the Re-colonization of West Papua.” *Journal of Genocide Research* 10 (4): 583–602.

———. 2016. *Decolonisation and the Pacific: Indigenous Globalisation and the Ends of Empire.* Cambridge: Cambridge University Press.

Barber, Paul, and Rosa Moiwend. 2011. “Internet Advocacy and the Mifee Project.” In *Comprehending West Papua,* edited by Peter King, Jim Elmslie, and Camellia Webb-Gannon, 37–49. Sydney: Centre for Peace and Conflict Studies, University of Sydney.

Bellanta, Melissa. 2014. “Uncle Tom in the White Pacific: African-American Performances of the ‘Slave Sublime’ in Late-Colonial Australasia.” *Journal of Colonialism and Colonial History* 15 (3): 1–15.

Bensa, Alban, and Eric Wittersheim. 2005. “Editors’ Introduction.” In *Kanaky, by Jean Marie Tjibaou,* edited by Alban Bensa and Eric Wittersheim, xiv–xxiii. Canberra: Pandanus Books.

Bertrand, Jacques. 2011. “‘Indigenous Peoples’ Rights’ as a Strategy of Ethnic

Accommodation: Contrasting Experiences of Cordillerans and Papuans in the Philippines and Indonesia." *Ethnic and Racial Studies* 34 (5): 850–869.

Biak Massacre Citizens' Tribunal. 2013. Centre for Peace and Conflict Studies, University of Sydney. https://www.biak-tribunal.org/.

Blades, Johnny. 2017. "Fiery Debate over West Papua at UN General Assembly." Radio New Zealand, September 17. https://www.radionz.co.nz/international/programmes/datelinepacific/audio/201860156/fiery-debate-over-west-papua-at-un-general-assembly.

Blaskett, Beverley. 1993. "Resistance Movement as Nationalist Force." In *Islands and Enclaves: Nationalisms and Separatist Pressures in Island and Littoral Contexts*, edited by Garry Trompf, 312–341. New Delhi: Sterling.

Blay, Sam. 2007. "Why West Papua Deserves Another Chance." *Inside Indonesia* 61. http://www.insideindonesia.org/why-west-papua-deserves-another-chance.

Bloch, Ernst. 1995. *The Principle of Hope*. Vol. 3. Translated by N. Plaice, S. Plaice, and P. Knight. Cambridge, MA: MIT Press.

Bob, Clifford. 2005. *The Marketing of Rebellion: Insurgents, Media and International Activism*. Cambridge: Cambridge University Press.

Boxill, Ian. 1996. "Atlantic Meets Pacific: Music as an Element of Struggle in Aotearoa/New Zealand." *Critical Criminology* 7 (2): 108–122.

Brown, Dominic, dir., prod. 2009. "Forgotten Bird of Paradise." London: Dancing Turtle Media. DVD, 27 min.

Brown, Peter, ed. 2004. *The Kanak Apple Season: Selected Short Fiction of Dewe Gorode*. Canberra: Pandanus Books.

Brundige, Elizabeth, Winter King, Priyneha Vahali, and Xiang Yuan. 2004. *Indonesian Human Rights Abuses in West Papua: Application of the Law of Genocide to the History of Indonesian Control*. Report prepared for the Indonesian Human Rights Network by the Allard K. Lowenstein International Human Rights Clinic, Yale Law School, 1–75. https://law.yale.edu/sites/default/files/documents/pdf/Intellectual_Life/West_Papua_final_report.pdf.

Budiardjo, Carmel, and Liem Soei Liong. 1983. *West Papua: The Obliteration of a People*. Surrey: Tapol.

Bujra, Janet. 1973. "The Dynamics of Political Action: A New Look at Factionalism." *American Anthropologist* 75 (1): 132–152.

Burton, John. 1990. *Conflict: Resolution and Prevention*. New York: St. Martin's Press.

Butt, Leslie. 2008. "Silence Speaks Volumes: Elite Responses to AIDS in Highlands Papua." In *Making Sense of AIDS: Culture, Sexuality, and Power in Melanesia*, edited by Leslie Butt and Richard Eves, 116–132. Honolulu: University of Hawai'i Press.

Byrd, Jodi. 2011. *The Transit of Empire*. Minneapolis: University of Minnesota Press.

Cabral, Amilcar. 1979. *Unity and Struggle: Speeches and Writings*. New York: Monthly Review Press.

Campbell, Horace. 1980. "Rastafari: Culture of Resistance." *Race and Class* 22 (1): 1–22.

Carr, James Revell. 2014. *Hawaiian Music in Motion: Mariners, Missionaries, and Minstrels*. Urbana: University of Illinois Press.

Césaire, Aimé. 1972. *Discourse on Colonialism*. New York: Monthly Review Press.

Chappell, David. 2005. "'Africanization' in the Pacific: Blaming Others for Disorder in the Periphery?" *Comparative Studies in Society and History* 47 (2): 286–317.

———. 2010. "A 'Headless' Native Talks Back: Nidoish Naisseline and the Kanak Awakening." *Contemporary Pacific* 22 (1): 37–70.

Charney, Jonathan. 2001. "Self-Determination: Chechnya, Kosovo and East Timor." *Vanderbilt Journal of Transnational Law* 34:455–467.

Chauvel, Richard. 2004. "Divide and Who Rules? Ethnic Nationalism under Siege in West Papua." *Inside Indonesia* 78. https://www.insideindonesia.org/divide-and-who-rules.

———. 2005. *Constructing Papuan Nationalism: History, Ethnicity, and Adaptation.* Policy Studies. Washington, DC: East-West Center.

———. 2006. "Australia, Indonesia and the Papua Crisis." APSNet Policy Forum. https://nautilus.org/apsnet/0614a-chauvel-html/.

———. 2008. "Rulers in Their Own Country?" *Inside Indonesia* 94. https://www.insideindonesia.org/rulers-in-their-own-country.

———. 2009. "Genocide and Demographic Transformation in Papua: A Response to Jim Elmslie and Stuart Upton." *Inside Indonesia* 97. https://www.insideindonesia.org/genocide-and-demographic-transformation-in-papua.

Clifford, James. 2001. "Indigenous Articulations." *Contemporary Pacific* 13 (2): 468–490. Accessed September 17, 2020. http://www.jstor.org/stable/23717600.

———. 2013. *Returns: Becoming Indigenous in the Twenty-First Century.* Cambridge, MA: Harvard University Press.

Crocombe, Ron. 1993. "Ethnicity, Identity and Power in Oceania." In *Islands and Enclaves: Nationalisms and Separatist Pressures in Island and Littoral Contexts,* edited by Garry Trompf, 195–223. New Delhi: Sterling.

Crowdy, Denis. 2016. *Hearing the Future: The Music and Magic of the Sanguma Band.* Honolulu: University of Hawai'i Press.

Dabbagh, Omar. 2016. "More than 1,700 Protestors Were Temporarily Detained as They Marked the Anniversary of the End of Dutch Rule." *SBS News.* https://www.sbs.com.au/news/assault-claims-during-mass-arrests-over-west-papua-independence-push.

Dawrs, Stuart. 2009. "Looking thru Those Eyeholes: Re-historicizing the OndoBondo Poster Poems." Master's thesis, University of Hawai'i, Honolulu.

Deloria, Vine, Jr. 1973. *God Is Red: A Native View of Religion.* Golden, CO: Fulcrum.

———. 2003. *God Is Red: A Native View of Religion.* New York: Putnam.

Denoon, Donald. 1999. "The Trouble with African Analogies." *Journal of Pacific History* 34 (3): 281–289.

Department of Foreign Affairs, Immigration and Trade, Federal Republic of West Papua. 2010. "Jacob Rumbiak on the Washington Solution." Address to seminar on Democracy and Human Rights in Asia and the Pacific: The Washington Solution, George Mason University, Virginia, November 9. https://dfait.federalrepublicofwestpapua.org/video/jacob-rumbiak-on-the-washington-solution/.

de Waal, Alex. 2015. "The Price of South Sudan's Independence." *Current History* 114 (772): 194–196.

Dickson-Waiko, Anne. 2003. "The Missing Rib: Mobilising Church Women for Change in Papua New Guinea." *Oceania* 74:98–119.

Dixon, Norm. 1996. "Melsol Discusses Its Future." *Green Left Weekly,* October 23. http://www.greenleft.org.au/node/13218.

Doherty, Ben, and Kate Lamb. 2017. "Banned West Papua Independence Petition Handed to UN." *Guardian,* September 27. https://www.theguardian.com/world/2017/sep/27/banned-west-papua-independence-petition-un.

Douglas, Bronwen. 2002. "Why Religion, Race, and Gender Matter in Pacific Politics." *Development Bulletin* 59:11–14.

———. 2007. "Christian Custom and the Church as Structure in 'Weak States' in Melanesia." In *Civil Society, Religion and Global Governance: Paradigms of Power and Persuasion,* edited by H. James, 158–174. London: Routledge.

———. 2008. "'Novus Orbis Australis': Oceania in the Science of Race, 1750–1850." In *Foreign Bodies: Oceania and the Science of Race, 1750–1940,* edited by Bronwen Douglas and Chris Ballard, 99–155. Canberra: ANU E Press.

Doumenge, Francois. 2002. "La Melanesie: 'Trou Noir' du Pacifique?" *Tahiti-Pacifique* 138:15–23.

Drooglever, Pieter. 2009. *An Act of Free Choice: Decolonization and the Right to Self-Determination in West Papua.* Oxford: Oneworld.

Du Bois, W. E. B. (1903) 2007. *The Souls of Black Folk.* Oxford: Oxford University Press. Citations refer to the 2007 edition.

Dummett, Kel. 2003. "Dirk Samuel Ayamiseba (1912–2003)." *Inside Indonesia* 77. https://www.insideindonesia.org/dirk-samuel-ayamiseba-1912-2003.

Dunbabin, Thomas. 1935. *Slavers of the South Seas.* Sydney: Angus and Robertson.

Dunham, Charlotte Chorn. 1998. "Generation Units and the Life Course: A Sociological Perspective on Youth and the Anti-war Movement." *Journal of Political and Military Sociology* 26 (2): 137–155.

Eagleton, Terry. 2015. *Hope without Optimism.* New Haven, CT: Yale University Press.

Eliezer, Christie. 2005. "West Papua Artist Rumwaropen Dies." *BillboardBiz,* May 23. https://www.billboard.com/articles/business/1411992/west-papuan-artist-rumwaropen-dies.

Elmslie, Jim. 2002. *Irian Jaya under the Gun: Indonesian Economic Development versus West Papuan Nationalism.* Adelaide, Australia: Crawford House.

———. 2009. "Not Just Another Disaster: Papuan Claims of Genocide Deserve to Be Taken Seriously." *Inside Indonesia* 97. https://www.insideindonesia.org/not-just-another-disaster.

Elmslie, Jim, and Camellia Webb-Gannon. 2013. "A Slow-Motion Genocide: Indonesian Rule in West Papua." *Griffith Journal of Law and Human Dignity* 1 (2): 142–165.

Elmslie, Jim, Camellia Webb-Gannon, and Peter King. 2011. *Anatomy of an Occupation: The Indonesian Military in West Papua.* Report prepared for the Centre for Peace and Conflict Studies, University of Sydney. https://www.academia.edu/25626470/Anatomy_of_an_Occupation_The_Indonesian_Military_in_West_Papua.

EMTV Online. 2016. *Black Brothers in PNG.* YouTube video, September 14. https://www.youtube.com/watch?v=NXn5E8fIG80.

Fanon, Frantz. 1963. *The Wretched of the Earth.* New York: Grove Press.

Far Eastern Economic Review. 2000. "Intelligence, Paramilitaries Gear Up." Kabar Irian e-mail network posting. http://www.angelfire.com/journal/issues/irian0420_3000.html.

Farhadian, Charles, and Stephan Babuljak. 2007. *The Testimony Project: Papua*. Jakarta: Suwaan Langoan Indah.

Federal News Service. 2010. *Preliminary Transcript of September 22, 2010 Congressional Hearing on West Papua*. Asia, Pacific and Global Environment Subcommittee of the House of Foreign Affairs Committee, East Timor Advocacy Network. http://www.etan.org/news/2010/09wpapuahearing.htm.

Feith, Annie. 2000. "Strategies of Rule, Strategies of Resistance: Women and the West Papuan Nationalist Struggle." Honors diss., Queensland University of Technology, Australia.

Fernandes, Clinton. 2006. *Reluctant Indonesians: Australia, Indonesia and the Future of West Papua*. Melbourne: Scribe Short Books.

Fest Napuan (website). 2010. "Tabura West Papua." Link no longer available.

Fifi'i, Jonathan. 1989. *From Pig-Theft to Parliament: My Life between Two Worlds*, edited by R. Keesing. Suva, Fiji: University of the South Pacific.

Fightback. 2014. "'One Ocean, One People'—Interview with Teresia Teaiwa on Self-Determination Struggles in the Pacific." https://fightback.org.nz/2014/10/29/one-ocean-one-people-interview-with-teresia-teaiwa-on-self-determination-struggles-in-the-pacific/.

Flassy, Angela. 2009. "Papua Activist Gets 3 Years for Peaceful 'Provocation.'" *Jakarta Post*, April 7. http://www.thejakartapost.com/news/2009/07/04/papua-activist-gets-3-years-peaceful-provocation039.html-0.

Franklin, Cynthia, and Laura Lyons. 2004. "Land, Leadership and Nation: Haunani-Kay Trask on the Testimonial Uses of Life Writing in Hawai'i." *Biography* 27 (1): 222–249.

Free West Papua (@FreeWestPapua). 2014. "Black Lives Matter. The People of West Papua Are Crying Out for Help. When Will the World Take Notice? Twitter, #genocide, December 13. https://twitter.com/freewestpapua/status/543891311359557632.

Free West Papua Campaign. 2017a. "Support for West Papua from Bob Marley's Band the Wailers." https://www.freewestpapua.org/2017/04/02/support-for-west-papua-from-bob-marleys-band-the-wailers/.

———. 2017b. "Westminster Declaration for West Papua Launched in Aotearoa New Zealand Parliament." https://www.freewestpapua.org/2017/05/11/westminster-declaration-for-west-papua-launched-in-the-aotearoa-new-zealand-parliament/.

Fullagar, Kate, ed. 2012. *The Atlantic World in the Antipodes: Effects and Transformations since the Eighteenth Century*. Newcastle upon Tyne, United Kingdom: Cambridge Scholars.

Galtung, Johan. 2000. "Conflict Transformation by Peaceful Means (the Transcend Method)." Participants' manual prepared for the United Nations Disaster Management Training Programme (DMTP). https://www.transcend.org/pctrcluj2004/TRANSCEND_manual.pdf.

Ganap, Vitor. 2006. "Krontjong Toegoe in Tugu Village: Generic Form of Indonesian Keroncong Music." Associação Cultural e Museu Cavaquinho. http://www.cavaquinhos.pt/en/CAVAQUINHO/Keroncong%20Indonesia%20History.htm.

Garae, Len. 2018. “Final Declaration.” *Vanuatu Daily Post,* February 10. http://dailypost.vu/news/final-declaration/article_cce0f97b-2c19-5a28-a484-aa4558145f02.html.

Gardner, Helen, and Christopher Waters. 2013. “Decolonisation in Melanesia.” *Journal of Pacific History* 48 (2): 113–121.

Geneva for Human Rights. 2018. “Indigenous Peoples: West Papua at the United Nations.” https://gdh-ghr.org/west-papua-project-ghr-wpp/west-papua-the-un-2000-till-now/.

Gilroy, Paul. 1993. *The Black Atlantic: Modernity and Double Consciousness.* London: Verso.

Glazebrook, Diana. 2004. “Teaching Performance Art Is Like Sharpening the Blade of a Knife.” *Asia Pacific Journal of Anthropology* 5 (1): 1–14.

———. 2008. *Permissive Residents: West Papuan Refugees Living in Papua New Guinea.* Canberra: ANU E Press.

Global Firepower. 2018. “Indonesia Military Strength.” https://www.globalfirepower.com/country-military-strength-detail.asp?country_id=indonesia.

Goa, Daniel. 2018. “New Caledonia at the Crossroads.” Public lecture, Lowy Institute, Sydney, July 12. https://www.lowyinstitute.org/news-and-media/multimedia/audio/daniel-goa-new-caledonia-crossroads.

Golden, Brigham. 2000. “Letter to the Editor.” *Van Zorge Report* 2 (20): 34. http://papuaweb.org/net/golden/2000-vanzorge-letter.pdf.

Goodman, Tom. 1998. “The Sosolot Exchange Network in Eastern Indonesia during the Seventeenth and Eighteenth Centuries.” In *Perspectives on the Bird’s Head of Irian Jaya, Indonesia: Proceedings of the Conference,* edited by J. Miedema, C. Odé, and R. Dam, 421–454. Amsterdam: Rodopi.

Grossberg, L. 1986. “On Postmodernism and Articulation: An Interview with Stuart Hall.” *Journal of Communication Inquiry* 10 (2): 45–60. doi:10.1177/019685998601000204.

Guiart, Jean. 1951. “Forerunners of Melanesian Nationalism.” *Oceania* 22 (2): 81–90.

HaLevi, Ezra. 2007. “West Papua Delegation Donates Gold for Holy Temple.” *Arutz Sheva Israel National News,* July 10. http://www.israelnationalnews.com/News/News.aspx/123837.

Hall, Stuart. 1985. “Signification, Representation, Ideology: Althusser and the Post Structuralist Debates.” *Critical Studies in Mass Communication* 2 (2): 91–114.

———. 1993. “Cultural Identity and Diaspora.” In *Colonial Discourse and Postcolonial Theory: A Reader,* edited by P. Williams and L. Chrisman, 222–237. New York: Harvester Wheatsheaf.

Harrison, Simon. 1993. “The Commerce of Cultures in Melanesia.” *Man* 28:139–158.

Harsono, Andreas. 2018. “Why Children Are Dying of Measles in Papua, Indonesia.” *Human Rights Watch Dispatches.* https://www.hrw.org/news/2018/01/26/why-children-are-dying-measles-papua-indonesia.

Hau’ofa, Epeli. 2008. “Our Sea of Islands.” In *We Are the Ocean: Selected Works,* edited by Geoffrey White, 27–40. Honolulu: University of Hawai‘i Press.

Hawai‘i Review. 2015. *Wansolwara: Voices for West Papua.* Manoa: Hawai‘i Review, University of Hawai‘i at Manoa. Accessed May 27, 2017. https://issuu.com/hawaiireview/docs/wansolwara_voices_for_west_papua.

HDC (Henry Dunant Centre for Humanitarian Dialogue). 2010. “Peacemaking

Analysis and Research: Peacemaking Research—Focus on Indonesia." Geneva: Centre for Humanitarian Dialogue.

Heine, Giddy. 2017. "How the Black Sistaz Are Fighting for a Better West Papua from Their New Home in Australia." *Beat,* May 26. https://www.beat.com.au/how-the-black-sistaz-are-fighting-for-a-better-west-papua-from-their-new-home-in-australia/.

Hernawan, Budi. 2018. *Torture and Peacebuilding in Indonesia: The Case of Papua.* New York: Routledge.

Higgins, Noelle. 2004. "The Application of International Humanitarian Law to Wars of National Liberation." *Journal of Humanitarian Assistance,* April 2004, n.p.

Hirschman, Charles. 1979. "Political Independence and Educational Opportunity in Peninsula Malaysia." *Sociology of Education* 52 (2): 67–83.

Huizinga, F. 1998. "Relations between Tidore and the North Coast of New Guinea in the Nineteenth Century." In *Perspectives on the Bird's Head of Irian Jaya, Indonesia: Proceedings of the Conference,* edited by J. Miedema, C. Odé, and R. Dam, 385–420. Amsterdam: Rodopi.

Human Rights Watch. 2010. "Prosecuting Political Aspiration: Indonesia's Political Prisoners." New York: Human Rights Watch. http://www.hrw.org/en/node/90960/section/1.

———. 2014. "Indonesia: Security Forces Kill Five in Papua." Press Release. Accessed October 3, 2018. https://www.hrw.org/news/2014/12/10/indonesia-security-forces-kill-five-papua.

ILWP (International Lawyers for West Papua) (website). 2009. http://www.ilwp.org.

International Coalition for Papua. 2017. *Human Rights in West Papua 2017.* October 26. http://www.humanrightspapua.org/images/docs/HumanRightsPapua2017-ICP.pdf.

International Crisis Group. 2001. *Indonesia: Ending Repression in Irian Jaya.* ICG Asia Report. Brussels: International Crisis Group. https://www.crisisgroup.org/asia/south-east-asia/indonesia/indonesia-ending-repression-irian-jaya.

———. 2010. "Indonesia: The Deepening Impasse in Papua." *Asia Briefing,* no. 108. https://www.crisisgroup.org/asia/south-east-asia/indonesia/indonesia-deepening-impasse-papua.

IPWP (International Parliamentarians for West Papua) (website). 2008. Accessed November 16, 2010. http://www.ipwp.org.

Jaggi, Maya. 2006. "Interview: Ngugi wa Thiongo: 'I Don't Think We Were Meant to Come Out Alive.'" *Guardian.* Accessed August 22, 2019. https://www.theguardian.com/books/2006/jan/28/featuresreviews.guardianreview13.

Joku, Franzalbert. 2007. "Problems and Prospects of the Special Autonomy Law." Paper presented at West Papua: Paths to Justice and Prosperity Conference, August 2007, Indonesian Solidarity and the West Papua Project, Centre for Peace and Conflict Studies, University of Sydney, Australia.

Jolly, Margaret. 2005. "Beyond the Horizon? Nationalisms, Feminisms and Globalization in the Pacific." *Ethnohistory* 52 (1): 137–166.

Junker, Laura Lee. 1999. *Raiding, Trading, and Feasting: The Political Economy of Philippine Chiefdoms.* Honolulu: University of Hawai'i Press.

Kabutaulaka, Tarcisius. 1994. "Cohesion and Disorder in Melanesia: The Bougainville

Conflict and the Melanesian Way." In *New Politics in the South Pacific*, edited by F. Alailima and P. Larmour, 63–82. Suva, Fiji: Institute of Pacific Studies, University of the South Pacific.

———. 2015. "RePresenting Melanesia: Ignoble Savages and Melanesian AlterNatives." *Contemporary Pacific* 27 (1): 110–146.

Kamma, F. C. 1972. *Koreri: Messianic Movements in the Biak-Numfoor Culture Area*. The Hague: Martinus Nijhoff.

Kareni, Ronny. 2018. "A Referendum in West Papua." Paper presented at Two Horizons: Pacific Studies in a Cosmopolitan World Conference, Australian Association for Pacific Studies, University of Adelaide, Australia, April 6.

Karoba, Sem. 1999. "Tribal Democracy for West Papua Government: A Rough Draft/ Proposal (Open for Discussion) (England, 1999)." *Sem Karoba* (blog). Accessed September 5, 2018. https://skaroba.wordpress.com/2009/10/07/tribal-democracy-for-west-papua-government-a-rough-draftproposal-open-for-discussion-england-1999/.

———. 2009. "What Is Tribal Democracy?" *Sem Karoba* (blog). Accessed September 5, 2018. https://skaroba.wordpress.com/2009/10/07/what-is-tribal-democracy/.

King, Joseph. 1909. *W. G. Lawes of Savage Island and New Guinea*. London: Religious Tract Society.

King, Martin Luther, Jr. 2010. "I've Been to the Mountaintop." *American Rhetoric*, October 27. http://www.americanrhetoric.com/speeches/mlkivebeentothemountaintop.htm.

King, Peter. 2004. *West Papua and Indonesia since Suharto: Independence, Autonomy or Chaos?* Sydney: UNSW Press.

———. 2008. "Lowying the Boom on West Papua." Papua Papers, West Papua Project, Centre for Peace and Conflict Studies, University of Sydney.

Kirksey, Eben. 2011. "Reclaiming the Messianic Promise." In *Comprehending West Papua*, edited by Peter King, Jim Elmslie, and Camellia Webb-Gannon, 278–293. Sydney: Centre for Peace and Conflict Studies, University of Sydney.

———. 2012. *Freedom in Entangled Worlds: West Papua and the Architecture of Global Power*. Durham, NC: Duke University Press.

Kirksey, Eben, and Jack Grimston. 2003. "Indonesian Troops for BP Gas Project." *New York Times*, July 20. https://www.thetimes.co.uk/article/indonesian-troops-for-bp-gas-project-30cfrwq7gh3.

Kirksey, Eben, and J. A. D. Roemajauw. 2010. "The Wild Terrorist Gang: The Semantics of Violence and Self-Determination in West Papua." *Oxford Development Studies* 30 (2): 189–203.

Kirsch, Stuart. 2010. "Ethnographic Representations and the Politics of Violence in West Papua." *Critique of Anthropology* 30 (1): 3–22.

Knauft, Bruce. 1999. *From Primitive to Postcolonial in Melanesia and Anthropology*. Ann Arbor: University of Michigan Press.

Kohn, Margaret, and Keally McBride. 2011. *Political Theories of Decolonization: Postcolonialism and the Problem of Foundations*. Oxford: Oxford University Press.

Koman, Veronica. 2016. "Papua—the Pricking of Indonesia's National Conscience." *Asia Pacific Report*. https://asiapacificreport.nz/2016/05/20/veronica-korman-papua-the-pricking-of-indonesias-national-conscience/.

Kraemer, Joseph. 1971. "Revolutionary Guerrilla Warfare and the Decolonization Movement." *Polity* 4 (2): 137–158.

Laguerre, Michel. 2006. *Diaspora, Politics, and Globalization.* New York: Palgrave Macmillan.

Laqueur, Walter Z. 1962. "The End of the Monolith: World Communism in 1962." *Foreign Affairs* 40 (3): 360–373. Accessed September 17, 2020. doi:10.2307/20029561.

Lawson, Stephanie. 2013. "Melanesia: The History and Politics of an Idea." *Journal of Pacific History* 48 (1): 1–22.

———. 2017. "Regionalism and Colonialism in Contemporary Oceania." *Round Table* 106 (2): 143–153.

Lear, Jonathan. 2008. *Radical Hope: Ethics in the Face of Cultural Devastation.* Cambridge, MA: Harvard University Press.

Lewis, M. Paul. 2009. "Ethnologue: Languages of the World." SIL International. Accessed November 7, 2011. http://www.ethnologue.com.

Lindstrom, Lamont. 1990. "Big Men as Ancestors: Inspiration and Copyrights on Tanna (Vanuatu)." *Ethnology* 29 (4): 313–326.

Lindstrom, Lamont, and Geoffrey White. 1990. *Island Encounters: Black and White Memories of the Pacific War.* Washington, DC: Smithsonian Institution Press.

Lini, Walter. 1980. *Beyond Pandemonium: From the New Hebrides to Vanuatu.* Wellington: Asia Pacific Books.

Linnekin, Jocelyn. 1990. "The Politics of Culture in the Pacific." In *Cultural Identity and Ethnicity in the Pacific,* edited by J. Linnekin and L. Poyer, 149–174. Honolulu: University of Hawaiʻi Press.

Lowe, Lisa. 2015. *The Intimacies of Four Continents.* Durham, NC: Duke University Press.

Lyons, Paul. 2016. Review of *The Black Pacific: Anti-colonial Struggles and Oceanic Connections,* by Robby Shilliam. *Contemporary Pacific* 28 (2): 499–502.

Mackley-Crump, Jared. 2015. "A 'Pacific Renaissance'? Exploring the Pacific Diaspora in Aotearoa New Zealand through the Evolution of Festivals and Popular Music." *Journal of New Zealand and Pacific Studies* 3 (20): 149–166.

MacLeod, Jason. 2009. "Nonviolent Struggle in West Papua: 'We Have a Hope.'" In *Nonviolent Alternatives for Change,* edited by R. V. Summy, 74–101. Oxford: EOLSS.

———. 2015. *Merdeka and the Morning Star: Civil Resistance in West Papua.* Brisbane: University of Queensland Press.

Magowan, Fiona. 2007. "Globalisation and Indigenous Christianity: Translocal Sentiments in Australian Aboriginal Christian Songs." *Identities* 14 (4): 459–483.

Mannheim, Karl. 1927. "The Problem of Generations." In *Essays on the Sociology of Knowledge,* edited by Karl Mannheim, 276–320. London: Routledge and Kegan Paul.

Matsuda, Matt. 2012. *Pacific Worlds: A History of Seas, Peoples and Cultures.* Cambridge: Cambridge University Press.

Matsuno, Akihisa. 1998. "Reading the Unwritten: An Anatomy of Indonesia Discourse on East Timor." In *The East Timor Problem and the Role of Europe,* edited by P. Liete, 195–210. Lisbon: International Platform of Jurists for East Timor.

———. 2010. "West Papua: 'Why Autonomy Is Failing.'" Paper presented at the International Peace Research Association Conference, Sydney, July 2010.

———. 2011. "West Papua and the Changing Nature of Self-Determination." In *Comprehending West Papua,* edited by Peter King, Jim Elmslie, and Camellia Webb-Gannon, 177–190. Sydney: Centre for Peace and Conflict Studies, University of Sydney.

May, R. J. 2004. *State and Society in Papua New Guinea: The First Twenty-Five Years.* Canberra: ANU E Press.

McGibbon, Rod. 2006. *Pitfalls of Papua: Understanding the Conflict and Its Place in Australia-Indonesia Relations.* Sydney: Lowy Institute for International Policy.

McNiven, Liz. 2010. "Curator's Notes: Pearls and Savages 1921." National Film and Sound Archive, October 23. http://aso.gov.au/titles/documentaries/pearls-and-savages/notes/.

Memmi, Albert. 1965. *The Colonizer and the Colonized.* Boston: Beacon Press.

Mietzner, Marcus. 2007. "Local Elections and Autonomy in Papua and Aceh: Mitigating or Fuelling Secessionism?" *Indonesia* 84:1–39.

Miller, Ben. 2009. "The Fantasy of Whiteness: Blackness and Aboriginality in American and Australian Culture." PhD diss., University of New South Wales.

Miller, J. Graham. 1978. *Live: A History of Church Planting in the New Hebrides, to 1880.* Sydney: Committees on Christian Education and Overseas Missions, General Assembly of the Presbyterian Church of Australia.

Mohanty, Chandra Talpade. 2003. *Feminism without Borders: Decolonizing Theory, Practicing Solidarity.* Durham, NC: Duke University Press.

Molisa, Grace Mera. 1987. *Colonised People: Poems.* Port Vila, Vanuatu: Black Stone.

Moore, Clive. 2003. *New Guinea: Crossing Boundaries and History.* Honolulu: University of Hawai'i Press.

Munro, Jenny. 2016. "Indigenous Women, Antenatal Care and Childbirth in Papua, Indonesia." State, Society and Governance in Melanesia in Brief 2016/22. http://bellschool.anu.edu.au/sites/default/files/publications/attachments/2016-10/ib-2016-22-munro.pdf.

Musgrave, Thomas. 2015. "An Analysis of the 1969 Act of Free Choice in West Papua." In *Sovereignty, Statehood and State Responsibility: Essays in Honour of James Crawford,* edited by C. M. Chinkin, Freya Baetens, and James Crawford, 209–228. Cambridge: Cambridge University Press.

Nairn, Allan. 2010. "Secret Files Show Kopassus, Indonesia's Special Forces, Targets Papuan Churches, Civilians. Documents Leak from Notorious US-Backed Unit as Obama Lands in Indonesia." *News and Comment* (blog), November 9. http://www.allannairn.com/2010/11/breaking-news-secret-files-show.html.

Nakagawa, Scott. 2012. "Blackness Is the Fulcrum." *Race Files* (blog), May 26, 2017. https://www.racefiles.com/2012/05/04/blackness-is-the-fulcrum/.

Narokobi, Bernard. 1983. *The Melanesian Way.* Port Moresby: Institute of Pacific Studies, University of the South Pacific.

Narokobi, Bernard, and his critics and supporters. 1980. *The Melanesian Way: Total Cosmic Vision of Life.* Introduced and arranged by Olela. Port Moresby: Institute of Papua New Guinea Studies.

National Parliament of West Papua. n.d. Accessed September 5, 2018. http://www.westpapuaparliament.org.

National PNG. 2008. "Editorial: Indonesia PNG." May 30. Link no longer available.

Neilson, David. 2000. "Christianity in Irian (West Papua)." PhD diss., University of Sydney.

Nersessian, David. 2005. "Rethinking Cultural Genocide under International Law." Carnegie Council for Ethics in International Affairs. https://www.carnegiecouncil.org/publications/archive/dialogue/2_12/section_1/5139.

Newton Cain, Tess. 2016. "The Renaissance of the Melanesian Spearhead Group." In *The New Pacific Diplomacy,* edited by Greg Fry and Sandra Tarte, 151–160. Canberra: ANU E Press.

Ngũgĩ wa Thiong'o. 1981. *Decolonising the Mind: The Politics of Language in African Literature*. Oxford: James Currey.

Nichols, Alan. n.d. *Escape from West Papua: How and Why Refugees Came to Australia*. Melbourne: Acorn Press.

Notley, Tanya, and Camellia Webb-Gannon. 2016. "Visual Evidence from Above: Assessing the Value of Earth Observation Satellites for Supporting Human Rights." *Fibreculture Journal* 27: n.p.

Ondawame, John Otto. 2010. *"One People, One Soul": West Papuan Nationalism and the Organisasi Papua Merdeka*. Belair, South Australia: Crawford House.

O'Neill, Peter, and David Lloyd, eds. 2009. *The Black and Green Atlantic: Cross-Currents of the African and Irish Diasporas*. London: Palgrave Macmillan.

OPM (Organisasi Papua Merdeka) Department for External Affairs. 2010. "The Political Mission of the OPM." YouTube video, June 7. http://www.youtube.com/watch?v=EutHVOkNpLg.

Osborne, Robin. 1985. *Indonesia's Secret War: The Guerrilla Struggle in Irian Jaya*. Sydney: Allen and Unwin.

Otto, Ton. 1997. "After the 'Tidal Wave': Bernard Narokobi and the Creation of a Melanesian Way." In *Narratives of Nation in the South Pacific,* edited by T. Otto and N. Thomas, 33–64. London: Routledge.

Pacific Institute of Public Policy. 2008. "MSG: Trading on Political Capital and Melanesian Solidarity." Port Vila, Vanuatu: Pacific Institute of Public Policy.

Papua National Consensus. 2009. *Papua National Consensus*. Jayapura: East Timor Action Network. http://www.etan.org/issues/wpapua/0905papconsensus.htm.

Papuan People's Consultative Assembly and Indigenous People of Papua. 2010. *Recommendations by Papuan People's Consultative Assembly and Indigenous People of Papua*. Papua Land of Peace Faith Based Network on West Papua. Accessed October 26, 2017. http://papua.2see.nl/news_release/recommendations_by_papuan_people_s_consultative_assembly_and_indigenous_people_of_papua.

Papuans Behind Bars. 2011. "Third Papuan People's Congress." Accessed October 3, 2018. http://www.papuansbehindbars.org/?case=third-papuan-peoples-congress.

Parameswaran, Prashanth. 2017. "Old Shadows in New Australia-Indonesia Military Spat." *Diplomat*, January 6. https://thediplomat.com/2017/01/old-shadows-in-new-australia-indonesia-military-spat/.

Paterson, Don, and Robert Early. 2006. "'Does Not Need To'—Discretionary Power or Non Discretionary Exemption? Ayamiseba V Attorney General." *Journal of South Pacific Law* 10 (2): n.p. http://www.paclii.org/journals/fJSPL/v0110n02/5.shtml.

Pickell, David. 2002. *Between the Tides: A Fascinating Journey among the Kamoro of New Guinea*. Hong Kong: Periplus Editions.

Pilcher, Jane. 1994. "Mannheim's Sociology of Generations: An Undervalued Legacy." *British Journal of Sociology* 45 (3): 481–495.

Post-Courier. 2017. "PNG's Embarrassing Failed Defence White Paper." December 13. https://postcourier.com.pg/pngs-embarrassing-failed-defence-white-paper/.

Pouwer, Jan. 1999. "The Colonisation, Decolonisation and Recolonisation of West New Guinea." *Journal of Pacific History* 34 (20): 157–179.

Prai, Jacob. 2004. "Letter to Mr. Bean H." Unpublished letter. Malmö Office, Organisasi Papua Merdeka.

Prai, Joseph. 2010. "Special Tribute to Late Kelly Kwalik." Stafaband (website), posted by Lewis Prai Wellip. http://cowo.men/search/west-papua-s-new-dawn.

Premdas, Ralph. 1987. "Melanesian Socialism: Vanuatu's Quest for Self-Definition." *Journal of Commonwealth and Comparative Politics* 25 (20): 141–160.

Qolouvaki, Tagi. 2015. "Dreaming Black Love." *Ke kaupu hehi ale* (blog), May 27. https://hehiale.wordpress.com/2015/08/10/dreaming-black-love/.

Radio New Zealand International. 2010. "Indonesian Police Praised for Showing Restraint So Far in Huge Papuan Demonstration." July 9. Link no longer available.

———. 2014. "Umbrella Papuan Group Suggested to Apply for MSG." *Pacific Islands Report,* January 22. Link no longer available.

———. 2016. "Pacific Peoples Lead Push for West Papuan Decolonisation." *Dateline Pacific,* October 18. http://www.radionz.co.nz/international/programmes/datelinepacific/audio/201820417/pacific-peoples-lead-push-for-papuan-decolonisation.

———. 2017a. "Cross-Party Support in New Zealand for West Papua Vote." May 11. https://www.radionz.co.nz/international/pacific-news/330597/cross-party-support-in-nz-for-west-papua-vote.

———. 2017b. "West Papuan Leader Sees Solidarity Grow in NZ." May 11. http://www.radionz.co.nz/international/pacific-news/330553/west-papuan-leader-sees-solidarity-grow-in-nz.

———. 2018. "MSG No Place for West Papua Talks—Director General." July 27. https://www.radionz.co.nz/international/pacific-news/362792/msg-no-place-for-west-papua-talks-director-general.

Reid, Anthony. 1998. "Merdeka: The Concept of Freedom in Indonesia." In *Asian Freedoms: The Idea of Freedom in East and Southeast Asia,* edited by D. Kelly and A. Reid, 141–160. Cambridge: Cambridge University Press.

Reilly, Ben. 2000. "The Africanization of the Pacific." *Australian Journal of International Affairs* 54 (3): 263–273.

Reynolds, Henry. 2005. *Nowhere People.* Sydney: Penguin Books.

Rich, Roland, ed. 2006. *Political Parties in the Pacific Islands.* Canberra: Pandanus Books.

Rintala, Marvin. 1963. "A Generation in Politics: A Definition." *Review of Politics* 25 (4): 509–522.

Robinson, Jennifer. 2009. "Justice for West Papua: Legal and Practical Issues." Public Lecture at the West Papua Project, Centre for Peace and Conflict Studies, University of Sydney, March.

———. 2010. "Self-Determination and the Limits of Justice: West Papua and East Timor." In *Future Justice,* edited by H. Sykes, 168–187. Sydney: Future Leaders.

Rodman, M., and Cooper, M., eds. 1979. *The Pacification of Melanesia*. Lanham, MD: University Press of America.

Rodney, Walter. 1972. *How Europe Underdeveloped Africa*. London: Bogle-L'Ouverture.

Rokolekutu, Ponipate. 2016. "Heterogeneity, Race and Genealogical Connection of Spiritual Hinterlands." *Robbie Shilliam* (blog). May 26. https://robbieshilliam.wordpress.com.

Rumakiek, Rex, and Jim Elmslie. 2017. "Interview with Jim Elmslie." August 31, Sydney, and November 1 and 2, Sydney, Australia.

Rumbiak, Jacob. 2017. Untitled conference paper. Paper presented at Beyond the Pacific: West Papua on the World Stage Conference, West Papua Project, University of Sydney, Australia, September 1.

Rutherford, Danilyn. 1999. "Waiting for the End in Biak: Violence, Order, and a Flag Raising." *Indonesia* 67:39–59.

———. 2003. *Raiding the Land of the Foreigners: The Limits of the Nation on an Indonesian Frontier*. Princeton, NJ: Princeton University Press.

———. 2012. *Laughing at Leviathan: Sovereignty and Audience in West Papua*. Chicago: University of Chicago Press.

Saltford, John. 2003. *The United Nations and the Indonesia Takeover of West Papua, 1962–1969: The Anatomy of Betrayal*. London: Routledge Curzon.

Saul, Ben. 2001. "Was the Conflict in East Timor 'Genocide' and Why Does It Matter?" *Melbourne Journal of International Law* 2 (2): n.p. Last accessed September 5, 2018. http://www.austlii.edu.au/au/journals/MelbJIL/2001/18.html.

Savage, Peter. 1978. "The National Liberation Struggle in West Irian: From Millenarianism to Socialist Revolution." *Asian Survey* 18 (10): 981–995.

Scheiner, Charles. 2006. "Self-Determination Requires More than Political Independence: Recent Developments in Timor-Leste." www.laohamutuk.org/reports/SDRequiresGen.pdf.

Schulze, Kirsten. 2003. "The Struggle for an Independent Aceh: The Ideology, Capacity and Strategy of GAM." *Studies in Conflict and Terrorism* 26:241–271.

Schwartz, Norman. 1969. "Goal Attainment through Factionalism: A Guatemalan Case." *American Anthropologist* 71:1088–1108.

Seroff, Doug, and Lynn Abbott. 2002. *Out of Sight: The Rise of African American Popular Music, 1889–1895*. Jackson: University Press of Mississippi.

Sharp, Nonie, in association with Markus Wonggor Kaisiepo. 1994. *The Morning Star in Papua Barat*. North Carlton, Melbourne: Arena.

Sharrad, Paul. 2001. "Out of Africa: Literary Globalization in the Winds of Change." *South Atlantic Quarterly* 100 (3): 717–728.

Shilliam, Robbie. 2015. *The Black Pacific: Anti-colonial Struggles and Oceanic Connections*. London: Bloomsbury.

Shore, Cris. 2014. "Anthropology." In *The Oxford Handbook of Political Leadership*, edited by R. A. W. Rhodes and Paul t'Hart, 176–194. Oxford: Oxford University Press.

Sidik, Raka. 2018. "Comment on Question: 'If Western Papua Got Their Independence in 1969, Would Today (2018) This Nation Be Better than Papua New Guinea? Would This Nation Unify with PNG after PNG's Independence in 1970s?' " Quora, August 13. https://www.quora.com/If-Western-Papua-got-their-independence-in

-1969-would-today-2018-this-nation-be-better-than-Papua-New-Guinea-Would-this-nation-unify-with-PNG-after-PNG-s-independence-in-1970s.

Siegel, Bernard J., and Alan R. Beals. 1960. "Conflict and Factionalist Dispute." *Journal of the Royal Anthropological Institute* 90:107–117.

Singapore Press Holdings. 2010. "The Road to Self-Governance." *Asia One*, September 28. Link no longer available.

Smith, Alan, Garry Trompf, and Kevin Clements. 1985. "Flight into Limbo: Refugees in Papua New Guinea." In *Plight of Papua: Religion and Politics in West Papua (or Irian Jaya)*, edited by J. Bieniek and G. Trompf, 137–141. Mount Hagen: Michaelite Communities in Papua New Guinea and Australia.

Sogavare, Manasseh. 2017. "In Conversation with Sogavare." Public address at the Lowy Institute, Sydney, August 14. https://www.lowyinstitute.org/news-and-media/multimedia/audio/conversation-solomon-islands-prime-minister-manasseh-sogavare.

Solis, Gabriel. 2012. "Artisanship, Innovation and Indigenous Modernity in the Eastern Highlands of Papua New Guinea: Ataizo Mutahe's Vessel Flutes." *MUSICultures* 39 (1): 83–110.

———. 2014. "The Black Pacific: Music and Racialization in Papua New Guinea and Australia." *Critical Sociology* 14 (2): 297–312.

———. 2015. "Transpacific Excursions: Multi-sited Ethnomusicology, the Black Pacific, and Nettl's Comparative (Method)." In *This Thing Called Music: Essays in Honor of Bruno Nettl*, edited by V. Levine and P. Bohlman, 354–365. Lanham, MD: Rowman and Littlefield.

Sopiee, Mohamed Noordin. 1973. "The Advocacy of Malaysia—before 1961." *Modern Asian Studies* 7 (4): 717–732.

Souter, Gavin. 1963. *New Guinea: The Last Unknown*. Sydney: Angus and Robertson.

Special MSG Leaders' Summit. 2014. "Communique." National Parliament, Port Moresby, Papua New Guinea, June 26. Link no longer available.

Spengler. 2008. "The Peculiar Theology of Black Liberation." *Asia Times Online*, March 18. https://historynewsnetwork.org/article/48488.

Spivak, G. C. 2012. *Outside in the Teaching Machine*. Oxford: Routledge.

Stasch, Rupert. 2014. "Powers of Incomprehension: Linguistic Otherness, Translators and Political Structure in New Guinea Tourism Encounters." *Hau Journal of Ethnographic Theory* 4 (2): 73–94.

Stott, David Adam. 2011. "Would an Independent West Papua Be a Failing State?" *Japan Focus: Asia-Pacific Journal* 9 (37): 1–41.

Strauss, William, and Neil Howe. 1991. *Generations: The History of America's Future, 1584–2069*. New York: William Morrow.

Swan, Quito. 2017–2018. "Melanesia's Way: Black Internationalism in Oceania." Radcliffe Institute for Advanced Study, Harvard University. https://www.radcliffe.harvard.edu/fellowship-program/research-partnership-opportunity/melanesias-way-black-internationalism-in-oceania.

———. 2018. "Blinded by Bandung? Illuminating West Papua, Senegal, and the Black Pacific." *Radical History Review* 131:58–80.

Sydney Morning Herald. 2018. "Amnesty Accuses Indonesian Forces of Unlawful

Killings in Papua." July 2. https://www.smh.com.au/world/asia/amnesty-accuses-indonesian-forces-of-unlawful-killings-in-papua-20180702-p4zp0c.html.

Teaiwa, Teresia, 2006. "On Analogies: Rethinking the Pacific in a Global Context." *Contemporary Pacific* 18 (1): 71–87.

Tebay, Neles. 2009. *Dialogue between Jakarta and Papua: A Perspective from Papua.* Aachen, Germany: Missio.

Thomas, Nicholas. 1994. *Colonialism's Culture: Anthropology, Travel and Government.* Princeton, NJ: Princeton University Press.

———. 2016. *The Voyages of Captain James Cook: The Illustrated Accounts of Three Epic Voyages.* London: Quarto Group USA.

Timmer, Jaap. 2005. "Decentralisation and Elite Politics in Papua." State Society and Governance in Melanesia Discussion Paper Series, Australian National University, Canberra.

Tinsley, Alex. 2012. "Benny Wenda's Plight Has Highlighted the Misuse of Interpol." *Guardian,* August 6. https://www.theguardian.com/commentisfree/2012/aug/06/benny-wenda-misuse-interpol.

Tjibaou, Jean-Marie. 2005. *Kanaky,* edited by Alban Bensa and Eric Wittersheim. Canberra: Pandanus Books.

Topping, Donald. 1977. "The Pacific Islands, Part II: Melanesia." *Southeast Asia Series* 25 (3): 1–33.

Trask, Haunani Kay. 1993. *From a Native Daughter: Colonialism and Sovereignty in Hawai'i.* Monroe, ME: Common Courage Press.

Trompf, Garry. 1979. *The Idea of Historical Recurrence in Western Thought.* Berkeley: University of California.

Tuhiwai Smith, Linda. 1999. *Decolonizing Methodologies: Research and Indigenous Peoples.* London: Zed Books.

ULMWP (United Liberation Movement for West Papua). 2015. *ULMWP—a Profile: The Unification and Reconciliation of the Melanesian People in West Papua.* Jayapura: United Liberation Movement for West Papua.

———. (website). 2016. Accessed September 2, 2018. https://www.ulmwp.org.

———. 2019a. "Press Release: West Papuan Military Factions Form Unified 'West Papua Army' in Historic Declaration (July 1, 2019)." https://www.ulmwp.org/press-release-west-papuan-military-factions-form-unified-west-papua-army-in-historic-declaration.

———. 2019b. "We Are Ready to Peacefully Reclaim Our Country from Indonesian Colonialism (July 3, 2019)." https://www.ulmwp.org/ulmwp-chairman-we-are-ready-to-peacefully-reclaim-our-country-from-indonesian-colonialism.

United Nations General Assembly. 1948. "Convention on the Prevention and Punishment of the Crime of Genocide." Resolution 260 (III) A.

———. 1960. "Declaration on the Granting of Independence to Colonial Countries and Peoples." Resolution 1514.

———. 1966a. "International Covenant on Civil and Political Rights." Resolution 2200A (XXI).

———. 1966b. "International Covenant on Economic, Social and Cultural Rights." Resolution 2200A (XXI).

Upton, Stuart. 2009. "A Disaster, but Not Genocide." *Inside Indonesia* 97. https://www.insideindonesia.org/a-disaster-but-not-genocide.

Van Heekeren, Deborah. 2011. "Singing it 'Local': The Appropriation of Christianity in the Vula'a Villages of Papua New Guinea." *Asia Pacific Journal of Anthropology* 12 (1): 44–59.

Vatsikopoulos, Helen. 2007. "Papua's Special Autonomy: Interview with Papuan Autonomy Advocate Franz Albert Joku." Australian Network—Asia Pacific Focus. Australian Broadcasting Commission. Link no longer available.

Waddell, Eric. 2008. *Jean-Marie Tjibaou: Kanak Witness to the World.* Honolulu: University of Hawai'i Press.

Wapedia. 2010. "Theys Eluay." October 23. Link no longer available.

Waters, Christopher. 2010. "Against the Tide: Australia Government Attitudes to Decolonisation in the South." Paper presented at the Australian Association for the Advancement of Pacific Studies (AAAPS) Conference, Melbourne, April.

Waziyatawin, and Michael Yellow Bird. 2012. *For Indigenous Minds Only: A Decolonization Handbook.* Santa Fe: School for Advanced Research Press.

Weaver, Jace. 2014. *The Red Atlantic: American Indigenes and the Making of the Modern World, 1000–1927.* Chapel Hill: University of North Carolina Press.

Webb, Michael. 2005. "Bembu Ben." *The Grove Dictionary of Musical Instruments.* 2nd ed. Oxford: Oxford University Press.

———. 2014. "Melanesia." *Continuum Encyclopedia of Popular Music of the World.* Vol. 5. London: Continuum.

Webb, Michael, and Camellia Webb-Gannon. 2016. "Musical Melanesianism: Imagining and Expressing Regional Identity and Solidarity in Popular Song and Video." *Contemporary Pacific* 28 (1): 59–95.

Webb-Gannon, Camellia. 2014. "Merdeka in West Papua: Peace, Justice and Political Independence." *Anthropologica* 56:355–369.

Webb-Gannon, Camellia, and Jim Elmslie. 2014. "MSG Headache, West Papuan Heartache: Indonesia's Melanesian Foray." *Japan Focus: The Asia-Pacific Journal* 12 (47): 1–23.

Webb-Gannon, Camellia, and Michael Webb. 2019. "'More than a Music, It's a Movement': West Papua Decolonization Songs, Social Media and the Remixing of Resistance." *Contemporary Pacific* 31 (2): 309–343.

Webb-Gannon, Camellia, Michael Webb, and Gabriel Solis. 2018. "The 'Black Pacific' and Decolonisation in Melanesia: Performing Négritude and Indigènitude." *Journal of the Polynesian Society* 27 (2): 177–206.

Webster, David. 2001–2002. "Already Sovereign as a People: A Foundational Moment in West Papuan Nationalism." *Pacific Affairs* 74 (4): 507–528.

Wenda, Benny. 2017. "West Papuan Human Rights Commissioner Tortured and Threatened by the Indonesian Police." Press release, Free West Papua Campaign, May 26. https://www.freewestpapua.org/2017/05/26/west-papuan-human-rights-commissioner-tortured-and-threatened-by-the-indonesian-police/.

Were, Samuel. 2006. *Bina Mene: Connecting the Hebrews.* Port Moresby: Bright Star Morning.

Westpapuambaham. 2010. "Pengembailan Otonomi Khusus Oleh MRP Dan Masyarakat Asli Papua." YouTube video. http://www.youtube.com/watch?v=eRes3cXmQpg.

West Papua National Leadership. 2010. "Pedoman Dasar: Constitution of the State of West Papua 1999." Unpublished document. Jayapura: West Papua National Leadership.

West Papua Unification Vanuatu. 2017. "VFWPA Short film." YouTube video, October 26. https://www.youtube.com/watch?v=k7hM-WyMZNM.

White, Geoffrey. 2008. "Foreword." In *We Are the Ocean: Selected Works,* edited by Geoffrey White, ix–xx. Honolulu: University of Hawai'i Press.

Widjojo, Muridan, Adriana Elisabeth, Cahyo Pamungkas Amiruddin, and Rosita Dewi. 2008. *Papua Road Map: Negotiating the Past, Improving the Present and Securing the Future.* Jakarta: Indonesian Institute of Sciences.

Wing, John, and Peter King. 2005. *Genocide in West Papua? The Role of the Indonesian State Apparatus and a Current Needs Assessment of the Papuan People.* Sydney: Centre for Peace and Conflict Studies, University of Sydney.

Wolfe, Patrick. 2006. "Settler Colonialism and the Elimination of the Native." *Journal of Genocide Research* 8 (4): 387–409.

Worsley, Peter. 1957. *The Trumpet Shall Sound: A Study of "Cargo" Cults in Melanesia.* London: Paladin.

Worth, Mark. 2004. *Land of the Morning Star.* ABC Television. Film, 55 min.

Wright, Stephen. 2019. "Papuans Get Independence Petition to UN Despite Obstacles." Associated Press, January 31. https://apnews.com/2c648a8e04a34c4b9f6c0a6e2d42e2ea.

Wright, Stephen, and Niniek Karmini. 2016. "West Papuans Protest against Indonesian Rule." *Oklahoman,* December 1. http://newsok.com/article/feed/1123163.

Zimmer-Tamakoshi, Laura. 1995. "Passion, Poetry and Cultural Politics in the South Pacific." *Ethnology* 34 (2): 113–127.

INDEX

About the Author

CAMELLIA WEBB-GANNON is an ethnographer and peace studies expert specializing in Oceanian politics of decolonization. Her research has concentrated on two areas: West Papua's self-determination movement and the role of the arts and technology in Pacific decolonization struggles. She teaches social advocacy and policy at the University of Wollongong in Australia and is the coordinator of the West Papua Project, also at the University of Wollongong.